MANPOWER ECONOMICS

MANPOWER ECONOMICS

EDWARD B. JAKUBAUSKAS, *University of Wyoming*
NEIL A. PALOMBA, *West Virginia University*

ADDISON-WESLEY PUBLISHING COMPANY
Reading, Massachusetts · Menlo Park, California · London · Don Mills, Ontario

MA 4/73 03284

Dedicated to:
Constantine Jakubauskas, Sr.
Mary Frances Palomba

PREFACE

During the 1940s and early 1950s, the major concern of labor economists was union—management relations. Collective bargaining, arbitration, and studies of union growth dominated the substance and formed the core of typical college and university labor courses. This was entirely appropriate for this period. The growth of unions and collective bargaining merited a focus upon forces which were truly revolutionary, and college textbook writers responded with the publication of a number of very excellent books which covered the labor relations field.

Beginning with the late 1950s, the focus of attention began to shift. Policymakers began to be greatly concerned with the development and utilization of workers as a manpower resource. Government intervened more actively in the labor market by promoting employment and training opportunities for a wide range of groups previously ignored. By the late 1960s programs had been designed to assist Blacks and other minority group workers, youth, women, older workers, the poor, etc. Training could be conducted in the classroom, on the job, or in centers away from home. Also, provisions existed for experimental and demonstration projects, and for relocating workers and families from labor-surplus to labor-shortage areas. Organizational changes paralleled program developments. The Manpower Administration emerged within the U.S. Department of Labor as a major force in the manpower field, and completely new actors—the Office of Economic Opportunity, and the Department of Housing and Urban Development—carved out parts of the action.

Labor economists responded by shifting the focus of their research toward manpower problems, but texts continued to be modeled in accordance with earlier priorities. College curricula changed slowly, and no text was developed in the 1960s which presented the study of manpower as an economic resource without appropriate chapters on labor—management relations. We feel that unions play an important role in manpower development—together with educators, civil rights groups, business associations, farm organizations, and many other groups. Special-purpose books on these institutions are in relative abundance. What has been lacking over the last decade has been a text which presented the process of manpower development and utilization—the study of the principles of manpower economics. This text is designed to meet this need.

The main outline for this book was prepared by the senior author at the University of Wisconsin in 1960 and 1961 while still a graduate student. This period saw the emergence of the Area Redevelopment Act, and much of the discussion of labor economists centered around the employment impact of technological change. To the professor at the University of Wisconsin and later at Iowa State University, the gap between course content in labor economics and the "action world" seemed to widen. Students completing the introductory economics courses had a theoretical background in micro- and macroeconomics, but little opportunity to see how these principles applied to policy changes taking place in the manpower field. Students completing the labor problems course had an understanding of labor—management relations but relatively little background on concepts which would help understand the truly revolutionary changes taking place in manpower, or in the basics of economic theory.

This text is designed to fill a number of needs. It can be used as part of a two-course sequence in labor economics—before or following the traditional treatment of unions, collective bargaining, and labor relations.

It is also designed to acquaint the intelligent layman with the field of manpower, and the principles of manpower economics. The growing field of adult education, and the expanding number of workers in the manpower field may gain better perspective of the economist's viewpoint of the manpower field.

We have resisted the temptation of including chapters within special areas of manpower—health manpower, problems of women, older workers, blacks, youth, etc. Excellent paperback monographs are in existence which provide good and timely supplements to our text. *Manpower Economics* constitutes an attempt to present the basic tools of analysis and the framework for the study of manpower, with some of the major policy trends.

We acknowledge the assistance of Dr. Catherine Palomba for many helpful comments, and also of Professor John Leyes, University of Wyoming, and of Professor J. Earl Williams, University of Houston. A special acknowledgment is due to the U.S. Department of Labor's Manpower Institutional Grant Program. Research generated under this program suggested many of the ideas and approaches used in this text. Special thanks are due to Mrs. Anne Culp, Mrs. Susan Wenell, and Mrs. Beverly Allfree, who devoted many hours to typing drafts of the manuscript.

Laramie, Wyoming   E. B. J.
Morgantown, West Virginia   N. A. P.
September 1972

CONTENTS

INTRODUCTION   Part I

Manpower economics is the study of how labor as a resource is utilized in the production of goods and services in organized society. Of concern to our study of manpower economics are such questions as who works at what occupations for whom, and at what level of remuneration. Manpower economics is also concerned with the aggregate level of employment in an economy, and the process of developing a more optimum and equitable system for developing, utilizing, and maintaining manpower resources.

MANPOWER PROBLEMS AND THE SCOPE OF MANPOWER ECONOMICS

1

1.1 THE SETTING FOR THE STUDY OF MANPOWER

Concern for manpower as a national issue developed very gradually in American society, and largely as a by-product of other social and economic concerns. Theory and practice conceptualized the economy as a self-regulating mechanism which called forth the resources required to produce what people were able and willing to buy, and decided who would work within specific occupations and industries.

Lags and imbalances in product and labor markets were considered temporary in nature, and self-correcting through wage and price cues received and acted upon by households and firms.

Gradually at first, and then in rising crescendo, public concern emerged for manpower-policy formulation in its own right. Fears and insecurities had periodically been generated by real or imagined effects of technological change, and in the last half-century old problems seemed to appear in more rapid succession. World War I required a balancing of military and civilian production and manpower. The 1920s accelerated technological change, and the Great Depression of the 1930s created much skepticism regarding the automaticity of market adjustments in production and manpower utilization.

At the termination of World War II, Keynsian economics was debated in academic and theoretical circles, although practitioners still talked about a balanced Federal budget as a desirable goal under all economic conditions. Certainly in the area of microadjustments of households and firms, theoreticians and practitioners seemed to be in agreement that market changes would create optimum adjustments in the use of capital and manpower resources.

By the mid-1950s, fears of widespread unemployment began to give way to a growing concern for "particularized," or class unemployment. The development of local and regional economies, and labor-market adjustments of groups previously ignored by Government policymakers began to receive growing attention. From 1945 to 1970, a profound and revolutionary change had taken place in economics and manpower policy. From an uneasy concern in the 1940s with a recurrence of the widespread unemployment of the 1930s, an active national manpower policy emerged covering a vast assortment of measures—all designed to intervene in some way with private decisions in the labor market. Training programs for youth, blacks, older citizens, and others on a wide spectrum of the labor force were introduced in rapid succession. Poverty was discovered as a national problem, and new terms were coined and introduced in our vocabulary such as "the disadvantaged," "automation," "outreach system," "depressed areas," and "human resources development." New Federal agencies entered the scene—Office of Economic Opportunity, Housing and Urban Development, Manpower Administration. Federal—state—local relationships were placed in organizational upheaval with an overgrowth of experimental and operational manpower programs. Presidents and Congressmen talked about designing new governmental relationships—"creative federalism"—and revenue-sharing with states and local communities.

Changes in academe paralleled social and economic forces. Economists building upon the pioneering work of John Maynard Keynes developed a body of literature which studied aggregate forces determining prices, employment, investment, money supply, etc. This formed the basis for macroeconomic theory and policy. A newer, and possibly equally revolutionary development was the evolution of "manpower economics" as an offshoot of traditional labor-relations-oriented labor economics. Manpower economics as a field of study emerged rapidly in the decades of the 1960s, and encompassed the study of macro- and microforces determining the level of employment, the process of deployment of manpower resources among geographical areas, occupations and industries. Manpower economics also was concerned with the systematic study and evaluation of private and public decision-making in providing for a socially and economically optimal utilization of manpower resources.

What is the scope of manpower economics? How is it defined, and what does it include as a subset of the science of economics? In this chapter we will discuss and conceptualize the area of manpower economics, and in the chapters that follow we will examine recent developments in the field in the context of economic theory and social and political developments.

1.2 MANPOWER ECONOMICS DEFINED

What is manpower economics? Since we know that it is a segment of economics, a starting point for defining manpower economics would be to define economics. At a very elementary level:

Economics is the social science that deals with the allocation of scarce resources to produce and distribute the goods and services to satisfy man's material wants.

To put it simply, economics deals with the three main economic questions of What, How, and For Whom. *What* refers to the question of what goods and services will be produced, and in what quantities will each of these products be produced. *How* refers to the specific combination of factors of production (land, labor, capital, and managerial skill) used to produce every good and service. *For Whom* refers to the distribution of the goods and services; who *receives* these products.

In manpower economics we are concerned with only *one* segment of economics.

Manpower economics is the subdivision of economics that deals with the forces operating within labor markets.

Thus manpower economics uses the tools of economic analysis to study the labor market by studying the labor-market characteristics of labor demand, labor supply, employment, and wages. We want to study the forces which determine the quantity and quality of labor which will be supplied by the members of our society, and will be demanded by business firms. Furthermore, we want to study the interactions of labor demand and supply. These interactions, we will discover, determine such important labor-market characteristics as wage levels and employment levels.

All of these labor-market characteristics can be examined at the micro- and macrolevel. The microlevel is concerned with individual business firms and individual occupations; the macrolevel is concerned with the aggregation of all the business firms and all the occupations in a region or in the entire nation. Both these levels hold vital information for those of us who are interested in studying labor-market processes— those of us who want to study manpower economics.

Another way of looking at manpower economics is from the factors of production point of view. Remember, factors of production are inputs which business firms combine, in varying proportions, to produce goods and services. The study of *all* these factors of production is known as economics; the study of the *human* factors of production is known as manpower economics.

TABLE 1.1 Factors of production

Nonhuman resources	Human resources
Land	Labor (manpower)
Capital	Managerial skill

Thus, manpower economics is concerned with the development and utilization of the human resources in an economy. As such this study centers on labor (or manpower) as the most important of the human resources. Anything that affects labor qualifies for examination under the general heading of manpower economics.

1.3 THE INSTITUTIONAL FRAMEWORK

In the study of the labor markets of an economy we cannot ignore the way the specific economy is organized. At one extreme is the planned economy. In a planned economy all the major labor-market decisions are made by some form of a central decision-making group. There is little if any reliance upon the market forces of labor demand and labor supply to determine the important questions of employment levels and wage levels. Thus a fully planned economy would decide the number of people there should be in each occupation, and then select the persons that the central planners think would be best qualified to be trained for that occupation. Of course, the central planners would also select the wage levels for each occupation.

On the other extreme of economic organization is the market economy. In such an economy the decision-making process is completely decentralized. There is complete reliance upon the market forces of labor demand and labor supply to determine the important questions of employment levels and wage levels. Thus the various labor markets in a market economy would decide the number of people in each occupation and their wage levels. Economic motives are most important in the decision-making process of market economy when it comes to labor-market questions; however, in a planned economy noneconomic motives play a far more important role.

Most real-world economies are mixed economies or a blend between the above two economic organizations. These economies have a mix between centralized decision-making and decentralized decision-making. The economic setting for most of this book will be the United States. Although the U.S. is a mixed economy, it leans very heavily toward a market economy in organization. Thus we will be able to analyze most labor-market questions from the point of view of a decentralized market economy.

1.4 MAJOR INSTITUTIONS

There are many important institutions which react within the various labor markets in any economy. These institutions would include households, business firms, and governments.

1.4.1 HOUSEHOLDS

Households are individuals and families which supply the factors of production to the business sectors in exchange for money payments. With these money payments (income) the households buy (demand) goods and services. Within these households we will be particularly interested in studying how the individuals choose an occupation, get the necessary training (or retraining), find their initial job, and change jobs. As we will discover, the manpower economist is concerned with the "world of work"— from the time an individual prepares for and enters the labor force until the individual leaves the labor force.

1.4.2 BUSINESS FIRMS

Business firms are business enterprises which demand factors of production from households and use them to produce goods and services for profit. It is the business firms which create the jobs for which the households train to fill. The manpower economist wants to study these firms in order to refine his knowledge of the determination of employments levels (and wage levels).

1.4.3 GOVERNMENTS

Governments are representatives of society and are grouped into various combinations (e.g., local, state, Federal). Government levels impose the various "rules of the game" on households and business firms. Moreover, in a mixed economy the Government does buy a certain amount of factors of production (thereby demanding and paying a certain amount of manpower), and they do produce some goods and services. In today's labor markets, the manpower economist must include the Government in his studies in order to fully understand the "world of work."

In addition to the above *major* institutions there are many other important institutions which have a bearing upon the study of manpower economics. Among these institutions are unions (combinations of labor); banks (suppliers of money and credit to business); and schools (educators of members of the population).

1.5 INTERACTION OF INSTITUTIONS

Before we go any further we will combine, in a very simplified manner, the most basic institutions into a circular-flow diagram (Fig. 1.1). The purpose of this diagram will be to picture how the economy combines its factors of production to produce goods and services—thereby determining employment and wage levels.

Of course the diagram is highly simplified and grows more complex as we add government, unions, banks, schools, etc. However, the essence of our circular-flow diagram will remain the same, and we will concentrate (in subsequent stages, each from a different point of view) on the utilization of human resources within the above framework.

1.6 SOME MANPOWER CONCEPTS

Before we actually begin the detailed study of manpower economics we should discuss some manpower concepts which are so basic that it would be beneficial for the reader to be familiar with them. These concepts will be dealt with again in much more detail as the book is developed.

1.6.1 LABOR FORCE

The labor force of an economy is composed of all the people in the economy (who are past some arbitrary age such as 14 or 16) who are either working or who are looking for work. The labor force is of course a function of the economy's population and of such economic forces as labor demand and wage levels. This concept can be broken into two major components; one being the civilian labor force, and the other noncivilian labor force.

As the name implies, the civilian labor force is composed of the total labor force

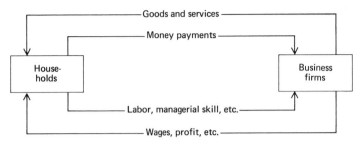

FIG 1.1　Simplified economic model

minus members of the armed forces; the noncivilian labor force is the remainder of the total labor force or the number of people in the armed forces.

In January 1971 the civilian labor force of the United States was 82,652,000 while the total labor force amounted to 85,628,000—meaning that there were 2,976,000 people in the U.S. armed forces. These figures can be broken down by sex, age, color, etc., depending on what the manpower economist wishes to study.[1]

1.6.2 EMPLOYMENT VERSUS UNEMPLOYMENT

The civilian labor force can be further divided into an employment category and an unemployment category. A member of the labor force is said to be employed if he (or she) has a job. In January 1971 of the 82,652,000 civilians in the U.S. labor force 77,238,000 (or 94%) had jobs.

The unemployment category would include any member of the civilian labor force who did not have a job but was looking for one (and was able and willing to take it if a job offer was made to him). In January 1971 this category contained 5,414,000 persons, or about 6% of the labor force.

In subsequent chapters we will discuss unemployment in detail, and try to discover its causes, costs, and possible remedies. One of the facts we shall discover is that unemployment varies with age, years of education, and occupation among other variables. The reader will probably not be very surprised to discover that a person with many years of education and a professional or managerial job has much less unemployment in his lifetime than a person with little formal education and a semiskilled or unskilled job.

Although we can divide the civilian labor force among the employed and unemployed, we will not find it interesting to do the same for the noncivilian labor force. Why? Because in the armed forces there is no unemployment—everyone has a job.

---

[1]See monthly series reported in *Employment and Earnings*, U.S. Department of Labor, Bureau of Labor Statistics, Washington, D.C.

1.6.3 LABOR-FORCE PARTICIPATION RATE

The labor-force participation rate (LFPR) is the percentage of the population which is in the labor force (either employed or unemployed) at a given period of time. Thus if there were 80 million people in the total labor force and 160 million people in the population (over the arbitrary age) then the LFPR would be 80/160 or 50%.

In actual numbers, the LFPR of the U.S. in January 1971 was 60.5% or 85,628,000 people in the total labor force out of an adult population of 141,500,000. This figure can also be broken down by age, sex, or color depending on the manpower question to be answered.

TABLE 1.2 A conceptual labor force

Occupation group	Civilian population		
	Civilian labor force		Not in labor force
	Employed	Unemployed	
Professional & technical	******* ******* ******* *******	*	******** *******
Managerial	****** ****** ****** ******	**	*******
Skilled	***** ***** ***** *****	***	******* *******
Semiskilled	******** **** ****	****	******* *******
Unskilled	*** *** *** ***	*****	********

Although Table 1.2 is only a hypothetical example, it should be useful in visualizing the basic manpower concepts. As we develop the book we will become more detailed in our discussion of these concepts, and real-world data will be used as examples periodically.

1.7 SOCIAL AND INSTITUTIONAL ASPECTS OF LABOR

The production process of creating goods and services by combining the factors of production—land, labor, capital, and enterprise—generates social and institutional problems. Decisions as to who shall work at what tasks and for how long, with what tools and at what wage level, must be made in any type of economic system geared to carry on production of goods and services. The problems which evolve from the work situation as to the control over the work environment are numerous and varied. It ranges from unilateral control exercised under slavery and serfdom in authoritarian societies, to various shades of relationships expressed in contractual arrangements in more democratic societal systems.

1.7.1 WORK RULES

A pluralistic society in an advanced and complex industrial economy generates various arrangements and degrees of control. This implies control from the public area by various governmental agencies, and also worker associations both formal and informal. Employer specifications and regulations play a most important role in the process of manpower application to the production process. Consequently, specific and implied work rules are applied within the shop environment, modified and superimposed by Governmental labor standards and regulations which limit the discretionary powers of one or both private groups—unions and management groups —involved in production and manpower regulation. The purpose of work rules in a society is to provide a balance between the disciplinary needs of orderly control in production, whereby manpower of various quantities must be supplied at various points of time, and the needs of workers in maintaining control over job opportunities (promotions, layoffs, retirements, etc.) and conditions of work with standards of dignity, democratic procedure, and in general, control over uncertainty.

The system of work rules which evolves on the work scene, therefore, is partially a result of collective bargaining between unions and management, and also is related to Governmental standards and informal worker arrangements. In general, the system of work rules provides an orderly process for production. Production is carried on with a minimum of interruption and inconvenience to workers and management.

Worker associations, formal and informal, interacting with employer organizations—and these, within the basic Governmental framework—determine for labor market purposes the following relationships:

1. The nature of the labor force which is employed, that is, the age, sex, race composition of the employed labor force.
2. The hours worked, wages on the job, training and skill standards.
3. Layoffs and retirements from the labor force.

The nature of the labor force of an economy is a function of demographic conditions which determine population growth and composition, and also it is due to custom, the actions of government, worker decision-making through unions, and work procedures of management.

Society as a whole and the actors in society—unions, managers, and workers—determine the basic answers to manpower questions of labor force participation, training and skill development, and retirement and layoff from the labor force. Within the framework of a democratic society an attempt is made to have a high degree of labor-market choice by workers in terms of occupational, industrial, and regional attachment. Policies are designed to permit flexibility of labor mobility within the context of maximum individual decision-making. Greatest reliance is placed upon economic factors—wages and other conditions of work—to facilitate the movement of workers, but Governmental programs are designed to permit more equality of opportunity among workers. These governmental programs imply, among other things, an attempt to equate opportunity among workers to have access to training and retraining opportunities through a recognition of the social benefits of general and vocational education.

1.8 CURRENT LABOR-MARKET PROBLEMS

But changing labor-market conditions generate problems depending upon the rate of technological advance and cyclical and secular conditions in output growth levels. Currently, the most pressing labor-market problems include:

1. The problem of lack of skill on the part of many workers. Workers find themselves with skills which were adequate a decade or so in the past but which are no longer useful in changing labor-market conditions. This is especially true when rapid movements out of primary to secondary industries—and today, to the service industries—take place.

2. Entry of workers much later into the labor force, with more and more preparation for work life, but with earlier retirement.

3. The marked increases in the labor-force participation of women particularly since the end of World War II.

4. The rapid transformation of skill requirements and increased rate of occupational obsolescence.

5. The earlier retirement of workers coupled with greater longevity.

There are many solutions to the five labor-market trends and problems outlined above. In general, varying degrees of dependence are placed upon economic factors such as supply and demand, income and investment changes, and upon social and Governmental aspects of political action. The application of manpower to other factors of production in economic activity must first begin with the decision-making process involving the determination of the size and nature of the labor force, the supply of labor forthcoming in the labor market under varying conditions, and employer demand for manpower of various skills and quantities. Given this static and skeletal framework of the basic economic variables, labor-market adjustments are made by workers in response to economic and noneconomic variables. Workers move among occupations, industries, and regions. The study of labor mobility is therefore a first step in understanding the dynamics of the labor market.

Manpower adjustments, however, work with varying degrees of smoothness and roughness. Time-lags are most often involved. Labor-market imbalances take place in terms of unemployment and/or underemployment of manpower. In addition, the chronically depressed area or industry appears to develop even in a growing economy. To facilitate the process of manpower adjustment to rapidly changing requirements, governmental policies are fashioned to deal directly with placement of workers, training and education, and revitalization of economically depressed regions. Superimposed upon this, we have private means developed within industry and also between union and management organizations in facilitating the adjustment of workers to changing economic conditions.

Manpower problems are complex and interrelated with the whole fabric of society as outlined in this chapter. The scope of this book will be limited essentially to the economics of the labor market—to manpower as a factor of production in the economic process. As a further limitation in scope, our discussion will relate primarily to the United States, though the experiences of other nations will be presented at times to illustrate alternative approaches and trends. Finally, our approach will be mainly a presentation and exploration of *concepts* of labor-market analysis. Empirical data will be used sparingly and only to illustrate specific concepts in our study of the "Economics of the Labor Market."

SUMMARY

Manpower economics is the subdivision of economics that deals with the forces operating within labor markets. It is concerned with the development and utilization of the human resources in an economy. In the United States most labor-market questions can be analyzed from the point of view of a decentralized market economy. There are many important institutions which react within the various labor markets in any economy. These institutions would include households, business firms, and Governments.

The labor force of an economy is composed of all the people in the economy past some arbitrary age (16 years in the United States) who are either working or are looking for work. The civilian labor force (labor force less the armed forces) can be divided into an employment and an unemployment category. A member of the labor force is employed if he or she has a job. The unemployment category would include any member of the civilian labor force who did not have a job and was looking for one. The LFPR is the percentage of the population (past the arbitrary age) which is in the labor force (either employed or unemployed) at a given period of time.

A listing of current labor-market problems would include the problem of lack of skill on the part of many workers; the entry of workers much later into the labor force with more education; the marked increases in the labor-force participation of women; the increased rate of occupational obsolescence; and earlier retirement of workers coupled with longer life expectancies.

To summarize, manpower analysis is the study of the preparation, application, and retirement of workers in the labor force as they produce goods and services and augment the wealth and well-being of a society and the individuals in society.

BIBLIOGRAPHY

Sanford Cohen, *Labor in the United States,* Charles E. Merrill Books, Inc., Columbus, Ohio (1970)

Eli Ginzberg, *Manpower Agenda for America,* McGraw-Hill, New York (1968)

Stanley H. Ruttenberg, *Manpower Challenge of the 1970's: Institutions and Social Change,* Johns Hopkins Press, Baltimore, Md. (1970)

Employment and Earnings, U.S. Department of Labor, Bureau of Labor Statistics, Washington, D.C., Vol. 1—17

MANPOWER AND
HUMAN CAPITAL FORMATION

2.1 MANPOWER UTILIZATION AND SOCIAL WELFARE

Man participates in economic society both as a factor of production, a producer of goods and services in the economic process, and also as a consumer and recipient of the benefits and burdens generated by the production process. He is born with certain hereditary characteristics, is educated and trained as a citizen in society and as a worker in the labor force. For all except a few individuals, virtually all members of society must develop work skills of a marketable nature, find jobs within the labor force, adapt to social and technological constraints on the work scene, and eventually leave the work force through death or retirement. Over the working years of a member of the labor force, he will change jobs and locations of work in response to economic and noneconomic considerations, experience unemployment, and in numerous ways will be influenced by policies of Governments, unions, and private firms.

From the point of view of society, the degree of participation of the population in the labor force has a vital role in the determination of the social and economic welfare of society as a whole. The larger the labor force, given the capital, natural resources, and technology, the greater will be an economy's capacity to produce goods and services. This in turn provides the means for further increasing the educational level of the population, raising the cultural level of society, increasing health and medical standards, or providing the basis of military might and political power on the world scene.

The efficient development and utilization of manpower in an economic system facilitates the attainment of goals and values established by a society. Conversely we can also say that the values of society are influenced by production processes, consumer aspirations, and the nature of labor's participation in economic activity. In a democratic system, goals and values imply the importance, worth, and dignity of the individual. In an authoritarian system, values imply the enhancement of the position of an ideology, a dictator, or a ruling elite. In the study of labor-market process and change the ends are inseparable from the means used to develop manpower within an economic system. In a democratic society, economic values imply that each individual will be given the opportunity to develop according to his abilities and desires. It also involves the orderly settlement of industrial conflict through organizations of workers, managers, and the public interest represented by Governments. A democratic system in essence implies not only the removal of handicaps imposed in an arbitrary fashion by other groups in society, but also a positive effort in creating an environment which will be favorable to the development of the abilities and motivations of workers.

A healthy and democratic system necessitates a mobile and fluid labor force which is alert to emerging job opportunities. This, however, loses its meaning if the institutions of society do not create better knowledge of job opportunities through employment services, or if entry into an occupation is restricted without regard to skill or ability. Moreover, geographical, industrial, and occupational mobility must be accompanied by some degree of social mobility as well. In addition to a highly mobile society cognizant of job opportunities, a democratic society must provide the conditions which will maintain reasonably full employment of manpower and other economic resources to prevent economic waste through underutilization and to insure the stability of a free and democratic system. Further, beyond economic stability and the lessening of fluctuations in output and employment, a democratically oriented society must achieve economic growth within the framework of often conflicting goals of its various subgroups. The political process, therefore, becomes firmly blended with the process of economic stability and growth. Some planning may be consistent with a democratic system. This planning, however, takes place of necessity through complex forces of supply and demand within the marketplace as well as through the ballot box in the political arena.

2.2 HUMAN CAPITAL

When we talk about manpower utilization and manpower development it becomes very useful to talk about manpower as a form of capital—i.e., human capital. Just as an economy can achieve a higher level of gross national product (GNP) by technological advances which improve physical capital,[1] an economy can improve its human capital and increase GNP. People can increase their capabilities as producers by investing in themselves.

Adam Smith and other writers of the classical economics period have recognized the capital nature of labor. Smith indicated further that the *Wealth of Nations* was largely dependent on the number of workers in an economy as well as the level of skills in ex-

---

[1] By physical capital we of course mean goods which are used in the production of other goods and services.

istence. Modern writers have gone even further. Professor Theodore Schultz[2] and others have recognized explicitly that human resources are a form of capital and that more should be considered in manpower analysis than merely the number of workers in existence. Various attempts have been made to relate the returns to education and the growth of national income and progress.

The nature and size of the labor force of an economy depends upon the state of technological development, the volume and nature of natural resources, population size, and the extent of the market. The latter factor permits the specialization of the labor force. This acts as a permissive variable. Whether labor skills are developed depends further on the social and cultural development of an economy. Progress in the manpower field, therefore, should be viewed as continuous. Old skills are made obsolete, and capital values destroyed. New skills appear. A full analysis of the manpower of a nation must include a study of all levels of education—formal education at the primary, secondary, and college levels, as well as vocational educational programs and training and apprenticeship relationships on the job.

Our human resources are, of course, the people who live in a nation. They are essential in the production of goods and services. But the number of workers represents only one of many dimensions. Quality, effort, and coordination must be considered in conjunction with numbers in the labor force.

The above propositions can be demonstrated by imagining an economy with the land, physical capital, and technology of the United States of today, but which attempted to produce goods and services with a labor force which had no schooling, no on-the-job training, no labor-market information (outside the immediate locality) and a 40-year life expectancy. What would that economy produce as compared to the U.S. economy of today? Surely, GNP would be much lower without a trained, educated, informed, and healthy labor force. The exact opposite case was probably true in West Germany and Japan after World War II with a large stock of human capital relative to their physical capital; and so the rate of return to investment in nonhuman capital appeared to be very high in these countries after World War II.[3]

Human capital can be improved by formal education, on-the-job training, fuller information about job opportunities, migration, and better health care. Thus each of these activities can be examined as investments in human capital. Looking at these investments from the worker's point of view, they each, ideally, have the same effect, and this effect is shown in Fig. 2.1.

In Fig. 2.1, the NN curve represents the lifetime earnings profile of a worker who did not invest in his "capital." Age A represents the beginning of his working life and

---

[2]The current literature on the capital nature of manpower is extensive. Suggestive of current approaches is an article by Professor Theodore W. Schultz, "Investment in Human Capital," *Amer. Econ. Rev.*, **51**(1), March (1961).

[3]See Theodore W. Schultz, "Reflections on Investment in Man," *J. polit Econ.*, Supplement, p. 1–8, October 1962. This entire supplement consisted of eight articles on the topic of Investment in Human Beings.

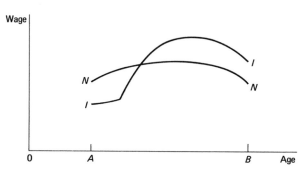

FIG 2.1   Investment in human capital

age *B* represents retirement. Now if this worker were to invest in improving his productivity (such as going to school, or undergoing on-the-job training), he would probably have a lifetime earnings curve similar to *II* in Fig. 2.1. Most investments in human capital cause the worker to earn less during the first few years of his working life, but then his lifetime earnings will rise above the noninvestment profile. The exact relationship between *NN* and *II* depends on the particular investment. A migration investment would cost the worker a "loss" (the cost of moving) the first year, but would probably yield a quick return right after that,[4] and investing in a college degree (instead of stopping at a high-school education) would cost the worker four years of foregone income plus tuition plus books, but would probably yield a much higher return than simply a job change.

2.3 RATES OF RETURN

Once we look at education, training, etc., as investments in human capital, the next step is to talk about the rates of return these investments earn. These rates of return can be calculated on a private basis or on a total basis. When the returns are calculated on a private basis, then all costs not borne by the private individual (such as that portion of the education costs that are paid by society and not the individual user) are excluded from the rate-of-return calculation.

These rates of return can be viewed as the percentage return that the money value of a particular investment yields over the lifetime of the worker. Thus, if a move from one job to another costs $500 but yields a salary increase of $525 in one year, it has a rate of return of 5%.[5] Once a worker knows the private costs and private lifetime bene-

---

[4]We are assuming rational workers; that is, workers who invest only when they expect a positive return in excess of the investment costs.

[5]Of course, very few investments have a pay-off lifetime of only one year. But the principle is the same for a 20-year investment as for a 1-year investment. Thus, if *C* is the cost of an

fits of each possible investment, he can make a rational decision about which investments he should undertake to improve his human capital. Moreover, a society interested in developing its human resources in an efficient manner would want to know the total costs and total benefits (or total rates of return) on every possible form of investment in human capital, so that it could select the best investment programs.

Although it is fairly easy to indicate in general how the rates of return are calculated, we do not want to imply that the actual calculations are simple. Both the private and total costs of any investment are usually not too difficult to estimate, but the future benefits may be very difficult. On the private level, the worker has to estimate what each investment will pay over his lifetime. We all know how difficult this can be in the real world. On the total or social level there are even larger problems. How does one calculate the benefits that society reaps from education or training which increase literacy, help people communicate with their neighbor, develop a sense of citizen duty, etc.?[6]

2.4 SOME RECENT EMPIRICAL ATTEMPTS TO MEASURE HUMAN CAPITAL

Professor Gary Becker has made some recent attempts to measure what is probably the largest type of investment in human capital in the United States—returns on investments for advanced education.[7] Becker estimated a return of 14.5% in 1939 and 12.7% in 1949 for white males investing in a college education. The rate of return for nonwhites in 1939 was about 2 percentage points lower for those living in the South, and about 6 percentage points lower for nonwhites living in the North. Becker hypothesized that this situation was due to a greater white/nonwhite wage differential in the South for workers who did not attend college. The rate of return for a college education in the 1940–1955 period appeared to be about 12% before tax, and about 9% after tax.

(Footnote 5 *continued*)

investment and R is the annual yield from the investment, the following relationship is true:

$$C = \frac{R}{(1 + r)} + \frac{R}{(1 + r)^2} + \cdots + \frac{R}{(1 + r)^n},$$

where r is the rate of return and n is the number of years the investment yields a return. A good discussion of rates of return applied to one form of investment in human capital (education) can be found in W. Lee Hansen, "Total and Private Rates of Return to Investment in Schooling," *J. polit. Econ.* 128–140 (April 1963).

[6]See Burton A. Weisbrod, "Investment in Human Capital," *J. human Resources*, 5–21 (Summer 1966). For an application of the human capital concept to international development, see Frederick Harbison and Charles A. Myers, *Education, Manpower and Economic Growth; Strategies of Human Resource Development*, McGraw-Hill, New York (1964).

[7]See Gary S. Becker, *Human Capital*, National Bureau of Economic Research Study, Columbia University Press, New York (1964); and Gary S. Becker, *Investment in Education*, National Bureau of Economic Research, New York (1965).

Professor Becker has also calculated rates of return from high-school education. The returns seem to be 16% in 1939 and 20% in 1949. It seems that the rates of return for high-school and college education for all groups in the U.S. economy declined gradually from 1900 to 1940, and has risen somewhat since World War II.

Estimates such as the above are very valuable, but they have major limitations. Studying yields on investment in human capital is very difficult since it takes the better part of a lifetime to accurately determine the return of those who went to college a generation earlier. Moreover, one cannot clearly attribute the superior income performance of college graduates over high-school graduates only to the education received. College in some ways is a screening device which separates out those with greater than average intelligence, diligence, and aspirations, and one would expect such persons to earn more income in later life whether or not they had gone to college.

Of course, the choice of attaining more education is not purely an economic choice, and so its justification should not rest only on an economic cost-benefit calculus. For example, if education can lead to a fuller life and enjoyment of literature and the arts, then an individual must consider these benefits as well as any economic benefits when he is deciding the optimal amount he should invest in education.

Professor Jacob Mincer has looked at another form of investment in human capital and found results similar to the above returns for education.[8] Mincer estimated the return to on-the-job training in 1950 to be 9.0 to 12.7% when looking at total costs. The return is about 8.5 to 11.3% when looking at private costs after tax.

We will look at the costs and benefits of some manpower programs in the United States, both from the theoretical and the empirical points of view, in Chapter 15. While a large amount of good research has been done in the area of investment in human capital, a great deal more work (both theoretical and empirical) needs to be done. We need better methods of accurately measuring costs and benefits before we can get better data on rates of return on investments in human capital.

2.5 THE NATIONAL STOCK OF HUMAN CAPITAL

Professor Theodore Schultz has estimated the United States' accumulated wealth in the form of human capital by looking at the replacement cost of formal education (which includes income foregone during the years of schooling).[9] In 1929, the amount of human capital was 24% of the amount of physical capital ($208 billion versus $872 billion in 1968 dollars); however, by 1970 human capital was projected to be 54% of physical capital ($1090 billion versus $1980 billion in 1968 dollars). The annual rate of growth of human capital is 4.1% for the labor force, and the rate is 2.0% per year for physical

---

[8]See Jacob Mincer, "On-the-Job Training: Costs, Returns and Implications," *J. polit. Econ.*, Supplement (October 1962).

[9]Theodore W. Schultz, *The Economic Value of Education*, Columbia University Press, New York (1963). For a concise review of this and other mentioned works in the area of human capital see Allan M. Cartter, "The Economics of Higher Education" in Neil W. Chamberlain (Editor), *Contemporary Economic Issues*, Richard D. Irwin, (Homewood, Illinois, 1969).

capital. The period of most rapid growth in human capital investment in the United States seems to have been since World War II.

2.6 IMPLICATIONS OF THE HUMAN-CAPITAL CONCEPT

In the remainder of this text we believe it would be helpful to think of manpower as a human form of capital. Thus, when we talk about unemployment, we will be talking about idle capital; when we talk about training or educating workers, we will be talking about improving capital; and when we talk about better job-market information, we will be talking about improving capital by moving it into a position where it is more productive.

One last point should be made now. When we are dealing with human capital (manpower) we must always keep in mind that many of the benefits of investing in human capital cannot easily be measured, but this cannot stop economists from estimating what are the best manpower programs (investments) for employing our idle human capital and constantly upgrading our human capital.

SUMMARY

The degree of participation of the population in the labor force has a vital role in the determination of the social and economic welfare of society as a whole. The larger the labor force (given the capital, natural resources, and technology) the greater will be an economy's capacity to produce goods and services.

In discussing manpower utilization and manpower development, we find it useful to talk about manpower as a form of capital—human capital. Human capital can be improved by various investments. These investments would include formal education, on-the-job training, fuller job-market information, and better health care.

Most investments in human capital cause the worker to earn less during the first part of his working life, but then his lifetime earnings will rise above the noninvestment level. Once we look at education, skill training, etc., as investments in human capital, we can then talk about the rates of return earned by the average person on these investments.

From this point forward we can talk about manpower as human capital. Thus unemployment can be viewed as idle capital; skill training can be viewed as improving capital; and better job-market information can be viewed as moving capital into a more productive position.

BIBLIOGRAPHY

Gary Becker, *Human Capital*, Columbia University Press, New York (1964)

W. Lee Hansen, "Total and Private Rates of Return to Investment in Schooling," *J. polit. Econ.* (April 1963)

"Investment in Human Beings," *J. polit. Econ.*, Supplement (October 1962)

Burton A. Weisbrod, "Investment in Human Capital," *J. human Resources* (Summer 1966)

EMPLOYMENT AND
MANPOWER UTILIZATION   Part II

At the macroeconomic level employment is determined by the aggregate decisions of households to purchase goods and services, decisions of firms to produce goods and utilize resources, as well as the multiroles of Government as a consumer, producer, and intervenor in the economy. Trade-offs, priorities, and goals are determined in the aggregate by millions of decisions made by individuals and groups.

At the microeconomic level, manpower utilization is determined by the forces of supply and demand, operating with cues from wages, prices, and output decisions. Manpower and other economic resources are managed by firms in producing goods and services. Workers respond to wage and income cues in the labor market and choose occupations and areas of residence, and other decisions relating to labor-force participation.

THE DETERMINATION OF
THE GENERAL LEVEL OF EMPLOYMENT   3

3.1 THE THEORY OF INCOME (EMPLOYMENT) DETERMINATION

We will begin our discussion of manpower economics by discussing the factors which determine the general or aggregate level of employment in an economy.[1] Before the reader can be concerned with employment and unemployment levels in specific industries and occupations, he must have some idea of how the employment and unemployment levels are set in the nation—which is the *aggregate* of all the specific industries and occupations. The questions we will be concerned with are what determines GNP, and what relationship exists between employment (and its counterpart—unemployment) and GNP.

3.1.1 A CIRCULAR FLOW DIAGRAM

Before we go into the theoretical model which will help us to understand the determination of aggregate employment levels, we should look at a simplification of the economy (in the form of a circular flow diagram) in order to set the stage for a study of this model. We will look at an economy composed of a public sector, a business sector and a Government sector.

In Fig. 3.1 we can see that both the Government and business sectors demand labor[2] (for which they pay wages) from the household sector. This labor is used to produce goods and services (which are purchased for money payments by the household and Government sectors).

What we want to determine now is how the level of goods and services is set

---

[1]At this point a review of some basic macroeconomic principles would be desirable. The reader's attention is directed to P. A. Samuelson, *Economics*, McGraw-Hill, New York (1967), Chapters 10–13, for the necessary proofs of the following macroeconomic model.

[2]There are of course other factors of production (capital, land, etc.), but we are concentrating on the labor (or manpower) factor of production.

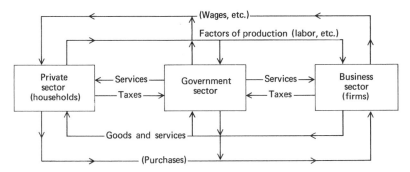

FIG. 3.1 Diagram of a hypothetical economy

by the economy, and what this level means in terms of employment (the demand for labor).

The following theoretical model is derived for an economy with a public sector which can consume (spend for goods and services) or save (refrain from using for goods and services) every dollar of its income; which the households earn by selling their labor, etc., on the market; a Government sector which taxes the economy and spends the money on Government expenditures; and a business sector which produces goods and services to sell and which invests (spends money to acquire capital goods such as plant and equipment) part of its income in order to be able to produce more products in the future.

Thus such an economy can be identified as a $C + I + G$ economy—where C stands for consumption, I stands for planned investment, and G stands for Government expenditures. As we shall see, $C + I + G$ are the total expenditures which take place in an economy, in any given period of time, and they play a key role in determining GNP—and thus in determining the nation's aggregate employment level.

3.2 THE THEORETICAL MODEL

In order to determine an economy's level of GNP we are really determining its equilibrium level of GNP. The equilibrium level of GNP is the only level of GNP which is maintainable—it is the level of GNP an economy will come to rest at (given its natural resource level and technology) in a given period of time.

We can start deriving our model with the use of a schedule (or table) and a diagram.

Figure 3.2 is a diagrammatic representation of Table 3.1. Together they answer the question of what will be the equilibrium (or maintainable) level of GNP for the hypothetical economy represented in Table 3.1. As the reader can see, the hypothetical economy has a business sector which plans to invest $60 billion (regardless of the current level of GNP), and a Government sector which will spend $90 billion on expenditures. Although there is no column marked Taxes in Table 3.1, the assumption is that taxes will be equal to $90 billion (this is the assumption Table 3.1

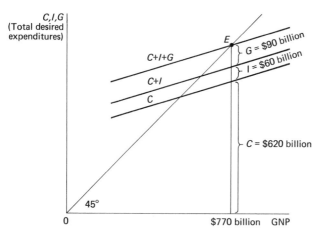

FIG. 3.2 Diagrammatic interpretation of Table 1

is built upon—however, this assumption could be changed without changing any of the theory). Finally, our hypothetical economy has a household sector which will consume its net income (gross income minus taxes) as shown in column 2 of Table 3.1, and save as shown in column 3 of Table 3.1 ($C + S$ = net income).

What is the equilibrium level of GNP? It is $770 billion. Why isn't it at some other level of GNP? The reason it is *not* at some other level of GNP is that the equilibrium condition is satisfied *only* at the $770 billion level.

We know from macroeconomics that the equilibrium GNP condition is that planned total expenditures ($C + I + G$) must equal current GNP. Checking Table 3.1, we see that $C + I + G$ is equal to GNP only at $770 billion. For all levels of GNP below $770 billion, $C + I + G$ (or total desired expenditures) is *greater* than current

TABLE 3.1 Hypothetical $C + I + G$ economy and
equilibrium GNP

GNP*	C*	S*	I*	G*	Change in GNP
$620	$500	$30	$60	$90	GNP rises
670	540	40	60	90	GNP rises
720	580	50	60	90	GNP rises
770	620	60	60	90	No GNP change; equilibrium
820	660	70	60	90	GNP falls
870	700	80	60	90	GNP falls
920	740	90	60	90	GNP falls
970	780	100	60	90	GNP falls

*In billions of dollars.

GNP. This means that the total demand for goods and services $(C + I + G)$ is greater than the current level of production of goods and services (GNP). Because of this strong demand, businessmen will find their inventories declining, and since inventories are part of investment, they will not be able to maintain their planned investment (I) at the current level of GNP. Wanting to profit from this demand businessmen will expand production—meaning GNP will expand or rise. For all levels of GNP above \$770 billion, $C + I + G$ is *less* than current GNP. This means that the total demand for goods and services $(C + I + G)$ is less than the current level of production of goods and services (GNP). Because of this weak demand, businessmen will find their inventory building and they will not be able to maintain their planned investment at the current level of GNP. Not wanting to be forced to hold high levels of unsold goods, businessmen will contract production—meaning GNP will contract or fall.

Thus, only when $C + I + G$ = GNP (or total desired expenditures equals current output) will the economy be at the equilibrium level of GNP. Now that we have solved this problem with Table 3.1 we can do it again but this time using Fig. 3.2 (which is simply the diagrammatic interpretation of Table 3.1). The reason for using a diagrammatic approach is that it gives us the same correct answer to our question, but does it in a simpler manner than the table approach.

Looking at Fig. 3.2 we see that the vertical axis is used to measure C, I and G, or total desired expenditures when these three figures are added together, and the horizontal axis is used to measure levels of GNP. The 45° line is just a construction line which aids us in determining the equilibrium level of GNP (point E in Fig. 3.2). The 45° line (by definition) is equidistant from the vertical and horizontal axis. This means that every point on the 45° line is a point where the level of $C + I + G$ (total desired expenditures) is equal to the level of GNP.

In Fig. 3.2 when we construct the consumption curve (a diagram of the consumption schedule—column 2 of Table 3.1) we get an upward-sloping line. If we add I and G to C we get the $C + I + G$ (or total desired expenditures) curve. When the $C + I + G$ curve intersects the 45° line (point E) we are at the equilibrium level of GNP. Why? Because when the $C + I + G$ curve intersects the 45° line we know that at that point $C + I + G$ equals GNP, and that is the equilibrium GNP condition.

Looking again at Fig. 3.2, we see that for all levels of GNP below equilibrium (to the left of point E) total desired expenditures are greater than GNP, and this strong demand will lead businessmen to expand production (or GNP); whereas for all levels of GNP above equilibrium (to the right of point E) total desired expenditures are less than GNP, and this weak demand will lead businessmen to contract production (or GNP).

3.3 EMPLOYMENT–GNP RELATIONSHIP

No level of output or GNP can be produced without inputs—and the labor of manpower input is what we want to concentrate on. For every level of GNP there is some level of labor (N) which, in combination with the other inputs, is required to produce the output or GNP.

In order to simplify our model we will combine all types of labor together into one labor market.[3] In the next two chapters we will discuss the demand for labor (D_N) and the supply of labor (S_N) in detail, but for now we need only to know that the aggregate D_N is downward sloping (meaning that as the price of labor decreases the quantity demanded of labor will increase) and the aggregate S_N is upward sloping (meaning that as the price of labor increases the quantity of labor supplied will increase).

Combining Figs. 3.3 and 3.4, we see that in order to have full employment (no person who is able to and willing to and is looking for work is without a job) the D_N must equal the S_N, or we must be at point E_1 in Fig. 3.4. Now every level of employment (N) is associated with a level of GNP. That is, *given* our other factors of production, each level of N will combine with them to produce a different level of GNP. In symbols, GNP $= f(N)$; so that $GNP_1 = f(N_1)$. Thus, in order to achieve N_1 in the labor market, the economy must achieve GNP_1 as its equilibrium GNP level in the commodities market.

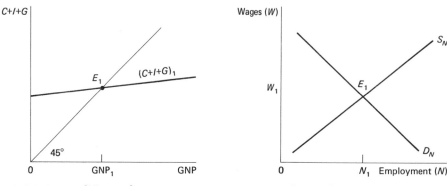

FIG. 3.3 Commodities market   FIG. 3.4 Labor market

If the real world existed exactly as diagrammed in Figs. 3.3 and 3.4, then we would never have to worry about unemployment. Why? Because without rigidities in the above markets the D_N will adjust to achieve full employment.

If $(C + I + G)_1$ is the correct total desired expenditures curve in the commodities market, then D_{N_1} will be the demand for labor in the labor market,[4] and GNP_1 will be the equilibrium level of GNP (point E_1 of Fig. 3.5) and N_1 will be the equilibrium level of employment (point E_1 of Fig. 3.6). If there was to be an increase in worker (and/or capital) productivity so that $(C + I + G)_2$ is the correct total desired expenditures curve in the commodities market, then D_{N_2} will be the demand for labor in the labor market, and GNP_2 will be the equilibrium level of GNP (point

---

[3]This assumption can be weakened without changing any of our major conclusions.

[4]As we shall discover in Chapter 4, the D_N is a *derived* demand—derived from the demand for goods and services.

E_2 of Fig. 3.5) and N_2 will be the equilibrium level of employment (point E_2 of Fig. 3.6).

    Thus, we have exposed the basic N–GNP relationship. The aggregate employment level in an economy depends on the aggregate level of production (GNP), since the D_N is derived from the demand for goods and services ($C + I + G$).

3.4 REAL-WORLD RIGIDITIES

The above N–GNP relationship is valid in the real world, but is further complicated by the possibility of unemployment in the labor market due to real-world rigidities.

    In the real world there probably exists in the labor market a "floor on wages" as diagrammed in Fig. 3.8 (the horizontal portion of the S_N curve). This "floor" means that labor will not work for wages *below* W_1. The "floor" can be due to many reasons including minimum wage laws, union collective bargaining agreements, and society's custom as to what labor should work for (as a minimum wage), but no matter what the reasons the "floor" allows the development of unemployment.

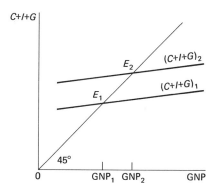
FIG. 3.5 Commodities market

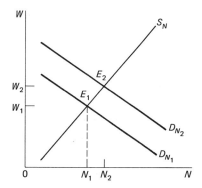
FIG. 3.6 Labor market

    Thus, if $(C + I + G)_1$ is the correct total desired expenditures curve, then GNP$_1$ will be the equilibrium level of GNP. Furthermore, D_{N_1} will be the demand curve for labor, and N_1 will be the equilibrium level of employment. However, there is no guarantee that $C + I + G$ will be at the correct level to achieve full employment in a real-world economy with rigidities in the labor market. So, if for some reason (such as a decrease in I on the part of the business sector, due to lack of confidence in the business sector) the total desired expenditures curve were $(C + I + G)_2$, then the equilibrium level of GNP will be GNP$_2$ (point E_2 of Fig. 3.7). Moreover, since the general demand for labor has declined, the corresponding D_N curve in the labor market is D_{N_2}. The full-employment point would now be E_3; however, if unions (or some other group) could resist any cut in the wage level, they would introduce a wage rigidity in Fig. 3.8 as shown. Due to the rigidity in the labor market, this lower D_N curve will mean unemployment. The unemployment is N_1 minus N_2—N_1 being the supply of workers looking for jobs at the prevailing wage (W_2) and N_2 being the level of employment available given the GNP level (GNP$_2$).

Once we introduce the idea of wage rigidities into the labor market, it is not surprising that unemployment becomes an important problem. With rigidities, it would be a rare coincidence if every year the level of $C + I + G$ would be just enough to lead to a GNP equilibrium which translates into full employment in the labor market. This is especially true since at least one component of total expenditures, investment (I), tends to be highly volatile. Thus, if businessmen believe, for any reason, that the future will not be very profitable for new investments, they may cut the level of I. In the absence of other compensating expenditure changes the level of aggregate demand ($C + I + G$) will thus fall, assuming rigidities in the labor market, and cause unemployment to develop.

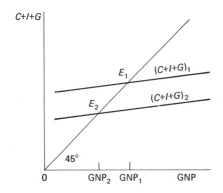

FIG. 3.7 Commodities market

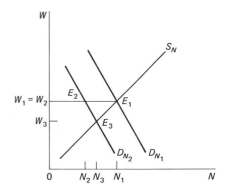

FIG. 3.8 Labor market

Once unemployment develops, the Government sector can intercede with monetary and/or fiscal policies to raise aggregate demand in the commodities market. The fiscal policies would consist of the Government sector increasing its level of expenditures (G) or cutting its taxes (to put more money into the hands of consumers). The monetary policies work through their effect on the money supply. In a recession (*low* aggregate demand and resulting unemployment) the money supply could be increased to lower interest rates and thereby encourage more investment thus raising aggregate demand. In an inflation (*high* aggregate demand and resulting price increases) the money supply could be decreased to raise interest rates and thereby discourage investment, thus lowering aggregate demand.[5]

In our hypothetical case of Figs. 3.7 and 3.8, if the aggregate demand was $(C + I + G)_2$ we already know that the economy would have $(N_1 - N_2)$ unemployment.

---

[5]For a discussion of monetary policies and their effect on GNP, see P. A. Samuelson, *Economics*, McGraw-Hill, New York (1967), Chapters 16–18.

However, now the government could use monetary and/or fiscal policies to raise aggregate demand in Fig. 3.7 from $(C + I + G)_2$ to $(C + I + G)_1$, and thereby raise the D_N in Fig. 3.8 from D_{N_2} to D_{N_1}. Employment will rise from N_2 to N_1—ending unemployment.

One final note. Unemployment can be due to reasons other than a low level of I. For example, the level of aggregate demand may be adequate to have full employment with the S_N shown in Fig. 3.8, but there may be a large increase in the supply of available workers (young people, women, etc.) without a similar rise in aggregate demand, leading to an unemployment problem. Moreover, unemployment can come about due to so-called structural changes (such as automation) which must be approached in a different manner than unemployment due to insufficient aggregate demand.

What we have done so far is set forth the theoretical model which has exposed the determinants of equilibrium GNP—which in turn determines the economy's aggregate level of employment (and unemployment). What we would like to do now is examine some empirical evidence concerning the determination of the general (or aggregate) level of employment.

3.5 SOME EMPIRICAL EVIDENCE

Now that we have examined the theoretical model relating aggregate production (GNP) to the aggregate level of employment, it would be beneficial to apply our theory to some real-world data. We will examine the period from 1948 to 1964 in the United States.[6]

3.5.1 THE DATA
The data are given in Table 3.2.

3.5.2 THE ANALYSIS
Looking at the first time interval (1948—1953) in Table 3.2 we notice a relatively high rate of growth in GNP, and a low unemployment rate. The two were the consequence of a good demand for goods and services by consumers (following the World War II years during which consumers could not freely consume due to rationing), and very heavy Government spending (especially the Federal Government) for the Marshall Plan and during the Korean war. Investment by U.S. business firms was low due to the expanded plant capacity of the World War II era, but the Government's fiscal policy of high expenditures provided the stimulus to keep GNP growing at a rate which kept unemployment below 4%. Moreover, there was a low rate of entry

---

[6]For a good discussion of the current U.S. business expansion contrasted to recent economic expansions and contractions, see R. A. Gordon and M. S. Gordon, *Prosperity and Unemployment*, Wiley, New York (1966), Part I.

TABLE 3.2 Economic change in the U.S. economy—selected time intervals

Variables	1948–1953	1953–1957	1957–1960	1960–1964
	Annual percentage rates of change—1954 prices			
Total GNP	4.7	2.6	2.5	4.1
Consumption (C)	3.4	3.6	3.2	3.9
Gross investment (I)	0.3	3.5	1.2	4.2
Government expenditures (G): total	14.9	−2.7	1.9	3.8
Federal	20.8	−7.4	−0.7	3.3
State & local	5.8	6.0	5.3	4.4
Exports	2.2	10.4	0.7	7.6
Imports	6.2	4.5	4.0	5.5
	Average annual percentage			
Total unemployment	3.7	3.9	5.6	5.8
	Change from beginning to end of interval—millions			
Youth (18 to 24 years) in civilian labor force	−2.2	0.7	1.0	1.4

Sources: R. A. Gordon and M. S. Gordon, *Prosperity and Unemployment*, Wiley, New York (1966), p. 18; and U.S. Department of Labor, *Manpower Report of the President*, U.S. Government Printing Office, Washington, D.C. (April 1967), pp. 203–217.

of young people (age 18–24) into the labor force—in fact, the number of young people in the civilian labor force fell from 1948–1953 by 2.2 million.[7]

The middle two time intervals (1953–1957 and 1957–1960) were periods of very slow-growing GNP, and therefore fairly rapidly rising unemployment. Although consumption continued at a good pace, the Federal Government decreased its expenditures drastically. In the 1953–1957 period there was an investment boom which offset a large part of the decrease in Government expenditures, but was not large enough to keep the unemployment level from going up. However, in the 1957–1960 period the investment boom ended, but the government continued to spend at a low level. This combination helped put the unemployment level up to 5.6%. Added to the insufficient aggregate demand (or total desired expenditures) was the high entry of young people in the 1953–1957 and 1957–1960 intervals. An expanding labor supply and a slow-growing demand for goods and services made these eight years ones of stagnation as far as the level of GNP and aggregate level of employment were concerned.

Finally, the fourth time interval in Table 3.2 shows the U.S. economy beginning to rebound from the stagnation of the late 1950s. Consumption, investment, and

---

[7] A low rate of entry of young people into the labor force of course helps to maintain low unemployment levels, since fewer jobs need be provided by the economy.

Government expenditures were high enough to lead to a rising GNP level and, although GNP did not go high enough to eliminate the high level of unemployment, GNP was high enough to stabilize the level of unemployment. Many young people continued to enter the labor force, and the economy could not create enough jobs to get unemployment below 4%.

If we were to follow the progress of the U.S. economy for 2 more years we would see a high-rising level of GNP and a rapidly decreasing level of unemployment (as aggregate employment grew in spite of a continued rise in the entry of young people into the civilian labor force). What occurred in 1964 was the Kennedy–Johnson Administration tax cut, which helped increase GNP from $632 billion in 1964 to $732 billion in 1966. This GNP level was accompanied by an ever-decreasing level of unemployment—5.2% in 1964, 4.6% in 1965, and 3.9% in 1966.

What we have done above is take the relationships that we learned from our theoretical model, and use them to explain the trends in GNP and unemployment that we observed in the U.S. data. This same thing could be done for any economy and for any period of time.

In the next section we will examine the characteristics of the U.S. employment level as it has been in recent history, and as it probably will be in the next few years.

3.6 PAST, PRESENT, AND FUTURE U.S. AGGREGATE EMPLOYMENT LEVELS

There are many ways in which we can analyze and study the level and composition of aggregate employment. We can look at its age, color, and education, or we can study patterns of change in geographical composition. Of particular interest to manpower economists is the study of the attachment of workers by industry and occupation. This section will discuss some of the major trends in U.S. aggregate industrial and occupational employment.

3.6.1 PAST AND PRESENT INDUSTRIAL ATTACHMENT OF WORKERS

In general, all economic societies develop their extractive and agricultural industries first. Direct subsistence through hunting eventually is replaced by agriculture, and in turn emphasis gradually moves to the production of nondurable and durable goods in various industries of manufacturing. In the United States the period from the end of the Civil War in 1865 to the 1920s saw a dramatic shift out of employment in farm work to employment in the production of goods in manufacturing. From roughly the 1900s to 1950 high levels of agricultural productivity coupled with industrial and technological developments in the manufacturing industries brought about major shifts in the deployment of workers in the labor force.

The decade of the 1950s brought about continued reductions in agricultural and mining employment, with only a moderate increase in manufacturing. In contrast, trade, service, government, finance, insurance, and real estate grew rapidly. Over the decade of the 1950s service-producing industries exceeded goods-producing industries in employment. In 1960 goods-producing employment had declined to 26 million and 44.7% of total employment in relation to service-generated employment of 34 million jobs and 55.3% of the total.

All the above is demonstrated in Table 3.3. Moreover we can see the trends continuing into the 1960s. From 1960 to 1970 agricultural and mining employment decreased again, whereas manufacturing and contract construction employment rose moderately. The service-producing industries again grew faster than the goods-producing industries (from an employment point of view). Within the service-producing sector the fastest-growing segments were finance, insurance, real estate, service and miscellaneous, and Government (particularly state and local).

The shift of employment from primary industries to goods-producing, and eventually to the service-generating activities of an economy is but one aspect of the changing industrial attachment of the labor force. In addition, qualitative changes take place in the ratio between production and nonproduction employment. More accurately, employment becomes more roundabout. Fewer and fewer workers are directly involved in the production process, and greater numbers of workers are assigned to planning, research, development, and supervisory roles. Over a longer time period, from 1947 to 1963, the ratio of nonproduction employment to production employment in manufacturing changed from 16.4% of total employment to 26.1%.

TABLE 3.3   U.S. employment by major industrial division 1950, 1960, and 1970 (in thousands) (establishment data)

Industry division	1950 annual average	1960 annual average	1970* annual average	1950– 1960 percent change	1960– 1970 percent change
Total	52,382	59,671	74,123	13.9	24.2
Goods-producing industries	25,635	25,851	26,822	0.08	3.8
Agriculture	7,160	5,458	3,462	−23.7	−36.6
Mining	901	712	622	−21.0	−12.6
Contract construction	2,333	2,885	3,347	23.7	16.0
Manufacturing	15,241	16,796	19,391	10.2	15.5
Service-producing industries	26,747	33,840	47,301	26.5	39.8
Transportation & public utilities	4,034	4,004	4,498	− 0.07	− 12.3
Wholesale & retail trade	9,386	11,391	14,948	21.4	31.2
Finance, insurance, & real estate	1,919	2,669	3,679	39.1	37.8
Service & miscellaneous	5,382	7,423	11,578	37.9	56.0
Government	6,026	8,353	12,598	38.6	50.8

*1970 data preliminary.

Source: *Employment and Earnings*, U.S. Department of Labor, Washington, D.C. (February 1971). Vol. 17, No. 8, p. 26 and p. 55.

These changes were particularly dramatic in printing and publishing, chemicals, petroleum, and ordinance, where nonproduction employment exceeded 30% of total employment. This pattern of employment growth of jobs removed from direct production was also experienced in industries such as lumber and wood products, textiles, apparel, and to a lesser extent leather products. As a general rule, capital-intensive industries tend to generate marked increases in the nonproduction type of employment characterized by planning, research, and maintenance, while labor-intensive industries tend to attach large numbers of direct production workers involved in the actual production process.

Employment patterns by industry attachment of workers for 1950, 1960, and 1970 are indicated in Table 3.3.

3.6.2 PAST AND PRESENT OCCUPATIONAL ATTACHMENT OF WORKERS

Parallel to the changes that have taken place (and are continuing into the future) in the industrial structure of the employed labor force, significant changes have also taken place in the occupational structure of the United States. In general, farm employment has declined sharply for farm laborers. In 1900, close to 40% of the labor force was in farm occupations. Farm workers were roughly divided into 50% farmers and farm managers, and 50% farm laborers and foremen. By 1950, farm workers accounted for only 12% of the nation's employed labor force. Two-thirds of these were farmers and farm managers, whereas farm laborers were only one-third.

A second change in industrial employment over the last 50 years has been a compositional decrease in the proportion of laborer and blue-collar employment, and rapid growth in professional and other white-collar employment. By the end of the decade of the 1950s white-collar employment exceeded the number of blue-collar workers. The gap widened even more over the 1960s, as professional and technical employment emerged as a major sector of employment opportunity for workers in the U.S. economy.

In general, as the structure of employment has shifted from the primary industries (agriculture, mining, fishing) to secondary (manufacturing) to tertiary service industries, simultaneous changes have occurred in the occupational composition—and this has implied a movement away from lesser-skilled laborer jobs to highly skilled professional types of jobs. Table 3.4 shows the continuation of these basic trends in the occupational structure from 1950 to 1970. (The data are *not* strictly comparable to Table 3.3. Industrial employment is obtained from establishments, while occupational data is accumulated from households.)

3.6.3 FUTURE INDUSTRIAL AND OCCUPATIONAL ATTACHMENT OF WORKERS

The trends in industrial and occupational employment outlined above are expected to continue and possibly accelerate in the future. Manpower experts anticipate that there will be a continuation of major structural changes in the industrial, occupational, and geographical distribution of manpower. Agricultural employment is expected

TABLE 3.4 U.S. employment by major occupational group 1950, 1960, and 1970 (in thousands) (household data)

Major occupation group	1950 annual average	1960 annual average	1970 annual average	1950– 1960 percent change	1960– 1970 percent change
Total	59,648	66,681	78,627	11.8	17.0
White-collar workers	22,648	28,726	37,997	26.8	32.3
Professional, technical & kindred	4,490	7,475	11,140	66.5	49.0
Managerial	6,429	7,067	8,289	9.9	17.3
Clerical & kindred	7,632	9,783	13,714	28.2	40.2
Sales	3,822	4,401	4,854	15.1	10.3
Blue-collar workers	23,336	24,211	27,791	3.7	14.8
Craftsmen, foremen, & kindred	7,670	8,560	10,158	11.6	18.7
Operatives & kindred	12,146	11,986	13,909	− 1.3	16.0
Laborers (except farm & mine)	3,520	3,665	3,724	4.1	1.6
Service (including private household)	6,535	8,349	9,712	27.8	16.3
Farm workers	7,408	5,395	3,126	−27.2	−42.1

to drop by about 100,000 per year during the late 1970s under the impact of rising productivity, and the elimination of less efficient marginal farms. Over the ten-year period from 1965 to 1975, it is expected that there will be close to one million fewer workers in agriculture (Table 3.5).

Among nonfarm industries, those furnishing services are expected to continue to grow at a much more rapid rate than those producing goods. If conditions of full employment are maintained in the economy, the service-producing industries are expected to supply three times as many jobs in the mid-1970s as the goods-producing sector—roughly about 1 million as compared with 300,000 jobs annually. Moreover, within the goods-producing sector, the trend will be toward the growth of jobs in planning, research, and maintenance—in general, removed from the direct production of goods (Table 3.5).

In occupational terms, the fastest-growing occupations will be in the professional and technical field, followed closely by clerical and sales. Among manual and blue-collar jobs, only the most skilled group (craftsmen, foremen, and kindred) will expand at a rate at least as rapid as total employment. Labor-market analysts predict that the number of semiskilled jobs will increase at two-thirds the rate of growth of total employment. The number of unskilled jobs in the laborer classification will remain about the same, continuing a long-term relative decline in their proportion of total employment. At the semiskilled level there will be some expansion of jobs, particularly those related to personal services (Table 3.6).

3.7 A SUMMARY OF OUR FUTURE EMPLOYMENT LEVEL

It is difficult to predict the nature of the employment level of some future period. But, assuming that past trends continue into the future, the profile of U.S. employment level appears to include prospects for change in at least the following directions:

1. Fewer workers will be employed directly in farm work, with some increases in manufacturing, and great growth of employment in the service industries.
2. In occupational terms, there will be more white-collar workers and fewer manual, unskilled, blue-collar workers. Some increases will take place for skilled craftsmen, but declines may even appear for unskilled laborer jobs.
3. Workers will in all likelihood be compelled to "retool" their skills, and change jobs more frequently during their working lives as a result of an accelerated pace of occupational obsolescence.

TABLE 3.5 Projected U.S. employment, by industry division, 1965–1975 (establishment data)

Employment (millions)		Industry	Percentage change									
1965	1975		−30	−20	−10	0	10	20	30	40	50	60
65.4	80.0	All industries						_____ 22.3				
7.7	11.4	State and local Government								_____ 47.8		
9.1	12.9	Services, personal, professional, business								_____ 42.5		
3.2	4.2	Construction							_____ 31.5			
3.0	3.7	Finance, insurance and real estate						_____ 23.2				
12.7	16.1	Trade						_____ 26.7				
18.0	19.7	Manufacturing					_ 9.2					
4.0	4.6	Transportation, communication and public utilities					_____ 13.5					
2.4	2.7	Federal Government					_____ 15.4					
0.63	0.62	Mining			−1.9_							
4.6	3.7	Agriculture		−18.3____								

Source: U.S. Department of Labor, *Statistics on Manpower: A Supplement to the Manpower Report of the President*, U.S. Government Printing Office, Washington, D.C., (March 1969), p. 83.

TABLE 3.6 Projected U.S. employment, by occupational division, 1965—1975
(household data)

Employment (millions)		Occupational group	Percentage change −30 −20 −10 0 10 20 30 40 50
1965	1975		
71.1	87.2	*All occupations*	———— 22.7
8.9	12.9	Professional and technical workers	——————— 45.2
8.9	12.0	Service workers	—————— 34.4
11.1	14.8	Clerical workers	—————— 32.5
4.5	5.6	Sales workers	———— 25.0
7.3	9.0	Managers, officials, proprietors	———— 23.3
9.2	11.4	Craftsmen and foremen	———— 23.1
13.3	14.7	Operatives, e.g. assemblers, truck drivers, bus drivers	— 10.5
3.7	3.6	Nonfarm laborers	−2.7—
4.1	3.2	Farm workers	−21.6————

Source: U.S. Department of Labor, *Statistics on Manpower: a Supplement to the Manpower Report of the President.* U.S. Government Printing Office, Washington, D.C. (March 1969), p. 83.

4. With the massive problem of absorbing large numbers of workers into the labor force coupled with a rapidly increasing demand for education resulting from a more affluent and technological society, the "educational industry" will experience significant growth in the area of adult education, if occupational "retooling" needs are to be met.

SUMMARY

We can demonstrate, with a basic macroeconomic model of the economy, the relationship between the aggregate employment level and the aggregate level of production. The equilibrium level of production will occur where total desired expenditures equals the level of production (GNP), and this level of GNP will generate a particular level of labor demand which can be less than the supply of labor leading to some unemployment.

In the event of unemployment, the Federal Government may find it possible to utilize monetary and/or fiscal policies to reduce this labor-market imbalance. The above analysis can be utilized in the real world to explain the trends in GNP, consumption, investment, unemployment, etc.

There are at least two ways of examining U.S. aggregate employment levels. We can look at the industrial attachment of workers, and we can examine the occupational attachment of workers. From the industrial point of view, employment has shifted from primary industries to goods-producing industries, and eventually to the service-generating industries. Parallel changes have taken place in the occupational attachment of workers. Farm employment, especially farm laborers, has declined sharply, and there has been a shift from unskilled laborer employment with sharp increases in the white-collar employment occupations.

The future profile of the U.S. employment level appears to include more white-collar workers and fewer manual, unskilled, blue-collar workers. Some increases will take place for skilled craftsmen, but declines may even appear for unskilled laborer jobs. Workers will be compelled to "retool" their skills and change jobs more frequently as a result of an accelerated pace of occupational obsolescence. There will be a great growth of employment in the service industries.

BIBLIOGRAPHY

R. A. Gordon and M. S. Gordon, *Prosperity and Unemployment*, Wiley, New York (1966), Part I

U.S. Department of Labor, *Manpower Report of the President*, U.S. Government Printing Office, Washington D.C. (March 1970)

Paul A. Samuelson, *Economics*, McGraw-Hill, New York (1967)

THE SUPPLY OF LABOR— VARIATIONS IN SIZE AND COMPOSITION OF LABOR FORCE 4

In order to talk about the supply of labor (S_N) in an economy, be it the S_N at the macro- (or aggregate) level or micro- (or individual industry) level, we must talk about the economy's population base, and the population's choice between work and leisure, as well as the worker's choice between alternative occupations. Only when we have talked about the latter three factors can we construct an aggregate supply curve of labor, and the individual industry supply curves of labor.

In this chapter we will discuss an economy's population and the role it plays in economic growth. Then we will turn our attention to the worker choice between work and leisure, labor-force participation rates, worker choice between occupations, and trends in LFPRs.

4.1 POPULATION AND ECONOMIC GROWTH

Changes in the size and nature of population have far-reaching effects on the welfare of an economy. First, the quantity and quality of a nation's population influences the quantity and quality of labor supply that will be forthcoming. Second, the quantity and composition (age, sex, average size of families) of a nation's population influence the amount and composition of the goods and services which that nation consumes. Third, important economic philosophers have claimed that the age structure and rate of growth or decline of population exert an influence on the quantity and composition of savings and investment. Fourth, population changes affect a nation's standard of living.[1]

For most economic analyses, particularly short-run studies, population can be considered as a given datum. This is due to the fact that it takes time for population

---

[1]See A. J. Jaffe and Charles D. Stewart, *Manpower Resources and Utilization: Principles of Working Force Analysis*, Wiley, New York (1951), Chapter 16.

changes to react back on the economy in response to income and other economic variables that have an influence on population growth. Demographers can attempt to estimate future population by considering estimates of fertility and birth rates, mortality, and migration rates and patterns. For longer analyses, however, economists must be concerned with the interaction of economic variables (income, mobility and migration patterns, standards of living) and the relationship of these variables to such things as education and the training of the labor force in facilitating economic growth.

It has been a fashion of social scientists to relate population changes with levels of wages and/or incomes. Well-known relationships have been established between economic and demographic phenomena in terms of per capita income and mortality experience.[2] Beyond this direct relationship, moreover, rising health standards of more industrialized nations are readily applied to underdeveloped nations. An input of even meager resources in public health and medicine can yield effective and impressive results in health standards through a reduction in mortality rates. Current soaring population trends in Africa, South America, and Asia appear to be largely related to significant reductions in death rates rather than in increases in births as such.

The best-known explicit model on the relationship between economic factors and population changes was stated by Malthus.[3] In its simplest form the Malthusian doctrine stated that within the limits of biological possibility, birth rates were an increasing function of per capita income. The doctrine, as expounded by Malthus, held that population tended to increase each generation according to geometrical progression, i.e., 1—2—4—8—16—32, etc., whereas at best food supply increased in an arithmetical progression, i.e., 1—2—3—4—5—6—7, etc. Checks such as war, famine, and pestilences kept population within the limits imposed by the food supply. The only alternative to these checks, according to Malthus, was sexual restraint or delayed marriage. This theory was a long-run relationship. In the short run, variations between income levels (food supply) and birth rates could exist because of time lags involved in the process of adjustment. In general and over long generations, there was an inexorable tendency for population growth to follow changes in income. Productivity increases, through better technology, could temporarily stem the tide of population pressure, but invariably and in time, birth rates would catch up with the increases in income.

To fully understand the population explosion we must look at the relative changes that have taken place in the world's population over time. Harold F. Dorn has presented data showing the number of years that it has taken the world's population to double. Population experts have estimated that about 2000 years ago the population of the world was about one-quarter billion. By 1650 the population had doubled to one-half billion. Currently it is estimated that the 1975 estimate of four billion persons will

---

[2]See J. J. Spengler, "Population Theory," in *A Survey of Contemporary Economics*, American Economic Association, Richard D. Irwin, Homewood, Illinois (1952), Volume II.

[3]Thomas R. Malthus, *An Essay on the Principle of Population* (Reeves and Turner, London, 1878, 8th edition).

double in only 35 years, to eight billion by the year 2010.[4] Dorn points out that this rapid acceleration has been due to dramatic declines in mortality rates with consequent sharp increases in the average expectation of life.

The Malthusian doctrine has been challenged by several writers. One point of view claims that income and population change are *inversely* related, rather than the other way around, for societies experiencing growth beyond the primitive, subsistence level. This is not immediately apparent, inasmuch as declines in death rates of growing and industrialized economies make it appear that population growth will remain unchecked. As the average calorie intake of the population increases, it appears that population begins to taper off, especially as this relates to birth rates. As birth rates and death rates reach a more stable level, population growth tends to taper off. It has been noted by various writers on population analysis that there are differential birth rates in existence in all countries between rural and urban regions. With shifts of population from agricultural–rural areas to manufacturing in urban places, birth rates have generally fallen.

The population question can best be analyzed by considering the nations of the world in three distinct groups. Group I consists of most of Western Europe, Australia, New Zealand, and North America. This group comprises about 20% of the world's population and is characterized by low birth rates, low death rates, high calorie intake (about 3000 per day), and a relatively stable population. The food problem of these countries is minor, and there seems to be no doubt of their ability to feed their people within the current or next generation. High agricultural productivity is generally coupled with high rates of productivity in manufacturing. Also, large segments of the population are enrolled in schools at all levels of education.

Group II represents another 20% of the world's population, and consists of Eastern and Southeastern Europe, Japan, Spain, and a few South American countries, such as Brazil and Argentina. Here there is a low but rising industrial productivity, a high but falling birth rate, and a medium but falling death rate. These areas have high rates of natural increase, largely because their birth rate is not falling as fast as the death rate. Since they enjoy a food level of 2300 to 2800 calories per day (somewhat better than subsistence), the food versus population problem in these countries will depend on how fast they industrialize and what measures are taken to increase their food supplies.

Group III constitutes the problem area. Taking in Asia and neighboring islands, most of Africa and South and Central America, this group contains 60% of the world's population, lives on a semistarvation level of about 2000 calories a day, and is most illustrative of the Malthusian pressure of population on the food supply. This area has a high birth rate, fluctuating (and currently, diminishing) death rate with periodic crises resulting from food shortages, and in the past, epidemics.

Changes in income and food supply appear to be significant in the early transitional

---

[4]Harold F. Dorn, "World Population Growth," Chapter 2 in *The Population Dilemma*, edited by Philip M. Hauser, Prentice-Hall, Englewood Cliffs, N.J. (1963).

stages of an economy's development from lower to higher levels of industrial development. Death rates decline sharply and birth rates continue to remain at high levels. Possibly within a generation or so, birth rates begin to decline as population migrates to urban areas of concentration which are noted for lower birth rates than are found in rural and agricultural regions.

One interesting theory of population attributes population growth differentials to density of population in particular regions.[5] Raymond Pearl, summarizing much research on growth and reproduction of several biological species—including humans—concludes that the rate of reproduction or fertility is negatively correlated with density of population. As people concentrate in close proximity there occurs a marked dampening of the growth of population. Unlike Malthus, Pearl concludes his study of the reproduction of biological species—particularly humans—on an optimistic note. He emphasizes the adaptive nature of man. To date the massive population explosion of man has not been accompanied by a lowering of living standards. Rather, the opposite has been more nearly correct.

4.2 POPULATION COMPOSITION AND ECONOMIC DEVELOPMENT

Size of population is only one factor of many in determining the size and effectiveness of the labor force, and in turn, economic growth and development. Even before training and education are evaluated (and also the health standards of the population) one must first begin with a consideration of the age—sex composition of the population. The age—sex composition of a region's population determines the nature and size of the labor force relative to population, and also the nature of goods and services that will be produced and consumed in an economy. A rapidly growing population usually indicates a disproportionate number of young persons not participating in the labor force. The labor-force dependency ratio—the ratio of the number of persons in the labor force to those not in the labor force—tends to be lower in a rapidly growing economy with a high proportion of young people. This would imply a high resource allocation to educational facilities to a society interested in developing its manpower resources for economic development. Given the basic nonhuman resources of an economy, a rapidly growing population provides a burden to development until workers reach the age at which they are able to enter the labor force and participate in the process of economic development. The development of manpower through the education of a nation's youth is tantamount to investment of resources in the development of "human capital." School buildings, materials, and teachers are allocated to the development of manpower by a society. Loss of youth after training, without a compensating in-migration of workers, constitutes a loss to the society or group involved in the process of education and training.

The early development of the United States economy illustrates well the relation-

---

[5]Raymond Pearl, *The Biology of Population Growth*, Alfred A. Knopf, New York (1925), Chapter IX.

ship of population changes and labor-force participation. In its early development, particularly between the Civil War and World War I, the United States received a high proportion of the young workers from European nations. In addition, about 80% of the immigrants from 1900 to 1920 were males.[6] This favorable influx of labor supply helped considerably in developing a rapid rate of industrial growth for the nation's economy.

For currently developing nations in the world this favorable position of having male, young workers entering the labor force is complicated by the initial problem of educating vast numbers of children prior to their participation in the labor force. For example, in Puerto Rico half the population is under the age of 19 and per capita income is $620.[7] Puerto Rico is faced with an enormous educational task and currently devotes more of its economic resources to education than any other country in the world. Similar problems of a large number of children in the population face other developing nations of South America, Africa, and Asia. The "dependency ratio" of developing nations is large, and acts as a brake on rapid development until a greater proportion of population enters the labor force. Conrad and Irene Taeuber have found that the development of the United States coincided with a falling dependency ratio from the early 1900s to the 1940s.[8] In 1915 the dependency ratio was 84; in 1935 it had fallen to 74 with declining birth rates, and in 1955, 100 persons in the labor force supported 81 who were not in the labor force.[9] It has been estimated that by 1975 the United States will have a dependency ratio of 98, because of the increased birth rates beginning with the late 1940s, and also as a result of the large number of older persons in the population.

The dependency ratio, however, is only a rough first approximation to the economic effectiveness of a nation's population. It must be kept in mind that a more affluent society is able to maintain a larger portion of its population in school, and moreover, retire workers sooner from active participation in the labor force. In general, given the level of technological development and basic resources, a nation is able to achieve a higher level of per capita growth of output if fewer members of the population are dependent on those who participate actively in the production of goods and services. Much of the economic growth of developing nations today is eroded by the necessity for allocating consumer resources to a large and growing proportion of the population not currently contributing to the growth of the GNP.

---

[6]See Harry Jerome, *Migration and Business Cycles*, National Bureau of Economic Research, New York (1926), p.40.

[7]Frederick Harbison and Charles A. Myers, *Manpower and Education: Country Studies in Economic Development*, McGraw-Hill, New York (1965), p. 114.

[8]W. W. Rostow, *The Stages of Economic Growth: A Non-Communist Manifesto*, Cambridge University Press, London (1960), p. 81.

[9]The dependency ratio is defined here as the number of non-working persons in the population per 100 workers in the labor force.

The recent changes in the United States economy since the end of World War II are noteworthy. High birth rates of the late 1940s created a massive demand for elementary- and high-school facilities in the 1950s and early 1960s. From the mid-1960s to about 1975 this group of young persons will enter the labor force in large numbers. Women are expected to comprise about 40% of the increase in the labor force. The U.S. Bureau of Labor Statistics estimates that much of this increase will be accounted for by women who have lived long enough to be beyond their child-bearing years, and who will be seeking to supplement family incomes. With a generally shorter work-week, labor-saving devices in the home, and less arduous industrial tasks, the competitive position of women will be enhanced. For men, the rate of growth was substantially greater for those in the younger age groups in the population, particularly for those in the age 25 and less segment from 1960 to 1970.[10]

Another important demographic change has been the great increase in the number of older persons in the population. Better health standards have increased the life expectancy of the population. At the same time pressures have developed for earlier retirement of workers from a rapidly changing industrial environment where high priority continues to be placed on youth, education, and adaptability to change. The number of people in the 65 and over group in the population has increased, and by the year 2000 this group is expected to grow to 29 to 35 million.[11] In contrast to the growth in the number of people age 65 and over in the population, fewer and fewer actually participate as workers in the labor force. In 1890, about 68% of all men 65 and over were in the labor force. In 1969, only 27% were so employed.[12]

4.3 TECHNOLOGY, POPULATION, AND ECONOMIC GROWTH

It has been previously mentioned that future population changes portend an explosion of population of unprecedented proportions in the world as a whole. Raw data on population trends fail to give a proper perspective to the issue. The key to increasing the per capita income of an economy lies in increasing productivity and production levels at a more rapid rate then population growth. Higher production and productivity levels, in turn, depend on the achievement of high rates of change in the application of technology, industrial growth, and an increasing level of education for the population as a whole.

---

[10]U.S. Department of Labor, *Manpower Report of the President*, U.S. Government Printing Office, Washington, D.C. (March 1970).

[11]U.S. Department of Health, Education, and Welfare, *Indicators* (April 1964), p. 1.

[12]U.S. Department of Labor, *Manpower Report of the President*, U.S. Government Printing Office, Washington D.C. (March 1970), Table A-2, p. 216.

The problem of population growth is therefore a relative question rather than an absolute problem in and of itself. The burden of population must be considered in terms of the resource patterns of a region, the level of technology, and the educational and skill level of the labor force. For some areas of Western Europe which have had a high density of population relative to area—such as Belgium and West Germany—shortages of workers have been the recent experience. Migrants have been attracted from Southern Europe to meet the needs of expanding and rapidly growing economies. The density of population of most nations of South America has been much less than that of Western Europe. Consequently, population has been a problem, since the rate of economic growth has not been rapid enough to absorb workers into the labor force.

4.4 CONCEPTUALIZING LABOR-FORCE PARTICIPATION

Given the size and composition of a country's population, what determines who will be in the labor force (employed or unemployed), and what will be the relative proportion of the population in the labor force (LFPR)? In this section we will present a framework for conceptualizing labor-force participation, and in Sections 4.5 and 4.6 our framework will be expanded to present work/leisure, and occupational-choice models.

Participation in the labor force depends upon a complex array of factors bearing upon and shaping:

1. Decisions of households to seek work, change jobs in response to monetary and nonmonetary cues in the labor market, or to withdraw from the labor force.

2. Decisions of firms to hire, promote, or layoff workers.

3. Decisions of Government which regulate the activities of households and firms in the employment process through labor-standards legislation, and other legal and economic security programs.

Conceptually we can visualize manpower in terms of both "stocks" and "flows." Individuals within the population can be placed in one of three categories: (1) employed, (2) unemployed, or (3) not in the labor force. Levels within each of the categories at any given time represent the manpower "stocks" employed in the production process, looking for work but unemployed, or not currently involved in the labor force.

The manpower economist is also concerned with changes in status—movements from one stock to another. These are termed "flows" and decisions to change status often involve complex social and economic factors.

There are also movements within stocks as workers move along the occupational ladder through higher levels of training and education. Movements within the category of "employed" involve changes in economic "resource value." In an economic sense a movement upward along the occupational ladder involves an increase in the marginal productivity of a worker's contribution to the production process.

The same analogy applies to other categories of status in the labor force. There are degrees of attachment to the category of "unemployed" as well as to "not in the labor force."

Figure 4.1 depicts a conceptual framework of the various categories within the labor force and population.

4.4.1 "EMPLOYED"

The layers within the group of employed represent varying degrees of attachment to the labor market. Levels E5 and E6 represent temporary attachment—part time, seasonal, etc. With a decrease in economic activity through a change in aggregate demand, movement accelerates within flows 2 and 3. Conversely, with an upswing in economic activity, the rate of flow of manpower is accelerated within flows 1 and 4, as workers change their labor-force status.

The category of "employed" includes those partially employed, as well as those working below their full potential. "Manpower development," therefore, is a process by which workers are moved along flows 1 and 4, and also from levels E6 toward E1—toward levels of highest resource value.

4.4.2 "UNEMPLOYED"

An individual who is unemployed must be available for work, and must be actively seeking a job. Just as we have degrees of attachment to the status of being "employed," there are similar degrees of attachment to the category of "unemployed." U4 represents temporary, short-duration, frictional unemployment, and U1 represents "hard-core," long-term, structural unemployment.

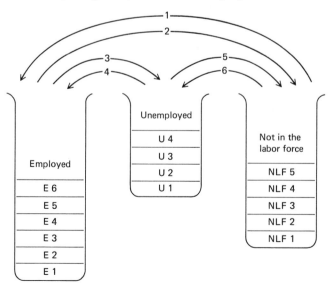

FIG. 4.1 Conceptual framework of population and labor force "stocks" and "flows"

Movement along flow 5 from level U1 has been studied by manpower economists as the "discouraged worker" hypothesis. Long-term unemployed workers find that barriers to employment prevent entry into the ranks of the employed. As the search process comes to an end, the worker exits from the labor force—he becomes a part of a group classified as "not in the labor force."

4.4.3 "NOT IN THE LABOR FORCE"

This category includes the residue of the population which is not currently employed, and not actively seeking work. Depending on particular circumstances, however, individuals in this group may enter the labor force. The "not in the labor force" group represents a wide range of individuals who constitute a labor reserve. Once again, as with the employed and the unemployed groups, there are degrees of attachment by individuals to this group.

4.5 THE WORK–LEISURE CHOICE

No matter how large an economy's population is or what its age–sex composition is, the amount of labor supplied will still be zero unless some members of the population choose to spend part of their time in the labor market performing work for pay or profit. If we take a theoretical view of the labor market, what can we say about the population's work–leisure choice?

4.5.1 THE BASIC TOOLS

In order to examine the work–leisure choice we will need an indifference map (which is a diagram showing several indifference curves), and a budget constraint.[13]

If we take a consumer and ask him to choose between various bundles of two commodities (X and Y), we can then record which bundles (combinations) of X and Y he prefers, and which bundles he considers inferior, and which bundles he is indifferent about. When we say that he prefers one bundle to another we mean that the preferred bundle yields more utility (satisfaction) than the inferior bundle. Thus, if our consumer is indifferent between two combinations of X and Y, then each combination yields the same utility.

In Fig. 4.2, every combination of X and Y which yields the same level of utility (let us say level U_1) is put together into an indifference curve. When all the consumer's indifference curves are derived we have the consumer's indifference map. Note that the indifference curves are concave from above. This shape is due to the so-called "law of substitution." This "law" states that if you are substituting between two commodities, the more you have of one commodity the lower its relative substitution value. We can see this by looking at curve U_1. Our consumer would be willing to go from point A to point B (since each point yields the same utility). This means he

---

[13]For a much fuller discussion of this technique, see Tibor Scitovsky, *Welfare and Competition*, Richard D. Irwin, Homewood, Illinois (1951), Chapter V.

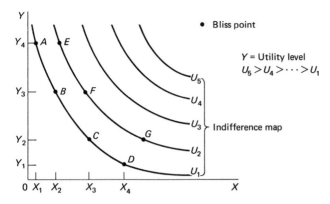

FIG. 4.2 Work-leisure choice

will trade a lot of Y $(Y_4 - Y_3)$ for a relatively smaller amount of X $(X_2 - X_1)$, since at point A the consumer had a large amount of Y relative to X. As we move down curve U_1, we see that as our consumer gets more X relative to Y, so now he will trade less Y for relatively more X. Going from point C to point D, our consumer will trade only $(Y_2 - Y_1)$ for an increase in X equal to $(X_4 - X_3)$. This type of substituting thus yields indifference curves that are concave from above.

Of course, a consumer who wants to maximize satisfaction will prefer bundles which contain more of both X and Y. Thus preference lies in a northeast direction— since a bundle which is northeast of another has more X and Y than the latter. Our consumer would go straight for his "bliss point" (point where he is satiated with X and Y) if he could; however, in a market economy, a consumer cannot get all the X and Y he desires. He must purchase X and Y with his income.

In Fig. 4.3 we see that the budget constraint constrains our consumer as to how much X and Y he can buy. The location of the budget constraint will depend on the consumer's income, the price of X (P_x), and the price of Y (P_y). Thus our

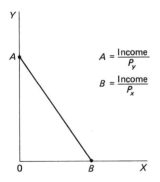

FIG. 4.3 Budget constraint

consumer could buy up to point A of Y if he spent all his income on Y, and he could buy up to point B of X if he spent all his income on X. So if our consumer's income was \$100, and the $P_x = \$5$ and the $P_y = \$2.50$, then A would equal 100/2.50 or 40 units of Y, and B would equal 100/5 or 20 units of X.

Our consumer (with P_X, P_Y, and his income level given) is thus constrained to buy only the combinations of X and Y on, or below, the budget constraint, but *not* above it. Since we are assuming that X and Y are all the commodities that our consumer will spend his income on, then our consumer will always be on the budget constraint—he cannot go above (unless P_X or P_Y or his income changes) and he will not go below (since this would mean unspent income).

We can now put Figs. 4.2 and 4.3 together in order to arrive at our consumer's equilibrium choice given his indifference map and his budget constraint. Our consumer will want to get as close as possible to the "bliss point" given his budget constraint.

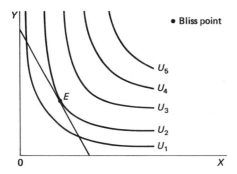

FIG. 4.4 Equilibrium choice

Our consumer will choose the X and Y combination shown by point E in Fig. 4.4, if the indifference map and budget constraint shown in Fig. 4.4 are drawn correctly. He cannot go to any point with an equal or higher utility level than point E because all such points are beyond his budget constraint, and he will not choose a point with less utility than point E because he is a satisfaction maximizer. Thus equilibrium occurs at the point where the budget constraint is tangent to an indifference curve.

4.5.2 WORKER'S EQUILIBRIUM CHOICE

Now that we have introduced the basic tools, we can apply them to the work—leisure choice. When we talk about the work—leisure choice, we are really talking about the choice that every member of an economy's population must make between working for a money income, and not working, or enjoying leisure. Thus we have to change our approach a little to allow for the fact that no one's time is unlimited, and that, by definition, the part of a person's time which is spent at work when added to his leisure time must add to 100% of the available time.

Let us look at the work—leisure choice from the point of view of one week. So the total amount of time available to be allocated is 7 × 24 or 168 hours. Every hour that a person spends working adds to his income and subtracts from the 168-hour total, whereas every hour he spends at leisure (not working) subtracts from his possible income and subtracts from the 168-hour total.

In Fig. 4.5 we put Leisure on the horizontal axis and money income on the vertical axis. The indifference map is thus our hypothetical worker's set of indifference curves between money income (wages earned from working) and leisure. The budget constraint in Fig. 4.5 depends on the level of wages (W) the worker receives for working and the amount of hours there are in a week to be allocated between work and leisure (168 hours).

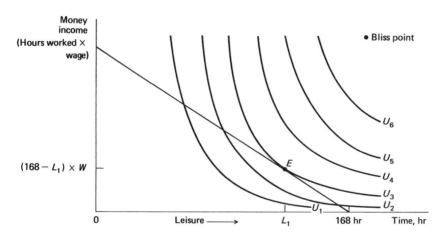

FIG. 4.5 Worker's choice between work and leisure

As in the previous section, the direction of preference lies in a northeast direction, meaning that our worker would prefer more of both Money income *and* leisure up to his "bliss point." However, our worker must observe his budget constraint. In one week he can only have a maximum of 168 hours of leisure—which would mean no work (and so no income) and this would be the horizontal axis point of the budget constraint. The vertical axis point of the budget constraint would occur if the worker worked all 168 hours (no leisure) and then his money income would equal 168 hours multiplied by his hourly wage rate.

Since our worker is restricted to remain on his budget constraint, and since he will want to get as close as possible to his "bliss point," the equilibrium point, or combination of work and leisure, will be point E in Fig. 4.5. At point E the amount of leisure our worker will want is L_1, meaning that he will work 168 hours minus L_1, and receive $(168 - L_1) W$ money income. What will happen to the amount

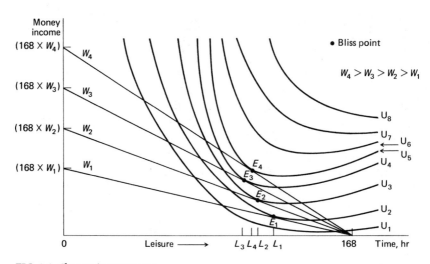

FIG. 4.6 Change in wage rate

of work offered on the labor market by our hypothetical worker if his wage rate
is increased?

In Fig. 4.6 we show an indifference map and four different budget constraints
(each one associated with a different wage level). As the wage rate increases, at
first the worker will work more (leaving less time for leisure). So at W_1 he will work
$(168 - L_1)$ hours in a week. If his wage level is raised from W_1 to W_2 he will work
more (L_2 is less than L_1, leaving more time for work). The same thing occurs for a
wage raise from W_2 to W_3 (less leisure, L_3 is less than L_2, and more work). However,
if wages go up to the W_4 level, our worker will offer fewer hours of work and therefore have more leisure (L_4 is greater than L_3).

Of course, the answers we got above (more work for higher wages at first, and
then less work for higher wages) depend entirely on the shape of the indifference
curves; thus it is possible that for some individuals wage increases will always
bring out more hours of work, and for other individuals the opposite may be
true. However, it is usually assumed that the results obtained in Fig. 4.6 are
the correct ones for the vast majority of people in a population such as the one
in the U.S.

Why does it happen that a worker may offer more hours of work as his wage is
raised, but at some high wage level he will begin to work fewer hours and take
more leisure? This seeming contradiction arises from the fact that there are two
"effects" at work in this work–leisure choice. These effects are the substitution
effect and the income effect.

Substitution effect As the price of a good increases, consumers tend to buy less
of that good. Thus, when the wage level increases, people will tend to substitute
away from leisure, since the price of leisure is the wage rate (each hour of leisure
costs you an hour of work, and so the price of leisure is W).

Income effect As income increases, consumers want to buy more of the so-called superior goods. Leisure being a superior good, as wage rates increase people see their income rising and want to buy more of the superior goods, including leisure.

The substitution effect works to get people to offer more hours of work (less leisure) when wages increase, and the income effect works to get people to offer fewer hours of work (more leisure) when wages increase. So now we can see that whether a worker offers fewer or more hours of work when his wage rate increases depends on the relative strengths of the two effects. If the substitution effect dominates, then a wage increase leads to more hours of work, but if the income effect dominates, then a wage increase leads to fewer hours of work. Our assumption that Fig. 4.6 is correct for most people can now be restated as the assumption that the substitution effect dominates at most wage levels, but at some high wage level (W_4 in Fig. 4.6) the income effect dominates.

The S_N is the diagrammatic representation of the relationship between the amount of work (N) forthcoming at the various level of wages. So, if we translate Fig. 4.6 into a S_N, we will have an upward-sloping supply curve of labor until W_4, and after W_4 the income effect dominates and we get the so-called backward-bending supply curve of labor.

One way to look at Fig. 4.7 is that the upward-sloping portion of the S_N is a short-run phenomena (as wages go up people work more hours each week), but in the long run, as wages and standards of living improve, the S_N "bends back" as workers want to enjoy more leisure (this is borne out by the historically declining work week in the U.S.). Of course, this means that Fig. 4.7 is not stationary, but will shift in the long run as wages and standards of living increase.

If all the people in a population were identical to the hypothetical person diagrammed in Fig. 4.6 and 4.7, then the S_N for the economy would be upward sloping and backward bending at relatively high levels of wages. However, not every person in a population has the same indifference map between work and leisure. What we must do now is to take an empirical (as opposed to a theoretical) view of labor-

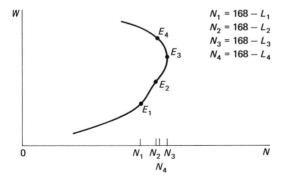

FIG. 4.7 Backward-bending supply curve of labor

force participation (work—leisure choice) before we can complete our treatment of the S_N.

4.6 ADDITIONAL-WORKER HYPOTHESIS VERSUS DISCOURAGED-WORKER HYPOTHESIS

One important question that has been debated recently and which has a bearing on the shape of the S_N is the additional-worker hypothesis versus the discouraged-worker hypothesis. The former argument states that during a recession there is an *inflow* of secondary (marginal) workers trying to supplement their family income— which was lessened due to the lay-off of the primary worker. The latter argument states that during a recession there is an *outflow* of secondary workers because they become discouraged due to the poor economic conditions.

Since this is a type of question that can only be answered empirically, there have been many attempts to measure the two arguments. The recent economic studies have used both time-series (quarterly and monthly) and cross-sectional (point in time) data.[14] The studies all agree that the discouraged-worker hypothesis dominates the additional-worker hypothesis. This results in a change in the labor force which varies *directly* with the employment level. One estimate of this effect (Strand and Dernburg, *Rev. Economics Stat.* [November 1964], 378—391) is that for every 100-person rise in the employment level there will be about a 50-person rise in the labor force, and vice versa for a decrease in the employment level.

Breaking the data down by age and sex and looking at the *net* "discouraged-worker effect," we can see that the greatest effect is on the secondary labor force (females, males under 25, and males over 54), and a small effect on the primary labor force (males age 25—54). We would expect this, since the secondary workers are more loosely attached to the labor force, and so can be expected to leave the labor force when jobs are scarce but return when jobs are plentiful.

4.7 AGGREGATE, INDUSTRY, AND FIRM SUPPLY CURVES OF LABOR

We are now in a position to combine our theoretical and empirical findings into a comprehensive treatment of the supply curve of labor.

---

[14]The time-series studies include K. Strand and T. Dernburg, "Cyclical Variation in Labor Force Participation," *Rev. Economics Stat.*, November 1964, 378—391; T. Dernburg and K. Strand, "Hidden Unemployment 1953—62: A Quantitative Analysis by Age and Sex." *Amer. econ. Rev.*, March 1966, 67—95; A. Tella, "The Relation of Labor Force to Employment," *Ind. Labor Relations Rev.*, April 1964, 454—469; and A. Tella, "Labor Force Sensitivity to Employment by Age, Sex," *Ind. Relations*, February 1965, 69—83. The cross-sectional studies include W. Bowen and T. Finegan, "Labor Force Participation and Unemployment," in A. M. Ross (Editor), *Employment Policy and the Labor Market*, University of California Press, Berkeley (1965), pp. 115—161; and J. Mincer, "Labor Force Participation of Married Women," in *Aspects of Labor Economics*, in National Bureau of Economic Research, Princeton, N.J. (1962), pp. 63—97.

4.7.1 AGGREGATE SUPPLY CURVE OF LABOR

Combining all the above, we find that the short-run (that period of time during which the population is fixed) aggregate supply curve of labor is upward sloping.

We can look at curve SS in Fig. 4.8 as the short-run aggregate supply curve of labor. It is upward sloping because as wages increase secondary workers are attracted into the labor market, and because in the short run the substitution effect will usually dominate—leading to more hours of work from individual workers as the wage level rises.[15] What happens to the S_N in the long run when the population expands? We would expect the S_N to shift out to $S''S''$ in Fig. 4.8. This assumes an expanding economy—growing population and rising wage levels. However, if we assume that as wages go relatively high, the income effect causes workers to demand more leisure (a shorter work week), the S_N will not shift out all the way to $S''S''$; instead it will shift out only to $S'S'$ (in Fig. 4.8) as the population grows and the general wage level rises. At the new higher population and general wage level, the S_N will again be upward sloping as the substitution and discouraged-worker effects dominate again.

To summarize we can consider the aggregate S_N to be upward sloping, with shifts occurring due to population shifts and downward shifts in the work week (as workers periodically demand a shorter work week due to the income effect).

4.7.2 INDUSTRY SUPPLY CURVES OF LABOR

What we have done above for the aggregate S_N we could now do for individual industry supply curves of labor.[16] However, now we would have the element of occupation choice to add to the foregoing. Moreover, we must remember that all the individual supply curves of labor must sum to the aggregate S_N.

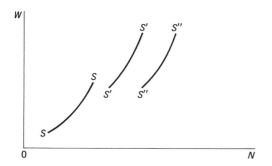

FIG. 4.8 Aggregate supply curve of labor

---

[15] Even if we assume that the substitution and income effects cancel out, the discouraged-worker effect will cause the S_N to be upward sloping.

[16] "Industry" is here to be taken to mean a labor market—or a group of firms demanding the same type of workers.

We will not say much here about occupation choice, except that it is really the outcome of investment in human capital. If a worker is unwilling or unable to undergo the training for a particular occupation, then he cannot become part of the S_N for that occupation. One final note: The individual industry or market supply curves of labor will be upward sloping; only now, the individual occupations can draw S_N from other occupations as well as from people not currently in the labor force. The shifting between occupations occurs due to relative wage (and nonwage) differentials.

4.7.3 FIRM SUPPLY—PERFECT COMPETITION

If the aggregate S_N and the industry S_N are upward sloping, what will the firm S_N look like? Looking at one business firm in a perfectly competitive industry the S_N for that firm will be perfectly elastic at the market wage rate (as diagrammed in Fig. 4.9).

The reason for the above is that one firm in a perfectly competitive industry is too small to effect the price of the labor it uses, and consequently it can get as much or as little labor as it needs at the going market wage (W_0 in Fig. 4.9). A horizontal S_N curve shows this geometrically—no matter what the level of N hired by the firm, the wage rate remains the same.

In a perfectly competitive industry,[17] if one firm tries to pay wages *below* the market wage rate then its S_N will fall to zero, since the workers would move to other firms in the same competitive industry. If the firm were to raise its wage *above* the market wage rate, then its S_N would be unlimited—as workers from other firms tried to get employment at the high-wage firm. However, since the perfectly competitive firm can get all the labor it requires at the market wage rate, there is no rational reason to pay wages above the market rate. Thus for all practical purposes the S_N does not exist below or above the market wage rate for the perfectly competitive firm.

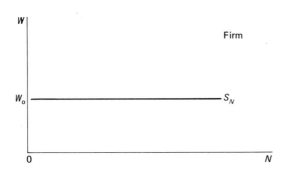

FIG. 4.9 Perfectly competitive firm supply curve of labor

---

[17] A perfectly competitive industry is one composed of a large number of firms—each one so small, relative to the total industry, that it cannot effect the price of inputs (labor, capital, etc.) or of its output.

4.8 A MODEL OF OCCUPATIONAL DECISION-MAKING

A first step in the development of a model of occupational decision-making is the specification of choice among alternatives, and a criterion for selection.[18] The alternatives specified are different occupational opportunities, and the criteria are the costs and benefits (monetary and nonmonetary) of the occupations within the range of an individual's scope of decision-making.

In theory there are many thousands of occupational choices available to an individual. In actual practice, however, choices are narrowed down to a relatively small number of alternatives by various constraints which limit choice to a fairly narrow band of occupations. These constraints include (but are not limited to) such things as an individual's socioeconomic status, physical and mental capabilities, and the costs of obtaining information on (and access to) the various occupations.

Figure 4.10 conceptualizes the problem of occupational choice. There is a narrow band of occupations both known and available to an individual. Surrounding this band is another cluster of occupations which are known to an individual, but which are not available to him for choosing because of problems of entry or cost constraints. At the outer perimeter are a vast number of occupations which are unknown to the individual, and therefore not a relevant part of his framework for decision-making (Fig. 4.10).

Knowledge of occupations and costs of information are of great importance in occupational decision-making.

If channels of information or entry are unknown or costly to the individual, the spectrum of occupational choice is diminished. Conversely, reducing costs of information or entry makes it possible to widen the field of occupational choice facing an individual. Also, it should be kept in mind that decision-making patterns of other individuals (or groups) have the effect of narrowing or widening the choices available

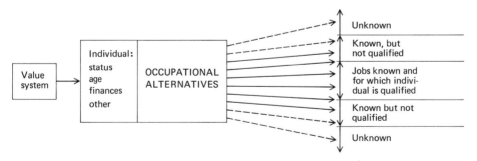

FIG. 4.10 Occupational choice and available occupational opportunities

---

[18] For an interesting analysis of occupational choice, see Donald R. Kaldor and Donald G. Zytowski, "A Maximizing Model of Occupational Decision-Making," *Personnel Guidance J.* (April 1969).

to a particular individual. The existence of patterns of discrimination against women, blacks, older workers, etc., have the effect of narrowing alternatives which may otherwise be available. Apprenticeship rules, restricted admissions to educational and training programs and even Government-established labor standards (child labor, employment of women, etc.) have significant effects on the quality and quantity of occupational alternatives available to an individual.

Given the relatively narrow band of occupational alternatives facing an individual (which are known to him and for which he may be qualified), what determines the selection of a specific occupation at a particular point in time? Choice emerges as an attempt to optimize a selection process which weighs the benefits (monetary and nonmonetary) of alternative courses of action, including such variables as:

1. Level of beginning earnings
2. Earnings over time
3. Stability of earnings
4. Fringe benefits
5. Status level
6. Social environment at work
7. Utility of physical and/or mental activity

From the cost side, the variables an individual have to evaluate include:

1. Training and education costs
2. Costs of entry
3. Costs of information and placement
4. Costs of commuting (or relocation)

In Fig. 4.11 all occupations lying between O and F yield greater benefits than costs to the individual. Beyond OF, occupational choice is not optimal, given the positions of the marginal cost and marginal revenue curves (costs will exceed benefits). An occupation at point F would give the individual the greatest benefit-in-excess-

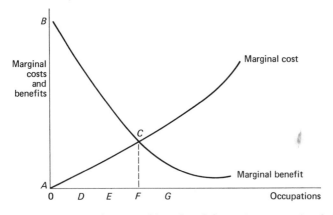

FIG. 4.11 Marginal costs and benefits of alternative occupational choices

of-cost choice. Total benefits would be *OFCB*, while costs incurred would be *OCF*. Would, in fact, the individual be able to choose an occupation at point *F*? He may not be able to if he is not able to meet the costs of the occupation (*OCF*). He may have to settle for a less-than-optimal choice (at say *D*, or *E*) and not be able to realize his full potential. If he were able to meet the costs of entry (borrowing, subsidy, etc.) he would be "investing" in his ability to choose an optimal occupation.

Are the marginal-cost and marginal-benefit curves fixed? No. If greater efficiencies are developed, costs of entry, training, information, etc., can be reduced. We would then have a downward shift in the marginal-cost curve, and occupation beyond *OF* would yield a greater total benefit versus total cost position. In the same manner, the marginal-benefit curve can shift if earnings, status, or satisfactions change.

4.9 SOME DYNAMICS OF OCCUPATIONAL CHOICE

The analysis in Section 4.6 is static in nature—it does not introduce a time dimension, nor does it say anything about the effects of choosing a first job on future job choices. Over time the marginal-benefit and marginal-cost curves do change and the individual incurs "capital gains" or losses over his work life. In addition to this, most career choices act as stepping stones to future jobs. Horatio Alger myths notwithstanding, very few workers entering the labor market as laborers have a very favorable probability of developing into corporation presidents. Very few college professors can aspire to careers as bricklayers or plumbers. Career choices follow a sequence or pattern, and by the time a worker reaches the age of 45 (or sooner in many cases) he becomes locked into an occupational "track." Changes between tracks are not impossible, but should be viewed in a probability sense. As workers age and acquire experiences and skills, the probability of a change between tracks diminishes. Comparatively little research has been conducted in this area, yet this concept is of great importance to our study of manpower economics.[19] Figure 4.12 shows a schematic framework for conceptualizing occupational choices and career tracks over time. At t_1 the individual faces a choice among three occupations. His choice of 1 permits him to choose between 4, 5, and 6 at t_2. This, in turn, leads to choices 9 at t_3, 12 at t_4, and 13 at t_5. If the individual has chosen 3 at t_1, he would have been precluded (low probability) from moving along the career track 1, 4, 9, 12, and 13.

We should keep in mind that career choices of an individual do not necessarily reflect his total desires. Discrimination patterns may "force" him to select an occupation within a narrow band, and this, consequently, may launch him along a less desirable "track." Conversely, an individual born into a high socioeconomic class has a broader range of selection, as well as adequate financial resources to move along a higher "track."

---

[19]For two interesting empirical studies, see John J. Corson, *Men Near the Top*, Johns Hopkins Press, Baltimore (1966), and Eli Ginzberg, *et al.*, *Talent and Performance*, Columbia University Press, New York (1964).

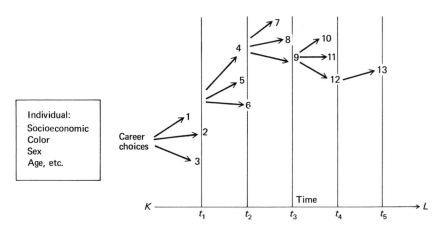

FIG. 4.12 Dynamics of occupational choice and career tracks

4.10 TRENDS IN LFPRs

We should make explicit here the definition of the number which is used to measure labor-force participation phenomena. This number is the LFPR, and it is derived by dividing the number of people age 16 and over in the labor force (both employed and unemployed) by the number of people age 16 and over in the population.[20] Of course, the above number would be the total LFPR for an economy. This number could easily be (and usually is) refined by looking at the LFPRs for only males, or only females, or only males age 25 through 54, etc. That is, the LFPR can be disaggregated by age, sex, and race. Moreover, we can talk about the total labor force and population (including armed forces), or just the civilian labor force and population— giving us another way to present the LFPR figures.

4.10.1 TRENDS IN OVERALL LFPRs

Over the course of the last two decades the total LFPR of the U. S. labor force has remained remarkably stable. In 1947 the total LFPR was 58.9% in comparison with 60.4% in 1958, and 61.1% in 1969. The percentage of those age 16 years and above who were in the labor force has stayed within about one percentage point of 60.0% for the past 20 years.

Although the LFPR has remained stable as a whole, the changes within various groups has been noteworthy. Essentially, the primary labor force consisting of males age 25 to 54 years has not varied considerably over this period. For those in the primary labor force, the LFPR has been between 95% and 98% with small variations from 1947 to 1969. Within other age and sex categories, however, significant changes

---

[20] As mentioned before, the lower age limit for the inclusion of persons in labor-force statistics was raised from 14 years to 16 years of age with the publication of data for January 1967.

have taken place. There have been long-run declines for males age 14 to 19 years as a result of increased educational standards and demands. A second major change occurred in the LFPR of men age 65 and over. Close to half the men age 65 years and over were in the labor force in 1957 (47.8%) in contrast to less than one-third in 1969 (27.2%).

One of the most dramatic changes in labor-force participation patterns has been the large-scale entry of women into the labor force, beginning with the World War II period and continuing to the present time. In 1947, 31.8% of women age 16 years and over were in the labor force, and 22 years later this figure had grown to 42.7%; with most of this increased participation rates for women concentrated in the age group 35 to 64 years.

In summary it appears that, although overall labor-force participation has not changed appreciably for the total population age 16 years and above since 1947, this stability has concealed a number of significant structural changes. Males tend to enter the labor force at a later stage in their life and exit at an earlier age than previously. The former is due to the trend for more formal education and training. A college degree is coming to have the same importance as a high-school diploma in the 1900s. Meanwhile, exit from the labor force takes place sooner due to the trend toward earlier retirement and better pension and social security payments. This decline in male participation has been balanced by the greater entry of women into the labor force in the middle age years 35 to 64. The LFPR of women, always a highly volatile element, appears to be bi-modal for the future—entry upon completion of high school, exit from the labor force during the child-bearing years, and entry once again in the middle-age years of 35 to 64.

Tables 4.1 and 4.2 present detailed data on U.S. LFPRs from 1947 to 1969.

TABLE 4.1 LFPRs (for noninstitutional populations) for persons (including armed forces) 16 years and over, by sex and age: annual averages, 1947–1969.

Sex and yr	Total, 16 years and over	16 and 17 yrs	18 and 19 yrs	20 to 24 yrs	25 to 34 yrs	35 to 44 yrs	45 to 54 yrs	55 to 64 yrs	65 years and over	14 and 15 yrs
Female										
1947	31.8	29.5	52.3	44.9	32.0	36.3	32.7	24.3	8.1	11.2
1948	32.7	31.4	52.1	45.3	33.2	36.9	35.0	24.3	9.1	12.2
1949	33.2	31.2	53.0	45.0	33.5	38.1	35.9	25.3	9.6	11.8
1950	33.9	30.1	51.3	46.1	34.0	39.1	38.0	27.0	9.7	12.7
1951	34.7	32.2	52.7	46.6	35.4	39.8	39.7	27.6	8.9	11.9
1952	34.8	33.4	51.4	44.8	35.5	40.5	40.1	28.7	9.1	11.1
1953	34.5	31.0	50.8	44.5	34.1	41.3	40.4	29.1	10.0	10.8
1954	34.6	28.7	50.5	45.3	34.5	41.3	41.2	30.1	9.3	11.3
1955	35.7	28.9	51.0	46.0	34.9	41.6	43.8	32.5	10.6	11.3
1956	36.9	32.8	52.1	46.4	35.4	43.1	45.5	34.9	10.9	12.9

(continued on next page)

TABLE 4.1 (continued)

Sex and yr	Total, 16 years and over	16 and 17 yrs	18 and 19 yrs	22 to 24 yrs	25 to 34 yrs	35 to 44 yrs	45 to 54 yrs	55 to 64 yrs	65 years and over	14 and 15 yrs
Female										
1957	36.9	31.1	51.5	46.0	35.6	43.3	46.5	34.5	10.5	12.5
1958	37.1	28.1	51.0	46.4	35.6	43.4	47.9	35.2	10.3	12.1
1959	37.2	28.8	49.1	45.2	35.4	43.4	49.0	36.6	10.2	12.9
1960	37.8	29.1	51.1	46.2	36.0	43.5	49.8	37.2	10.8	12.6
1961	38.1	28.5	51.1	47.1	36.4	43.8	50.1	37.9	10.7	13.1
1962	38.0	27.1	50.9	47.4	36.4	44.1	50.0	38.7	9.9	13.2
1963	38.3	27.1	50.6	47.6	37.2	44.9	50.6	39.7	9.6	11.8
1964	38.7	27.4	49.3	49.5	37.3	45.0	51.4	40.2	10.1	12.0
1965	39.3	27.7	49.4	50.0	38.6	46.1	50.9	41.1	10.0	12.2
1966	40.3	30.7	52.1	51.5	39.9	46.9	51.7	41.8	9.6	13.5
1967	41.1	31.0	52.3	53.4	41.9	48.1	51.8	42.4	9.6	14.7
1968	41.6	31.7	52.5	54.6	42.6	48.9	52.3	42.4	9.6	14.8
1969	42.7	33.7	53.5	56.8	43.8	49.9	53.8	43.1	9.9	14.8
Male										
1947	86.8	52.2	80.5	84.9	95.8	98.0	95.5	89.6	47.8	27.7
1948	87.0	53.4	79.9	85.7	96.1	98.0	95.8	89.5	46.8	27.5
1949	86.9	52.3	79.5	87.8	95.9	98.0	95.6	87.5	46.9	27.4
1950	86.8	52.0	79.0	89.1	96.2	97.6	95.8	86.9	45.8	28.7
1951	87.3	54.5	80.3	91.1	97.1	97.6	96.0	87.2	44.9	27.7
1952	87.2	53.1	79.1	92.1	97.7	97.9	96.2	87.5	42.6	25.9
1953	86.9	51.7	78.5	92.2	97.6	98.2	96.6	87.9	41.6	24.6
1954	86.4	48.3	76.5	91.5	97.5	98.1	96.5	88.7	40.5	24.7
1955	86.2	49.5	77.1	90.8	97.7	98.1	96.5	87.9	39.6	24.0
1956	86.3	52.6	77.9	90.8	97.4	98.0	96.6	88.5	40.0	26.6
1957	85.5	51.1	77.7	89.8	97.3	97.9	96.4	87.5	37.5	25.1
1958	85.0	47.9	75.7	89.5	97.3	98.0	96.3	87.8	35.6	23.8
1959	84.5	46.0	75.5	90.1	97.5	97.8	96.0	87.4	34.2	24.2
1960	84.0	46.8	73.6	90.2	97.7	97.7	95.8	86.8	33.1	22.3
1961	83.6	45.4	71.3	89.8	97.8	97.7	95.6	87.3	31.7	21.8
1962	82.8	43.5	71.9	89.1	97.4	97.7	95.6	86.2	30.3	21.6
1963	82.2	42.7	73.1	88.3	97.3	97.6	95.8	86.2	28.4	20.9
1964	81.9	43.6	72.0	88.2	97.5	97.4	95.8	85.6	28.0	20.8
1965	81.5	44.6	70.0	88.0	97.4	97.4	95.6	84.7	27.9	21.4
1966	81.4	47.0	69.0	87.9	97.5	97.3	95.3	84.5	27.0	21.6
1967	81.5	47.5	70.9	87.5	97.4	97.4	95.2	84.4	27.1	22.2
1968	81.2	46.8	70.2	86.5	97.1	97.2	94.9	84.3	27.3	22.1
1969	80.9	47.7	69.6	86.6	96.9	97.0	94.6	83.4	27.2	22.0

Source: U.S. Department of Labor, *Manpower Report of the President*, U.S. Government Printing Office, Washington D.C. (March 1970), p. 216.

TABLE 4.2 Employment status of the noninstitutional population 16 years and over: annual averages, 1947—1969 (numbers in thousands)

Year	Total noninstitutional population	Total labor force including armed forces		Civilian labor force		Not in labor force
		Number	Percent of noninstitutional population	Employed	Unemployed	
1947	103,418	60,941	58.9	57,039	2,311	42,477
1948	104,527	62,080	59.4	58,344	2,276	42,477
1949	105,611	62,903	59.6	57,649	3,637	42,708
1950	106,645	63,858	59.9	58,920	3,288	42,787
1951	107,721	65,117	60.4	59,962	2,055	42,604
1952	108,823	65,730	60.4	60,254	1,883	43,093
1953	110,601	66,560	60.2	61,181	1,834	44,041
1954	111,671	66,993	60.0	60,110	3,532	44,678
1955	112,732	68,072	60.4	62,171	2,852	44,660
1956	113,811	69,409	61.0	63,802	2,750	44,402
1957	115,065	69,729	60.6	64,071	2,859	45,336
1958	116,363	70,275	60.4	63,036	4,602	46,088
1959	117,881	70,921	60.2	64,630	3,740	46,960
1960	119,759	72,142	60.2	65,778	3,852	47,617
1961	121,343	73,031	60.2	65,746	4,714	48,312
1962	122,981	73,442	59.7	66,702	3,911	49,539
1963	125,154	74,571	59.6	67,762	4,070	50,583
1964	127,224	75,830	59.6	69,305	3,786	51,394
1965	129,236	77,178	59.7	71,088	3,366	52,058
1966	131,180	78,893	60.1	72,895	2,875	52,288
1967	133,319	80,793	60.6	74,372	2,975	52,527
1968	135,562	82,272	60.7	75,920	2,817	53,291
1969	137,841	84,239	61.1	77,902	2,831	53,602

Source: U.S. Department of Labor, *Manpower Report of the President*, U.S. Government Printing office, Washington D.C. (March 1970), p. 215.

4.10.2 TRENDS IN FULL-TIME AND PART-TIME LABOR-FORCE PARTICIPATION

We have previously mentioned that workers are attached to the labor force in varying degrees of participation. The "hard-core" participants are males, roughly age 25 to 54 years, and some females in the age group 35 to 55. Others enter the labor force under certain circumstances, either on a part-day, part-week, or part-year basis. These have a temporary attachment to the labor force, and are commonly designated as "secondary" workers.

In 1968, for example, a little more than 90 million people participated in the employed labor force. Only 52 million worked full-time (35 hours or more a week) for a full 50—52 weeks (including vacations and sick leave). About 20 million worked full-time, though for less than 50 weeks, while close to 17 million were part-time workers during the year. Over the past 15 years there has been a significant growth of employment for part-time workers.[21] Table 4.3 indicates the change in full-time versus part-time employment from 1950 to 1968.

The extent to which part-time employment has grown in the economy has important implications for social and economic factors. To the extent that this trend will continue into the future, we can anticipate that work (as it has been known in the past) may experience far-reaching qualitative changes. Leisure activities will assume greater importance, as well as various combinations of work/education, or work/recreation, which have been heretofore unknown. A quasi-leisure class may appear, based not on wealth or tradition, but rather one of high labor productivity with shorter hours of work for a large segment of the population. The potential for social and cultural development will be much greater than in the past, though much speculation will ensue as to the possible uses of leisure time. Certainly from an economic point of view there will be a more elastic labor supply, highly responsive to changing requirements for labor in relation to basic economic conditions.

4.11 PROJECTIONS OF LABOR-FORCE GROWTH TO 1980

As we have discussed before, population changes will have an important effect on the changes in the pattern of labor supply. Between 1960 and 1970 the most dramatic

TABLE 4.3 Persons with work experience during the year, 1950 and 1968 (thousands of persons)

	1950	1968
Total who worked during the year	68,876	90,230
Full-time:	58,181	73,266
50—52 weeks	38,375	52,285
27—49 weeks	11,795	11,115
1—26 weeks	8,013	9,866
Part-time:	10,695	16,964
50—52 weeks	3,322	5,769
27—49 weeks	2,214	3,720
1—26 weeks	5,162	7,475

Source: U.S. Department of Labor, *Manpower Report of the President*, U.S. Government Printing Office, Washington D.C. (March 1970), p. 260.

[21]There has been a long-run trend in the number of part-time jobs, with some acceleration since the end of World War II. It is important to note that the hours worked by full-time workers have also decreased over time. This would further emphasize the greater trend toward leisure versus labor-force participation on a full-time basis.

TABLE 4.4 Changes in the total labor force, by sex and age, 1950—1980 (numbers in thousands)

Sex and age	Actual		Projected		Number change			Percent change		
	1950	1960	1970	1980	1950—60	1960—70	1970—80	1950—60	1960—70	1970—80
Both sexes										
16 years and over	63,858	72,104	84,617	99,942	8,246	12,513	15,325	12.9	17.4	18.1
16 to 24 years	12,440	12,720	18,921	22,554	273	6,208	3,633	2.2	48.8	19.2
25 to 44 years	29,263	31,878	33,442	43,407	2,615	1,564	9,965	8.9	4.9	29.8
25 to 34 years	15,145	15,099	16,957	24,937	−46	1,858	7,980	−0.3	12.3	47.1
35 to 44 years	14,118	16,779	16,485	18,470	2,661	−294	1,985	18.8	−1.8	12.0
45 years and over	22,156	27,506	32,254	33,981	5,350	4,748	1,727	24.1	17.3	5.4
45 to 64 years	19,119	24,127	29,055	30,545	5,008	4,928	1,490	26.2	20.4	5.1
65 years and over	3,037	3,379	3,199	3,436	342	−180	237	11.3	−5.3	7.4
Male										
16 years and over	45,446	48,933	54,960	64,061	3,487	6,027	9,101	7.7	12.3	16.6
16 to 24 years	8,045	8,101	11,746	13,888	49	3,652	2,142	0.6	45.1	18.2
25 to 44 years	20,996	22,394	22,993	29,674	1,398	599	6,681	6.7	2.7	29.1
25 to 34 years	11,044	10,940	12,063	17,590	−104	1,123	5,527	−0.9	10.3	45.8
35 to 44 years	9,952	11,454	10,930	12,084	1,502	−524	1,154	15.1	−4.6	10.6
45 years and over	16,405	18,438	20,221	20,499	2,033	1,783	278	12.4	9.7	1.4
45 to 64 years	13,952	16,013	18,113	18,403	2,061	2,100	290	14.8	13.1	1.6
65 years and over	2,453	2,425	2,108	2,096	−28	−317	−12	−1.1	−13.1	−0.6
Female										
16 years and over	18,412	23,171	29,657	35,881	4,759	6,486	6,224	25.8	28.0	21.0
16 to 24 years	4,395	4,619	7,175	8,666	224	2,556	1,491	5.1	55.3	20.8
25 to 44 years	8,267	9,484	10,449	13,733	1,217	965	3,284	14.7	10.2	31.4
25 to 34 years	4,101	4,159	4,894	7,347	58	735	2,453	1.4	17.7	50.1
35 to 44 years	4,166	5,325	5,555	6,386	1,159	230	831	27.8	4.3	15.0
45 years and over	5,751	9,068	12,033	13,482	3,317	2,965	1,449	57.7	32.7	12.0
45 to 64 years	5,167	8,114	10,942	12,142	2,947	2,828	1,200	57.0	34.9	11.0
65 years and over	584	954	1,091	1,340	370	137	249	63.4	14.4	22.8

Source: U.S. Department of Labor, *Manpower Report of the President*, U.S. Government Printing Office, Washington D.C. (March 1970), p. 297.

change involved an increase in the number of people under 25. In absolute terms there was an increase of about 6.2 million persons in this group between 1960 and 1970, in comparison with an increase of just under 0.3 million during the previous decade. This under-25 age group will grow by about 3.7 million between 1970 and 1980, it is projected.

The age group 35 to 44 years actually experienced a decrease in number from 1960 to 1970, and will experience slightly under a 2-million-person increase from 1970 to 1980. In essence, from 1960 to 1980 it appears that a bi-modal labor force will emerge—high concentrations of workers in the younger age group as well as the older age group, with fewer workers in the middle age group of 35 to 44 years. Table 4.4 summarizes the changes in the labor force by age groups, from 1950 to 1980.

In overall terms the total labor force in the United States increased by about 13 million people from 1960 to 1970, and will increase by 15 million people from 1970 to 1980. By way of comparison, the increase from 1950 to 1960 in the U.S. total labor force was only 8.3 million people.

SUMMARY

Changes in the size and nature of population can have far-reaching effects on the welfare of an economy. Population quality and quantity can affect the quality and quantity of the labor supply; population growth can exert an influence on the quantity and composition of savings and investment; and population changes can affect a nation's standard of living. The whole question of population growth is a relative question. The burden of population must be considered in terms of the resource patterns of a region, the level of technology, and the educational and skill level of the labor force.

In order to derive an individual worker's supply of labor, we can utilize an indifference curve analysis. In so doing, we discover that the amount of labor forthcoming from an individual worker at various wage levels depends on the substitution effect and the income effect.

The present-day concept of the labor force was developed on the basis of *current* activity in the labor force. The labor force consists of noninstitutionalized adults (16 years and over) who are either employed or unemployed. Employed people have a job for pay or profit (or in a family business or farm), whereas the unemployed are all jobless persons looking for work.

The shape of the supply-of-labor curve partially depends on the additional-worker hypothesis versus discouraged-worker hypothesis. Most economists agree that the latter dominates the former—with about a 50-person rise in the labor force for every 100-person rise in the employment level (and vice versa for a decrease in the employment level).

The aggregate supply-of-labor curve will be upward sloping, with shifts occurring due to population shifts and due to reduction of the average work week (as workers periodically demand a shorter work week due to the income effect). The supply-of-labor curve can also be derived at the market and firm levels.

Although the overall LFPR has not changed appreciably since the late 1940s, there have been a number of significant structural changes. Males tend to enter the labor force at a later stage in their lives and exit at an earlier age than previously. Moreover, females seem to have a bi-modal LFPR, with entry on school completion, exit from the labor force during the child-bearing years, and entry once again from age 35 to 64.

Between 1960 and 1980 it appears that a bi-modal labor force will emerge. There will be high concentrations of workers in the younger age group, as well as the older age group, and there will be fewer workers in the middle age group (35 to 44 years).

BIBLIOGRAPHY

Gertrude Bancroft, *The American Labor Force: Its Growth and Changing Composition*, Wiley, New York (1958)

W. Bowen and T. Finegan, *The Economics of Labor Force Participation*, Princeton University Press, Princeton, N.J. (1969)

T. Dernburg and K. Strand, "Hidden Unemployment 1953–1962: A Quantitative Analysis by Age and Sex," *Amer. Econ. Rev.*, March 1966

A. J. Jaffe and Charles D. Stewart, *Manpower Resources and Utilization: Principles of Working Force Analysis*, Wiley, New York (1951)

Tibor Scitovsky, *Welfare and Competition*, Richard D. Irwin, Homewood, Illinois (1951), Chapter V

John J. Corson and R. Shale Paul, *Men Near the Top*, Johns Hopkins Press, Baltimore (1966)

Eli Ginzberg *et al.*, *Talent and Performance*, Columbia University Press, New York (1964)

5.1 THE NATURE OF THE DEMAND FOR LABOR

From an economic point of view, the degree of participation of the labor force— given the capital and natural resources, and the state of the arts—determines the economic system's capacity to produce goods and services. At the macroeconomic level, fluctuations in the utilization of an economy's resources generate changes in the level of production of goods and services, which, in turn, determines the level of employment. Consequently, the demand for manpower is said to be a derived demand. It is derived from the final consumer demand for the products produced.

Over the course of time, changes in the nature of goods and services produced, as well as in the technology used in production, have complex relationships to the occupational and industrial attachment of workers in the labor force. In general, as an industrial society evolves from a primitive state in which self-sufficiency is the basic theme in economic activity, production moves from the extractive industries, such as agriculture, mining, and fishing, to such industries as the manufacture of tangible goods. In time, and with varying rates of change, production becomes more and more roundabout, and economic activity changes from the output of tangible goods to that of services rendered by such industries as insurance, finance, education, medical aid, and numerous governmental functions which result from a greater interdependence in a highly industrialized economic society.

The overall development of economic society, therefore, takes place within a general framework of long-term structural change represented by varying rates of change in technical knowledge and industrial development, whereas in the short run, levels of private and public expenditures, as well as complex relationships of expecta- tions, determine the degree of utilization of the economic resources of a society. Manpower, therefore, is subject to long-term as well as short-term changes of structure due to technology as well as the level of utilization of the labor force due to changes in the level of expenditures.

An economic society must adjust its educational system to these changing demands of industry to keep pace with society's changing needs. If an economy is subject to abrupt changes, such as severe depression or war, the educational system as a whole will be required to adjust rapidly to these changes. Defense needs require large numbers of technicians and specialists to plan programs and to produce rapidly changing methods and techniques of defense. These defense changes in turn influence the nature of change taking place in the private sector. New products are introduced, and new methods of producing old products emerge with implications for skill needs and training requirements.

Defense needs are but one facet of changing manpower needs. As an economic system develops out of the primary industry stage, not only are more workers trained and educated than ever before, but in addition, the training becomes more specialized and more intensive. In a primitive economic system it is quite adequate in many cases to have an average educational level of grade school or less. In an advanced economy, nothing short of a high-school education becomes adequate to meet the demands of industry. Those unable to keep up with this pace of manpower demand can scarcely find a place in a developed economy's labor force.[1]

Moving from the long-term structural changes in the labor force and its training and educational requirements—as well as the short-term cyclical fluctuations in labor demand—we have the microeconomic or allocative feature of manpower utilization. In the short run, in addition to the fluctuation in employment and production, there is the problem of allocating workers among many thousands of occupations, firms, and areas of an economy. Principal reliance in a capitalistic system is placed on the operation of the market mechanism to perform the allocative function. Just as the price of goods and services is determined by the forces of supply and demand, so in the case of labor, wages and income levels are basically determined by the number of workers willing to assume certain occupations and also the willingness of employers to utilize workers at various wage levels and at various tasks. The basic market mechanism is modified by the operation of political forces, such as the establishment of minimum labor standards of work, and limitations placed on child labor, hours worked, and minimum wages. Further governmental modifications take place in labor-management relations law and in the development of unions. These factors have all had far-reaching implications for the operation of labor markets.

Within the microeconomic allocative framework, employers hire workers within certain occupations, establish working conditions, provide for wage payments, and train and retrain workers to meet changing manpower needs. From the workers' standpoint, job changing occurs in response to wage and nonwage considerations. Labor mobility takes place in terms of industry, occupational, and regional attachment. Moreover, workers join labor unions for the purpose of attempting to direct the process of industrial application of manpower to the production of goods and

---

[1] For an interesting and up-to-date discussion of educational problems in developing nations, see Frederick Harbison and Charles A. Myers, *Education, Manpower, and Economic Growth: Strategies of Human Resource Development*, McGraw-Hill, New York (1964).

services. Superimposed on employer and worker decision-making patterns and choices are the governmentally established laws and rules of society.

Public education plays a most important role in providing basic education to the population at the elementary, secondary, and increasingly at higher levels. In addition to basic educational skills, vocational education is provided by public as well as private industry to meet the needs of economic society.

The allocative function is partially met through public employment services which assist the process of matching jobs with people, and numerous counseling and guidance services of educational institutions and private industry. Further, in an attempt to make the allocative function of the economy work more efficiently, much statistical data are collected by public agencies on wages, mobility patterns, and labor demand and supply. Changes of worker attachment take place with varying degrees of time lag, depending on knowledge of labor-market conditions, uncertainty, and employer policies toward hiring and layoff. In general, the allocative function works slowly, but over the course of time workers are sorted out according to their respective contributions to the economic process, and economic rewards of the market place respond to the demands of consumers' expenditures and the priorities of governments in providing goods and services. Certain pockets of inefficient labor-market operation remain, and governmental policies are developed to deal with these and to make the market mechanism operate more efficiently and equitably through the political process.

The foregoing discussion portraying some of the major factors affecting the demand for labor in an economic system is summarized in Table 5.1, which indicates the nature of economic change, the causes, and the resulting impact on manpower.

In this chapter we will be talking about the demand for labor of firms which are in perfect competition (as opposed to imperfect competition, or *monopsony*—one buyer of labor) in the labor market. This is a very good assumption for the present-day U.S. economy, since the existence of unions, Government regulation, and mobility possibilities have made the various U.S. labor markets much more competitive (and therefore much less in the control of any one buyer of labor).

5.2 LABOR DEMAND OF THE INDIVIDUAL FIRM

In a market economy in which business firms operate under the profit-maximization goal, the only economic reason for demanding labor (or any other factor of production) is to increase the firm's profit.[2] Thus, whenever an employer considers hiring an additional unit of labor (or firing a unit of labor), he wants to know how much production that individual unit of labor adds to his total production, *and* how much

---

[2] In this chapter we will only be concerned with labor demand (in contrast to the last chapter, in which we were concerned only with labor supply). Thus a *complete* demonstration of a firm's profit-maximization goal and its effects will have to wait until the next chapter, when we put labor demand and labor supply together.

TABLE 5.1 Factors affecting the demand for labor in an economy

Nature of economic change	Causes	Impact on manpower
Structural (macroeconomic)	a) Technological change b) Product development	1. Changing skill requirements 2. Changing occupational, industrial, and area attachment
Cyclical (macroeconomic)	a) Changes in expenditures (consumer, governmental, private investment)	1. Unemployment 2. Underempolyment
Allocative (microeconomic)	a) Changes in wages d) Changes in product demand c) Governmental wage and labor policies	1. Allocate labor to various occupations, industries, and regions through the process of labor mobility 2. Changing levels of income, hours of work, and leisure

revenue this additional production will bring into the firm. These two points are equally important to the employer. If an additional unit of labor (or any other factor of production) cannot contribute a positive amount of production, then a profit-maximizing employer will not want to employ that additional unit; however, even if this additional unit of labor can contribute positive production the employer cannot make a rational decision until he has looked at the monetary value of this production (or the additional revenue this production will bring into the firm).

When we are talking about the additional production one more unit of labor will contribute, we are talking about the marginal product of labor (MP_N). $MP_N = \Delta Q/\Delta N$, or the marginal product of labor is the additional output (ΔQ) that one additional unit of labor (ΔN) will produce when added to the existing level of inputs.

When we are talking about the additional revenue this added output will bring into a firm, we are talking about the marginal revenue of this output (MR_Q). $MR_Q = \Delta TR/\Delta Q$, or the marginal revenue of the output is the additional total revenue (ΔTR) that the additional output (ΔQ) will bring into the firm. (Of course, the additional output we are talking about is the output added by the one additional unit of labor we are concerned with.)

Thus, to determine the value of an additional unit of labor, an employer will look at the MP_N and value it by the MR_Q, or the employer will look at the marginal revenue product of labor (MRP_N). The $MRP_N = MP_N \times MR_Q = \Delta Q/\Delta N \times \Delta TR/\Delta Q = \Delta TR/\Delta N$, or the marginal revenue product of labor is the marginal product of labor multiplied by the marginal revenue of the output. (Which output? The output which the labor we are considering has contributed to production.)

An example will help clarify the above. Let us examine a firm which has a set amount of land, capital, and managerial skill, and see what happens as we look at varying amounts of labor.

TABLE 5.2 Firm A's input, output, and MRP_N data

Capital (K)	Land (L)	Managerial skill (E)	Labor (N)	Output (Q)	MP_N	MR_Q	MRP_N
5 units	2 units	3 units	3 units	40 units	*15 units	$50	$750
5 units	2 units	3 units	4 units	52 units	12 units	48	576
5 units	2 units	3 units	5 units	62 units	10 units	46	460
5 units	2 units	3 units	6 units	71 units	9 units	44	396
5 units	2 units	3 units	7 units	79 units	8 units	42	336
5 units	2 units	3 units	8 units	86 units	7 units	40	280

*An MP_N of 15 units for the third unit of labor means we are assuming that Q was 25 units when only 2 units of N were used with the fixed amounts of K, L, and E.

Looking at Table 5.2, we see what happens to the MP_N in Firm A as the amounts of N are varied with the other inputs. Knowing this, the employer can then look at what happens to the MR_Q as Q varies, and then calculate the $MRP_N (MP_N \times MR_Q)$ for each additional unit of labor. This MRP_N is the demand for labor (as long as we assume profit-maximizing firms in a perfectly competitive labor market).

The fact that the MRP_N is the demand for labor is easier to see when we remember that the business firm must equate marginal revenue (MR) to marginal cost (MC) in order to maximize profits. When the firm applies this profit-maximizing rule to the labor input it must look at the marginal cost of labor (MC_N) and the marginal revenue of labor (which is the MRP_N). As we saw in Chapter 4, the MC_N is the market wage of labor (for the perfectly competitive firm). Thus, at any given wage, the profit-maximizing firm determines its demand for labor by equating the wage to the MRP_N. Since a demand curve is the relationship between price and quantity demanded, the MRP_N curve (which provides this information for labor) is therefore the demand for labor curve.

Figure 5.1 is a graphical presentation of columns four and eight of Table 5.2. A little later we will have more to say about the downward-sloping shape of the MRP_N curve.

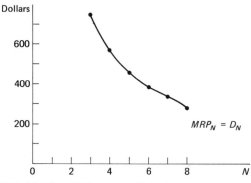

FIG. 5.1 Firm MRP_N curve: Firm A

5.2.1 DEGREE OF COMPETITION IN THE PRODUCT MARKET

The above is true whether the firm produces in a product market composed of only one firm (a monopoly) or a very large number of firms (perfect competition). However, there is one point that can be discussed which will differ depending on whether there is monopoly or perfect competition in the product market.

If there is imperfect competition in the product market, then the firm faces a downward-sloping demand curve for its product. Since the price of the product falls as more is supplied, the marginal revenue curve of the product will be downward sloping. The marginal revenue will fall as more product is supplied. The example shown in Table 5.2 and Fig. 5.1 is an example of a firm in imperfect competition in the product market. We know this because the MR_Q falls as Q increases (indicating that the firm faces a downward-sloping demand curve for its product.

If there is perfect competition in the product market, then the firm faces a horizontal (perfectly elastic) demand curve for its product. This means that the price of the product (to the perfectly competitive firm) remains constant as more is supplied by the firm, and this means that the marginal revenue of the product will be constant (and equal to the price of the product). At this point let us look at a firm in perfect competition in the product market. (Table 5.3 and Figure 5.2).

Thus, when a firm is in perfect competition in the product market, the $MR_Q = P_Q$ and is constant, but the rest of the analysis is the same in deriving the MRP_N (the demand curve for labor) as it is when the firm is in imperfect competition in the product market.

Since the $MR_Q = P_Q$ when a firm is in perfect competition in the product market, many economists refer to the MRP_N in such a case as the marginal value product of labor (MVP_N). The $MVP_N = MP_N \times P_Q$. We always talk about the demand curve of labor being the MRP_N, since $MVP_N = MRP_N$ when the firm is in perfect competition in the product market, and because when the firm is in imperfect competition in the product market it is the MRP_N (and *not* the MVP_N) which the profit-maximizing employer must know to make a rational decision.

At this point we can discuss the downward-sloping shape of the MRP_N curve. Looking again at Table 5.3, we see that the downward-sloping shape of the MRP_N curve comes from the fact that the MP_N is downward sloping. Why does the MP_N slope downward? This is due to the law of diminishing returns, which states that as more of

TABLE 5.3 Firm B's input, output and MRP_N data

Capital (K)	Land (L)	Managerial skill (E)	Labor (N)	Output (Q)	MP_N	$MR_Q = P_Q$	$MRP_N = MVP_N$
5 units	2 units	3 units	3 units	40 units	15 units	$45	$675
5 units	2 units	3 units	4 units	52 units	12 units	45	540
5 units	2 units	3 units	5 units	62 units	10 units	45	450
5 units	2 units	3 units	6 units	71 units	9 units	45	405
5 units	2 units	3 units	7 units	79 units	8 units	45	360
5 units	2 units	3 units	8 units	86 units	7 units	45	315

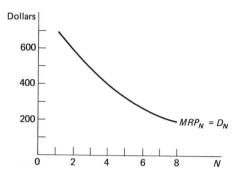

FIG. 5.2 Firm MRP_N curve: Firm B

a variable input is added to fixed inputs, the output produced will increase at a decreasing rate (see column 5 of Tables 5.2 and 5.3). Going back to Table 5.2, we see that the MP_N slopes downward (due to the law of diminishing returns) and the MR_Q slopes downward (due to the downward-sloping product demand curve), meaning that the MRP_N curve must slope downward.

Thus the D_N is downward sloping whether the firm is in perfect or imperfect competition in the product market.

5.3 SOME SPECIAL CASES OF LABOR DEMAND

So far we have been discussing demand curves of labor which are smooth and continuous. This is the typical case and will be the only one we concentrate on in this text. However, at this point we will discuss special cases in order to indicate how the above analysis can be modified.

If a firm produces only one product but can operate in three shifts, the MRP_N curve might look like the illustration in Fig. 5.3.

The three stages in Fig. 5.3 would be due to the three production shifts in the firm.

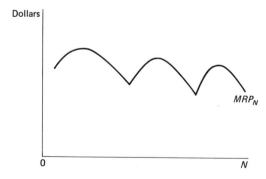

FIG. 5.3 Firm with a 3-shift operation plant

Although labor would probably be equally productive in each of the three shifts, the marginal revenue of increments of output will fall as output increases (assuming that the firm sells its product in an imperfectly competitive market).

A second special case could result if a firm (again in imperfect competition in the product market) experienced a MP_N curve which was nearly horizontal for a wide range of output but dropped sharply after capacity was reached.

Figure 5.4 illustrates this special case, with OA being the level of employment corresponding to the plant capacity.[3]

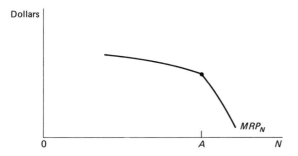

FIG. 5.4 Firm with flat cost curve to "capacity"

5.4 INDUSTRY LABOR DEMAND

Having discussed the individual firm's demand curve for labor we can now derive the industry demand curve. The industry D_N is the *aggregation* of the D_N for every firm in that industry. That is, in order to derive the industry D_N you add the amount of N each firm in the industry demands at each given wage rate.

In Table 5.4 and Fig. 5.5 we show an example of an industry consisting of three firms and derive its D_N^4.

The above example consists of a three-firm industry, but the analysis would be the same regardless of the number of firms (as long as the firms are in perfect competition in the labor market).

5.4.1 DEGREE OF COMPETITION IN THE PRODUCT MARKET

The above analysis is true whether the firms produce in a product market composed of only one firm (monopoly) or a very large number of firms (perfect competition).

---

[3]See Allan M. Cartter, *Theory of Wages and Employment*, Richard D. Irwin, Homewood, Illinois (1959), Part I.

[4]Of course, an industry in perfect competition in the labor market would consist of many more than three firms; however, for purposes of our example, we will consider the three firms as prototypes for a larger number of firms.

TABLE 5.4 Industry I, and Firms A, B, and C.

Wage*	D_N (Firm A)	D_N (Firm B)	D_N (Firm C)	D_N (Industry I)
$1.00	8 units	9 units	7 units	24 units
1.25	7 units	8 units	6 units	21 units
1.50	6 units	7 units	5 units	18 units
1.75	5 units	6 units	4 units	15 units
2.00	4 units	5 units	3 units	12 units
2.25	3 units	4 units	2 units	9 units

*The wage is an hourly rate, and so if we assume a 40-hour week, then each unit of labor costs 40 times its hourly wage rate each week.

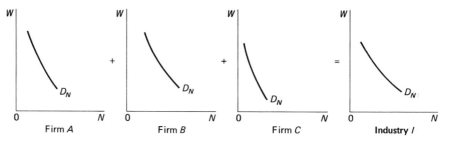

FIG. 5.5 Illustration of 3-firm industry

However, there is a refinement we can discuss when the firms are in perfect competition in the product market.

Going back to Table 5.3 and Fig. 5.2, we see that when a firm is in perfect competition in the product market we assume that the product price is constant for that firm. This assumption is entirely appropriate in the case of this firm, but it is not an appropriate assumption for the industry. The industry D_N must take into account the impact on product price caused by variation in industry output.

Looking at Fig. 5.6, the broken line $(D_{N'})$ is the industry D_N which is derived by simply summing the demand schedules of every firm, holding the price of the output (P_Q) constant (k). However, for the industry, we must allow for the fact that the P_Q is not constant. When we make this allowance we will arrive at D_N (the solid line). How? Along the solid line D_N there is a point at which P_Q (which we are allowing to to change as output changes) will be equal to k (the constant we assumed it to be equal to for the perfectly competitive firms). Thus at that point (point B in Fig. 5.6), the solid-line and broken-line D_N curves coincide. What happens if the wage rate (W) goes above W_B? The firms will demand less N and this means less product will be produced, which will increase the P_Q. This higher P_Q means a higher MRP_N than the broken-line D_N curve indicates, which in turn means that the solid-line D_N curve will be above the broken-line curve $(D_{N'})$. What happens if the wage rate goes below W_B? The firms will demand more N, and this means more product will be produced, which will decrease the P_Q. This lower P_Q means a lower MRP_N than the broken-line D_N curve

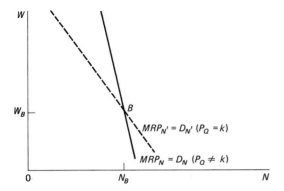

FIG. 5.6 Industry D_N with perfect competition in product market

indicates, which in turn means that the solid-line D_N curve will be below the broken-line curve ($D_{N'}$).

In other words, when the firms are perfectly competitive in the labor market *and* product market, the industry D_N cannot be simply summed from the firm demand curves. Instead, an allowance must be made for the fact that the P_Q varies with variations in the level of Q for the industry (even though it doesn't for the perfectly competitive firm); and when this allowance is made, the industry D_N curve becomes more vertical than the D_N curve without this allowance (D_N as compared to $D_{N'}$ in Fig. 5.6).[5]

5.5 ECONOMY LABOR DEMAND

We are now ready to derive the economy D_N. As in the case of the industry D_N, the economy D_N is an aggregation—an aggregation of industry D_N for every industry in the economy (Fig. 5.7).

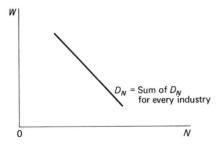

FIG. 5.7 Economy D_N curve

[5]See Neil W. Chamberlain, *The Labor Sector*, McGraw-Hill, New York (1965), Chapter 17.

5.5.1 PRODUCTIVITY CHANGES

We have already presented the economy D_N in Chapter 3, but now we are in a position to know where it came from and why it is downward sloping. Moreover, having examined the MRP_N at the firm level we can now understand what is meant by productivity changes in an economy, and their impact on the economy D_N.

Since the economy D_N is derived from the industry D_N, which in turn depends on the firm MRP_N, then the economy D_N will be affected by any change in the MRP_N. The MRP_N consists of the MP_N and the MR_Q. Thus a change in labor productivity means a change in the MP_N which shifts the economy D_N. In Fig. 5.8 we have illustrated a shift in the economy D_N which would result from an increase in the MP_N (an increase in labor productivity). In a growing economy we can expect periodic increases in labor productivity which will cause the D_N to expand—meaning a growth in available jobs, plus higher wage rates.[6]

5.6 D_N AS A DERIVED DEMAND

Elsewhere in this text we talked about the demand for labor being a derived demand. What did we mean by this statement? Having gone through the demand for labor analysis on the firm, industry, and economy levels, we are in a position to explain this statement.

The D_N is called a derived demand because it is derived (or depends on) the demand for the product which the labor is helping to produce. If there is no demand for a product, then there will be no demand for the labor which produces the product. Or if there is a high (low) demand for a product, then there will be a high (low) demand for the labor which produces the product.

The above follows directly from the fact that the D_N is the MRP_N, which in turn is the MP_N × the MR_Q. No matter how productive a particular type of labor is (MP_N), there will be a low or zero demand for labor unless the product being produced has a relatively high demand (reflected in the MR_Q). Of course, if a product has a high

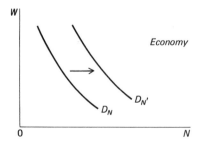

FIG. 5.8 Productivity changes and economy D_N

---

[6]Exactly how many more jobs and how high wages will go depends partly on the S_N.

demand, there can still be a low or zero demand for a particular type of labor if that labor is unproductive (low MP_N) in producing that product.

SUMMARY

The demand for labor is said to be a derived demand, since it is derived from the final consumer demand for the products produced. The demand for labor in an economy can be affected by structural changes (such as technological change), cyclical changes (such as major changes in expenditures), and allocative changes (such as changes in product demand or governmental wage and labor policies).

Business firms demand labor only if the labor will increase the firm's profit level. Thus, to determine labor demand, employers want to determine the monetary value each additional unit of labor would bring into the firm. This means that they look at the marginal product of labor and value it by the marginal revenue product of labor (MRP_N). The MRP_N curve is downward sloping for the firm in a competitive labor market, whether there is perfect or imperfect competition in the product market.

The industry (or labor market) demand for labor is the aggregation of the demand for labor for every firm in that industry. Thus, in order to derive the industry demand for labor, we add the amount of labor each firm in the industry demands at each given wage rate. In turn the economy demand for labor is derived by aggregating the industry demand for labor in every industry in the economy.

Having derived our various demand-for-labor curves, we can then talk about the effect of such economic factors as an increase (or decrease) in the productivity of labor. However, no matter how productive a grade of labor is, there must be a good level of demand for the product being produced or there will be a low (or even zero) demand for that grade of labor.

BIBLIOGRAPHY

Allan M. Cartter, *Theory of Wages and Employment*, Richard D. Irwin, Homewood, Illinois (1959), Part I

Neil W. Chamberlain, *The Labor Sector*, McGraw-Hill, New York (1965), Part IV

Frederick H. Harbison and Charles A. Myers, *Education, Manpower, and Economic Growth: Strategies of Human Resource Development*, McGraw-Hill, New York (1964)

Frederick H. Harbison, Joan Maruhnic, and Jane R. Resnick. *Quantitative Analyses of Modernization and Development*: Industrial Relations Section, Princeton University Press, Princeton, N.J. (1970)

WAGE DETERMINATION 6

In this chapter we will put together the material from Chapter 4 (S_N) and Chapter 5 (D_N) in order to develop a complete wage determination model. We will do this on the firm and industry level for the short-run and long-run time periods.[1]

6.1 MARGINAL PRODUCTIVITY THEORY OF WAGES AND PERFECT COMPETITION

We will begin our analysis of wage determination by first dealing with the case of perfect competition. We will do this for the short-run and the long-run periods.

6.1.1 SHORT-RUN PERIOD

A perfectly competitive firm faces a downward-sloping demand curve of labor and a horizontal supply curve of labor, while the industry faces a downward-sloping demand curve of labor and an upward-sloping supply curve of labor. Knowing this we can now construct a full wage-determination model.

In the typical perfectly competitive industry the market (or industry) wage is set by the interaction of D_N and S_N. The example in Table 6.1 and Fig. 6.1 demonstrates this interaction. The market wage rate (W_0 in Fig. 6.1) is set where D_N equals S_N. For any wage above W_0 the S_N is greater than the D_N and there will be pressure developed to lower the wage rate by this excess supply. For any wage below W_0 the D_N is greater than the S_N, and there will be pressure developed to raise the wage rate by this excess demand. Thus the equilibrium (or stable) wage rate occurs exactly where D_N equals S_N, for at that point there is no excess demand or excess supply to force the wage rate above or below this point. In Table 6.1 we

---

[1]The short-run period of time is that period during which the plant size of business firms is fixed—the firms cannot expand or contract their size. The long-run period of time is that period during which plant size can be expanded or contracted.

TABLE 6.1 Firm and industry wage data

Firm			Industry		
Wage rate	D_N (MRP_N)	S_N	Wage rate	D_N	S_N
$10	4 units	Unlimited units	$10	40 units	120 units
8	5 units	Unlimited units	8	50 units	100 units
6	6 units	Unlimited units	6	60 units	90 units
5	7 units	Unlimited units	5	70 units	70 units
4	8 units	0 units	4	80 units	55 units
3	9 units	0 units	3	90 units	45 units

see that the equilibrium wage rate will be $5, since at that wage the D_N and the S_N both equal 70 units.

Given the equilibrium market wage rate, what does this mean for the firm? The perfectly competitive firm is too small to affect the price of labor, and so all that is decided on the firm level is the equilibrium level of employment. Looking at Table 6.1 and Fig. 6.2, we see that this stable level of employment occurs where the D_N equals the S_N. Why? This follows from our assumption of profit maximization. If a business firm wants to maximize profits, then it must hire labor up to the point at which the MRP_N equals the MC_N (the marginal cost of labor).[2]

We derived the MRP_N in Chapter 5 for the perfectly competitive firm, but what about the MC_N? The marginal cost of labor is the additional cost of hiring an additional unit of labor. Since the perfectly competitive firm can hire any amount of labor it needs at the market wage,[3] then the additional or marginal cost of additional units of labor

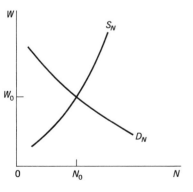

FIG. 6.1 Industry equilibrium

---

[2]In order to be at a point of maximum profits, the marginal profit must be zero. Marginal profit equals marginal revenue minus marginal cost, and when marginal profit equals zero, then marginal revenue must equal marginal cost. Looking at this from the labor-input point of view, maximum profits occur when the marginal revenue of labor (MRP_N) equals the marginal cost of labor (MC_N).

[3]The perfectly competitive firm can also hire any amount of labor at wages above the market wage, but since we are assuming profit maximization, no rational firm would pay a wage higher than it must to get labor.

is equal to the market wage rate. In Fig. 6.2 this means that the S_N curve is equal to the MC_N curve. Thus the profit-maximizing firm will hire labor up to the point at which the MRP_N equals the MC_N—which means the equilibrium level of N occurs where the firm D_N equals the firm S_N. In Fig. 6.2 the market wage rate (W_0) is given to the firm and the equilibrium level of employment (N_0) is set by the intersection of D_N with S_N. This same example in Table 6.1 shows the equilibrium wage to be \$5 and the firm equilibrium level of employment to be 7 units.

Summarizing what has gone before, we have seen that the equilibrium levels of wage and of employment are determined by the labor demand and supply curves of the industry and firm. The interaction of the industry demand and supply curves sets the equilibrium industry wage rate and the equilibrium industry level of employment. This market wage rate is given to every firm in the industry, and since each firm is too small to effect W, the firm labor demand and supply curves set only the equilibrium firm level of employment. Of course the derivations of the labor demand and supply curves were treated in detail in the previous two chapters.

At this point we can discuss, from another view, a statement that was examined in Chapter 5. There we said that the D_N for a perfectly competitive firm is the MRP_N, since the firm (being a profit maximizer) wants to know both the productivity of labor (MP_N) and the marginal revenue of the output produced (MR_Q) in order to rationally determine their demand for labor. Now that we have put the demand and supply sides together, we can demonstrate the above statement ($D_N = MRP_N$ for the firm) more directly. We know that a profit maximizer will hire labor at the point at which the MRP_N equals the MC_N, and also that the MC_N equals the industry wage rate for the perfectly competitive firm. Therefore, for any market wage, the firm will hire that amount of labor indicated by the MRP_N curve; and this is the definition of a demand curve—a demand curve is a diagram of the relationship between price (W in this instance) and the quantity demanded.

Although the circular-flow diagram in Fig. 6.3 is very simplified, it shows the two basic decisions and decision-makers which go into determining the wage rate under conditions of perfect competition. Of course, if the household sector and/or the busi-

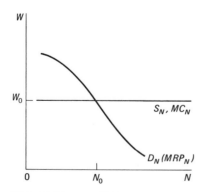

FIG. 6.2 Firm equilibrium

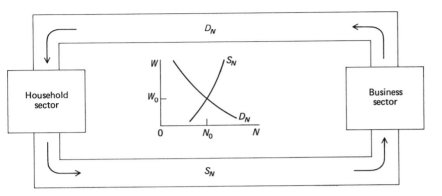

FIG. 6.3 A wage determination model

ness sector alter their decisions (causing the S_N and/or the D_N to shift), then a new wage rate will be set. The decision-makers can alter their decisions because of changes in government policies (taxation, spending, etc.), changes in productivity, changes in population, etc. Any changed decisions which increase the D_N given the S_N will increase W and N; and any changed decisions which increase S_N (given the D_N) will decrease W and increase N. The opposite of course is true—a decrease in D_N will decrease W and N; and a decrease in S_N will increase W and decrease N. All these cases are illustrated in Fig. 6.4 (from an industry viewpoint).

6.1.2 LONG-RUN PERIOD

In the long-run period of time, the same basic relationship determines wages and employment levels that determined them in the short-run. The only difference is that now the business firms can change their plant size (either expand or contract), and so excess profits will not exist.

If in the long run the business firms are making excess (greater than normal) profits[4] in a labor market, then there will be pressure for the existing firms to demand more of that labor (and for new firms to enter the industry), raising the industry D_N. This increased D_N will cause wages to rise, cutting into the excess profits, and this process will continue until the excess profit level is reduced to a normal profit level.

The converse is also true. Thus, if there are losses in the industry, then there will be pressure for the existing firms to demand less labor (and some firms may even exist the industry), lowering the industry D_N. This decreased D_N will cause wages to fall, cutting down the size of the losses, and this process will continue until the losses are converted into a normal profit level (or until the industry ceases to exist for that type of labor).

Figures 6.5 and 6.6 demonstrate the case in which the industry was in a short-run

---

[4]The term "normal profits" implies that the firm's total revenue covers all the costs of production, including a return to the entrepreneur which is equal (not greater or less) to the best alternative return the entrepreneur could earn elsewhere.

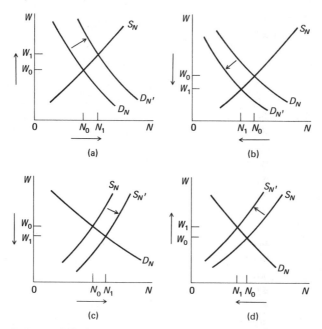

FIG. 6.4 Shifts in D_N and S_N due to altered decisions

equilibrium which generated excess profits, W_0, N_0 in the industry and W_0, N_0 in the firm. These excess profits can cause firms to expand in the long run (and will probably cause new firms to enter the industry—increasing the firm's D_N^5 and therefore increasing the industry D_N. The increased industry demand for labor (D_N), will raise wages to W_1 to the firms. This process will continue until the long-run equilibrium of normal profits (neither losses nor excess profits) is achieved.

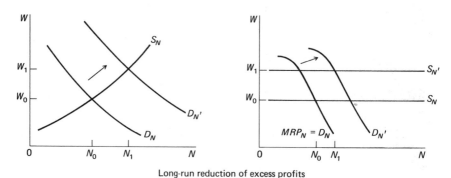

Long-run reduction of excess profits

FIG. 6.5 Industry   FIG. 6.6 Firm.

---

[5]The firm's increased plant size increases the firm's D_N because it increases the MP_N.

If the short-run equilibrium had been one of losses, then the reverse would take place. The decreased D_N would lower W until the losses were turned into normal profits—in the long run.

6.2 MARGINAL PRODUCTIVITY THEORY OF WAGES AND MONOPSONY

All the above has been based on perfect competition in the labor market. What changes would take place in the foregoing wage determination model if instead of perfect competition we had monopoly in the labor market? Monopoly in the labor market is the case of only *one* buyer of labor in the industry, and is known as *monopsony*. This section will be devoted to wage determination in a monopsonistic labor market.

6.2.1 SHORT-RUN PERIOD

Since a monopsonistic labor market is composed of only one buyer, the industry and firm analysis is the same—the firm is the industry. Thus the monopsonistic firm faces a downward-sloping industry MRP_N, and an upward-sloping industry S_N. We are still assuming profit maximization, and so the monopsonist will want to hire labor up to the point at which MRP_N equals MC_N. However, since the monopsonist *is* the industry, we can no longer say that the MC_N is the market wage rate. The monopsonist faces an upward-sloping S_N, not a horizontal S_N, and so he must pay a higher wage rate in order to hire additional labor.

In most real-world situations, when a firm has to raise its wage level to hire additional workers, it must then give this pay raise to its previous work force. Assuming this to be true, then the MC_N to a monopsonist will be upward sloping and greater than (above) the S_N. Why? If a monopsonist were demanding 5 units of labor[6] at $4 an hour and had to raise the wage rate to $4.25 an hour to get an additional unit of labor, what would the MC_N be? The marginal cost would be the wage ($4.25 × 40 hours) of the additional worker *plus* the increase in wage ($0.25 per hour) for the previous 5 units of labor (200 hours)—or ($4.25 × 40) + ($0.25 × 200) = $220. Thus the sixth unit of labor would have a W of $170 (for 40 hours) and a MC_N of $220 (assuming that the previous units of labor had to be paid at least the same wage increase as the new unit of labor). If we continued this analysis up the S_N curve (for higher and higher wage levels) we would construct the MC_N curve and see that it is upward sloping and above the S_N curve.

In Fig. 6.7 we see that the typical monopsonist faces a downward-sloping MRP_N, an upward-sloping S_N, and an upward-sloping MC_N (which is above the S_N). The monopsonist will determine the equilibrium level of employment (N_0) by equating the MRP_N and the MC_N (point E in Fig. 6.7). However, since the S_N and the MC_N

---

[6]A unit of labor here could be taken to mean one employee working a 40-hour week. Thus 5 units of labor would become 200 hours of work every week.

curves are no longer identical, the equilibrium wage level (W_0) is determined by point
A—the point on the S_N curve which corresponds to N_0.

Looking at Fig. 6.7, we see that N_0 amount of labor is employed at W_0, which is
below the marginal revenue product of labor (MRP_{N_0}). This has become known as the
"exploitation" of labor by monopsonistic firms, since in perfect competition labor
is paid its marginal revenue product.

6.2.2 LONG-RUN PERIOD

Unlike the case of perfect competition, there is not necessarily a movement to a normal
profit-level equilibrium in the long run with a monopsonistic labor market. By definition, the monopsonist controls the industry, and in order to stay a monopsonist he
must block entry to the industry by other firms.[7] If the monopsonist can block entry
in the long run, then he may be able to maintain a long-run equilibrium of excess
profits. Of course, if the monopsonist were operating at a loss (less than normal
profits), in the long run he would exit the industry. If the monopsonist is making an
excess profit rate in the long run and cannot block entry, then other firms will probably enter the industry, ending the monopsony situation and moving toward a situation of perfect competition (and normal profits).

Even if a monopsonist can keep other firms from entering the industry (and thus
ending the monopsony), some forces may arise to cut into any excess profits he is
earning. These forces can consist of either government minimum-wage legislation or
union wage bargaining. Minimum-wage legislation or union bargaining can put a
floor on the wage that a monopsonist can pay to the workers, and if the floor on
wages is not too high it can increase both the W and N equilibrium levels.

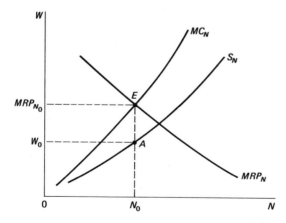

FIG. 6.7 Monopsony equilibrium: Firm = Industry

---

[7]This may be accomplished by being the only employer in a geographically isolated village, or
by controlling an exclusive patent, or by using illegal means to restrict entry by other firms,
etc.

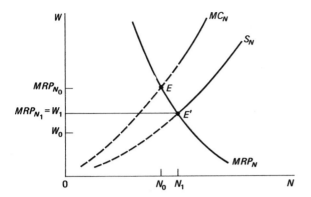

FIG. 6.8 Monopsony with a floor on wages

In Fig. 6.8, before a floor on wages is imposed, the monopsonist would hire N_0 units of labor and pay wage W_0. If the government or a union were to put a floor on wages at the W_1 level (no one could be hired for less than W_1), then the broken portions of S_N and MC_N would no longer apply; the MC_N and S_N curves would be identical up to point E' and then diverge (at wage levels above the floor). This floor on wages would cause the monopsonist to hire more labor ($N_1 > N_0$) at a higher wage ($W_1 > W_0$). Also, the so-called "exploitation" of labor ($MRP_{N_0} > W_0$) would be eliminated ($MRP_{N_1} = W_1$).

Thus, if a monopsony exists and is earning excess profits, it can usually expect competition from other firms, or union bargaining to raise wages, or government minimum-wage legislation to raise wages in the long run.

6.3 BARGAINING THEORY OF WAGES

The marginal productivity theory of wages has been accepted by many economists and goes far to shed light on the basics of wage and employment determination in an economy such as that of the United States. However, many economists have dealt with bargaining theories of wages in order to supplement the marginal productivity theory. We will here deal with three of these bargaining theories, and then attempt to homogenize them with the above sections of this chapter.

6.3.1 BARGAINING WITHIN A RANGE OF INDETERMINATENESS

One theory put forward by Professor A. C. Pigou[8] deals with a bargaining range of wages. Looking at Fig. 6.9, we have a diagram of Pigou's theory. The "range of indeterminateness" is bounded by a top wage (C) above which the firm would rather go out of business than pay (D_N falls to zero), and by a bottom wage (D) below which the workers would rather work elsewhere than work for that low a wage (S_N falls to zero). Within this range the union will have some "lower limit" (A)—a wage the union would

[8]See A. C. Pigou, *The Economics of Welfare*, Macmillan, London (1932).

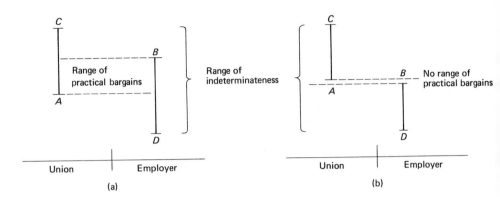

FIG. 6.9 Pigou's bargaining theory

rather accept than strike over. Conversely, the employer will have some "upper limit" (*B*)—a wage the firm would be prepared to accept rather than face a strike. These limits are their respective "sticking points."

If the "sticking points" (*A* and *B*) meet or overlap, then there is a "range of practical bargains" (as illustrated in Fig. 6.9(a)) and a bargain should be reached over the wage rate without a strike. If the "sticking points" do not meet or overlap, there is no range of practical bargains (see Fig. 6.9(b)) and a strike will occur—until or unless the sticking points are made to overlap or meet by union and/or management compromise.

6.3.2 CONCESSION AND RESISTANCE CURVES

Another bargaining theory was presented by Professor J. R. Hicks[9] and consists of concession and resistance curves. Each employer has a schedule of wage changes which he would be willing to pay rather than face a strike of some given length. The wage changes and expected strike durations would vary directly. That is, at a low wage only a very short strike would have to be expected before the employer decided that the costs of the strike equaled the costs of the wage; but at a higher wage a longer strike would have to be expected before the employer decided that the costs of the strike equaled the costs of the wage (at some very high wage the employer would rather face an indefinite strike than pay that high a wage). At each point on the employer's schedule (which is called a concession schedule), the anticipated costs of the expected strike and the anticipated cost of the wage concession balance.

A similar schedule can be drawn for the union, showing the length of time its members would remain on strike rather than allow their wage to fall below a corresponding wage rate. This is the union's resistance schedule.

The union's resistance curve shows that at a very high wage the union members would be willing to strike for only a short period of time; but as the proposed wage

---

[9]See J. R. Hicks, *The Theory of Wages*, St. Martin's Press, New York (1966).

drops the union members would remain on strike longer rather than have their wage fall any further. At some low wage rate the union members would rather strike indefinitely than sign a contract for such a low wage rate.

Figure 6.10 presents a typical concession curve and resistance curve. The optimal equilibrium would be point P (wage level W_P). At point P the union is willing to strike for a time equal to T_P in order to support wage demand W_P, and the employer considers a wage level of W_P equal in costs to a strike of duration T_P. Thus both sides would agree on W_P and avoid a strike. Any wage settlement above W_P would be a bad bargain for the employer, since the union members would have struck for a shorter period of time than the employer was prepared to hold out for. Any wage settlement below W_P would be a bad bargain for the union, since the union members would have struck for a longer period of time than the employer was prepared to withstand.

It is the task of the negotiators to identify point P and thus avoid any strike. If the curves do not intersect, or if one or both sides underestimate the other side, then a strike is likely. The concession and resistance curves are based on the *expectations* of both parties, and these expectations change throughout the period of any strike—thus shifting the curves.

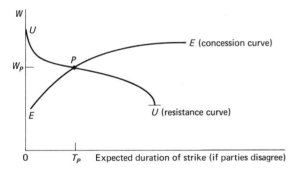

FIG. 6.10 Hicks' bargaining theory

6.3.3 COSTS OF AGREEING AND DISAGREEING

A third bargaining theory of wages has been presented by Professor N. W. Chamberlain[10] and involves the costs of agreeing and disagreeing. Chamberlain's theory looks at the union's bargaining power and management's bargaining power as the ratio of the costs of agreeing and disagreeing.

$$\text{The union's bargaining power} = \frac{\text{Management's costs of disagreeing}}{\text{Management's costs of agreeing}};$$

$$\text{Management's bargaining power} = \frac{\text{Union's costs of disagreeing}}{\text{Union's costs of agreeing}}.$$

[10]See N. W. Chamberlain and J. W. Kuhn, *Collective Bargaining*, McGraw-Hill, New York (1965) second edition.

The "costs" refer to both the pecuniary and nonpecuniary costs.[11] They take into account the total situation—not only the striking or resistance capacities of the parties, but also the economic, political, and social circumstances.

As the costs of disagreeing, relative to the costs of agreeing, increase for one party, the other party's bargaining power is enhanced. As the costs of agreeing, relative to the costs of disagreeing, increase for one party, that party's bargaining power is enhanced. In the typical bargaining case, each party tries to enhance its own bargaining power until a compromise solution is found.

The strike is the main union weapon for imposing costs of disagreeing upon the employer. The union strives to make a strike hit the employer at the peak season, and involve the whole work force or entire craft segment of the work force. The picket line can also be used to provoke sympathetic action by unionists in other establishments or trades.

The lockout is the employer's big tactic to increase the union's costs of disagreeing. Moreover, many industries have developed strike insurance; and ultimately the employer can try to replace striking workers and win the strike.

Bargaining power is relative to what is being bargained for. Thus, the higher the monetary demands, the higher the costs of agreement to the party on whom the demands are being made, and the weaker the bargaining power of the demanding party.

The union may increase its bargaining power either by increasing management's costs of disagreeing with the union's demands, or by decreasing management's costs of agreeing to the union's demand. Of course the management can increase its bargaining power in a similar manner.

No matter what theory is used, bargaining power is a highly complex and subjective concept.

6.4 SYNTHESIS

Can the marginal-productivity theory of wages and the bargaining theory of wages be brought together? The answer is a definite *yes*. The two theories of wage determination are really different aspects of the same problem. The marginal-productivity theory is the general approach to wage determination, and the bargaining theory of wages is the specific approach.

We can look at the marginal-productivity theory as being generally true for all firms in the U.S. economy, and as being the approach to use to get the approximate wage level at any profit-maximizing firm. However, if we wanted to predict the exact wage settlement of a specific business firm and labor union (at a particular point in

---

[11] Of course, management's costs of disagreeing is management's costs of disagreeing with the union demands; and management's costs of agreeing is management's costs of agreeing with the union demands. Similar definitions hold for the union's costs of agreeing and disagreeing.

time), we would supplement the marginal-productivity approach with the bargaining-theory approach. This latter approach would help explain the specific wage settlement that occurs within a range that is set by the marginal-productivity approach.

6.5 WAGE DETERMINATION—A SUMMARY

In general we can concern ourselves with the decisions made by the household sector, business sector, Government sector, and unions which effect the D_N and the S_N when we are trying to determine the equilibrium wage and employment levels.

The household sector supplied labor (unionized and nonunionized) to the government and business sectors; whereas the business and government sectors demand labor. Moreover, the government sector regulates union (right-to-work laws, strike regulation, etc.); households (compulsory education laws, child labor laws, etc.); and business firms (minimum-wage legislation, collective-bargaining regulations, etc.). These decision-makers and their decisions determine wage and employment levels, and the foregoing wages theories help shed light on the integrated process (Fig. 6.11).

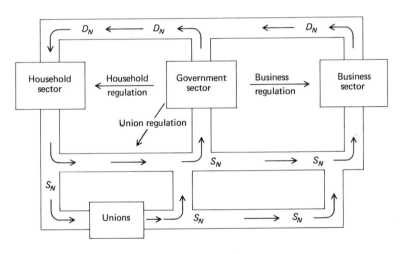

FIG. 6.11 Wage determination—decision makers

SUMMARY

In a competitive labor market the equilibrium level of wage and employment is determined by the labor demand and supply curves of the industry (market) and firm. The interaction of the industry demand and supply curves sets the equilibrium industry wage rate and the equilibrium industry level of employment. This market wage rate is given to every firm in the industry; and since each firm is too small to affect the wage rate, the firm labor demand and supply curves set only the equilibrium firm level of employment. In the long run this process will yield a normal profit equilibrium.

If only one firm dominates the labor market, then we have a monopsony. In such a case the labor-supply curve is upward sloping and so the marginal cost of labor curve will be upward sloping and above the supply curve. The monopsonist will normally hire less labor and pay a lower wage than the competitive labor market. Under certain conditions, the monopsonist can be pressured to raise employment and wages by government minimum-wage legislation or by union bargaining.

There are many bargaining theories of wage determination. Included among them would be Pigou's bargaining within a range of indeterminateness, Hicks' concession and resistance curves, and Chamberlain's costs of agreeing and disagreeing. We can look at the marginal-productivity theory of wages as the general approach to wage determination, whereas the bargaining theory of wages is the specific approach.

In general we can concern ourselves with the decisions made by the household, business, government, and union sectors which affect the D_N and the S_N when we are trying to determine the equilibrium wage and employment levels.

BIBLIOGRAPHY

Allan M. Cartter, *Theory of Wage and Employment*, Richard D. Irwin, Homewood, Illinois (1959), Part II

J. R. Hicks, *The Theory of Wages*, St. Martin's Press, New York (1966), Chapter VII

Campbell R. McConnell, *Perspectives on Wage Determination: A Book of Readings*, McGraw-Hill, New York (1970)

THE DEFINITION AND
STRUCTURE OF LABOR MARKETS 7

In the previous three chapters we discussed the supply of labor, the demand for labor, and their interaction, to determine the equilibrium level of wages and employment in a market economy. In this chapter we will discuss the labor market—the area in which the D_N and the S_N interact—in some detail. We will examine the various views of the labor market, the degree of structure of labor markets, and conclude with a discussion of wage differentials.

7.1 DIFFERENT VIEWS OF THE LABOR MARKET

Economists have viewed the labor market from many different angles. One possible definition is that the labor market is a process whereby the supplies and demands for a particular grade of labor are brought into balance. Another viewpoint, put forward by Professor Lloyd G. Reynolds, looks at the labor market as a geographical area. The labor market is a manufacturing and trading center plus the agricultural hinterland directly tributary to it.[1]

During World War II, the War Labor Board viewed the labor market as the area in which the wage structure and levels in an industry are fairly uniform. The War Manpower Commission had a still different definition. They looked at the labor market from the viewpoint of commuting patterns. The labor market was defined as the widest area in which employees with fixed addresses would accept employment.

---

[1]See Dale Yoder and Donald Patterson, *Local Labor Market Research*, University of Minnesota Press, Minneapolis (1948); Lloyd G. Reynolds, "Some Aspects of Labor Market Structure," in R. A. Lester and J. Shister, *Insights into Labor Issues*, Macmillan, New York (1948); and G. F. Bloom and H. R. Northrup, *Economics of Labor Relations*, Richard D. Irwin, Homewood, Illinois (1965), Chapter 8.

7.2 FIVE MODELS OF THE LABOR MARKET

It is the opinion of Professor Clark Kerr[2] that the term "labor market" has developed a double life. In one sense, the labor market is the totality of jobs for which the same wage is paid in equilibrium. It is the area within which the single wage pertains. The labor market sets the price. In the second sense the labor market is the area (occupational, industrial, and geographical) within which workers are willing to move and do move from one job to another. It is the mechanism which distributes jobs.

The above two processes (wage setting *and* job distributing) may or may not be closely connected, and it is out of their changing degree of association that confusion develops. Professor Kerr presents five general labor-market models which represent the differences among real-world labor markets.

7.2.1 THE PERFECT MARKET

This model is the perfect-competition labor market. Free entry and exit, complete knowledge, many small buyers and sellers, and the absence of collusion allows the perfect market to exist. The wage market *is* the job market, and the consumer reigns supreme in the allocation of resources. Demand and supply interact to clear the market and a single wage prevails.

7.2.2 THE NEOCLASSICAL MARKET

This model of the labor market recognizes some real-world imperfections. Workers differ, unions exist (but are not too strong), unskilled workers are at a disadvantage because of the perishability of their service, etc. Yet the labor market is the main determinant of wages, and workers are considered to be mobile. Over time, wages tend to the competitive level, resource allocation approaches the optimum, and the consumer retains his sovereignty.

7.2.3 THE NATURAL MARKET

Due to the great dispersion in wage rates discovered by economists during World War II and after, there is abundant evidence to testify that it would, in the absence of collusion, be almost more correct to say that wages tend to be unequal rather than the opposite. To the worker the job market is ill defined, since his information about alternative jobs tends to be very poor. The worker has a view of the market limited by lack of knowledge and a restricted conception of himself. Sovereignty is now jointly held by the consumer and the employer, wages are not set uniformly at the competitive level, and resources are not utilized to the best advantage. The operation of the job market doesn't set wages, but sets the limits within which wages are fixed and influences the specific wage levels within these limits.

---

[2]See Clark Kerr, "Labor Markets: Their Character and Consequences," in *Industrial Relations Research Association Proceedings* (1950).

7.2.4 THE INSTITUTIONAL MARKET

In this model of the labor market the policies of unions, employers, and government are substituted for the traditional action of market forces as the more significant source of wage movements. The wage market and the job market are disjointed, and can go quite separate ways. Labor is employed and unemployed in a restricted job market, but the wage market is an orbit of coercive comparisons. Institutional and leadership comparisons are substituted for physical movement as the main basis for the inter-relatedness of wage markets. The single wage now exists as a consequence of policy rather than market forces. The policies of unions and employer groups, as well as consumer choices, affect the distribution of resources.

7.2.5 THE MANAGED MARKET

This model of the labor market has been put forward recently by economists who believe the real-world labor markets to be too imperfect. There are basically two types of suggested managed markets. One is compulsory individualism—the labor market should be returned to competition by strictly limiting or abolishing trade unions, and by vigorous antitrust prosecutions to increase competition in the product market. The other type of managed market is collective determination—wage settlement by collective bargaining should be replaced by wage fixation by public authority. In either case state control replaces, in whole or in part, private control.

According to Professor Kerr, the institutional market is gaining in importance in the United States; since the first two markets are not currently obtainable in the U.S., the managed market is too unpopular, and the natural market is decreasing in importance as unions, large enterprises, and employers' associations grow. The insti-tutional market, although far from the best theoretical market form, is probably the best alternative; especially if it is modified whenever necessary to protect the legiti-mate welfare of individuals, groups, and the economy at large.

7.3 GEOGRAPHICAL LABOR-MARKET CONCEPTS

We have just discussed several definitions of the term labor market. Which one is the best? The asnwer to that question depends on the particular problem we are consider-ing.

For our purposes we can take the labor market to be the geographical area within which the suppliers of a particular grade (or kind) of labor came together with the demanders to buy and sell that grade of labor. Looking at this from the viewpoint of a circular-flow diagram, the labor market for a grade of labor (or particular occupation) bounds the particular set of households which supplies that grade of labor and the set of business firms which demands that grade of labor.

Of course, Fig. 7.1 is a simplification of the real world. For some occupations the labor market may bound a very small geographical area (such as the demand and supply of maids in a small city), whereas for other occupations the geographical area bounded is nationwide (such as the demand and supply of chemical engineers).

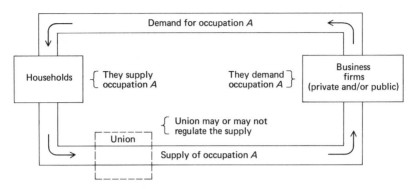

FIG. 7.1 Labor market for occupation *A*

There is one point that must be emphasized. In today's economy, no matter which definition of the labor market we begin with, the labor market is more complex than any product market. In a product market a good is bought and sold, and this is the end of the relationship (except where some warranty is involved); however, the buying and selling of labor involves a continuing relationship. The worker is interested in the totality of the job and not just the wage rate. Everything that goes into the personnel relationship on the part of the employer is of concern to the worker—especially where the worker is unionized and able to react to the employer's policies as part of a group as well as individually. The relationship between the demander and supplier of labor is far more intimate (and therefore more complex) than any similar relationship in a product or service market.

7.4 MEASURING THE LABOR MARKET

For most occupations and workers in even as mobile a nation as the United States, the appropriate labor market is somewhat less than nationwide. The costs (economic and psychological) of moving, the lack of knowledge by many workers of job opportunities outside their residence area, and the quality of existing transportation all have a part in making the appropriate labor market for most jobs and workers a local geographic labor market.

The U.S. Bureau of the Census has been measuring areas which can be said to approximate labor markets since 1910. In that year the Bureau of the Census introduced the *Metropolitan Districts* concept to its system of area classification.[3] The Metropolitan District of 1910 was defined for every city of over 200,000 inhabitants, and it

---

[3]For a brief discussion of this concept and the others we will be discussing in this section, see Brian J. L. Berry, Peter G. Goheen, and Harold Goldstein, *Metropolitan Area Definition: A Re-Evaluation of Concept and Statistical Practice*, U.S. Department of Commerce, Bureau of the Census, Working Paper 28 (June 1968).

tried to distinguish between urban population (whether located within the central city or adjacent to it) and the surrounding rural population. The same concept was used in 1920 and 1930.

In 1940, Metropolitan Districts were defined for each city having 50,000 or more inhabitants, and included adjacent and contiguous minor civil divisions or incorporated places having a population density of 150 (or more) persons per square mile. Although the Metropolitan District is not a labor market measure *per se*, we can look at it as the forerunner of some fairly adequate labor-market concepts. At the same time, the various Government agencies did not have a set of standardized areas for which they reported statistics. This meant that the statistical data gathered by these agencies were not comparable.

In order to remedy the above situation, the Metropolitan District concept was replaced by the *Standard Metropolitan Area* (SMA) in 1950. The SMA was defined so that a wide range of statistical data might be presented on a uniform basis, and it consisted of one or more contiguous counties containing at least one city of 50,000 inhabitants. Any additional counties had to meet certain criteria of metropolitan character, and social and economic integration with the central city in order to be classified within an SMA. This concept can definitely be considered a labor-market-area concept, since the SMA takes into account places of industrial concentration (labor demand) and of population concentration (labor supply).

In 1960 the *Standard Metropolitan Statistical Area* (SMSA) was developed as a slight refinement of the SMA. The SMA is currently the most widely accepted measure of local labor markets in the United States. It is used by various Governmental agencies to collect, analyze, and present data. Of course, no economist would argue that every SMSA defines a closed labor-market area and that no labor-market areas exist outside SMSA's; however, the SMSA concept is one very good approach to defining the major labor markets in the U.S., and it makes it possible for a wide range of data to be presented in a comparable form.

The definition of an individual SMSA involves two distinct considerations: first, a city (or cities) of specified population to constitute the central city and to define the county in which it is located as the central county; second, economic and social relationships with contiguous counties which are metropolitan in character, so that the boundaries of the specific metropolitan area may be determined.

Looking at the above two considerations in detail, we find that every SMSA must include at least one city with 50,000 or more inhabitants, or two contiguous cities (which constitute a single community for general economic and social purposes) with a combined population of at least 50,000 (the smaller city must have at least 15,000 inhabitants). Moreover, to determine whether additional counties should be included in the specific SMSA, they must meet criteria of metropolitan character and integration. The criteria of metropolitan character are that a minimum of 75 % of the labor force of the county must be in the nonagricultural labor force, and that the county must have a certain minimum population density (or meet an equivalent condition concerning its nonagricultural labor force).[4] The criteria of integration relate primarily to the extent of economic and social communication between the outlying counties and the central county (which contains the central city). A county is regarded as integrated with the county containing the central city of the SMSA if 15% of the workers living in the county work in the county containing the central city, or if 25% of those working in the county live in the county containing the central city.

Thus an SMSA includes the county containing a central city (or cities), and adjacent counties that are metropolitan in character and economically and socially integrated with the county of the central city. Figure 7.2 shows the SMSA's in the United States in 1960.

Over the years, the criteria used to define the SMSA have been subjected to much criticism. One of the alternative proposals for a new classification system to improve the SMSA concept is the *Functional Economic Area* (FEA).[5] The FEA attempts to set out the labor-market areas of central cities by defining around them a set of small towns, villages, and farms which comprise the area of active commuting to the central city. We can look at the FEA as a low-density city characterized by definite interaction of the various parts with the center. The proponents of the FEA maintain that the United States (outside the largest metropolitan areas) can be divided into a series of FEA's which will approximate relatively closed labor-market areas.

Using the journey-to-work data available from the 1960 Bureau of the Census, a set of definitions has been developed to identify FEA's. First, a *labor market* is composed of all counties sending commuters to a given central county. Second, a *central county* is the designated workplace area for definition of a labor market. And third, the *central city* is the principal city located in a central county. Using these three definitions, the FEA is defined as all those counties within a labor market for which the proportion of resident workers commuting to a given central county exceeds the proportion commuting to alternative central counties. Thus there are as many FEA's as there are central counties. Moreover, if two or more FEA's have at least 5% of the resident workers of the central county of one commuting to the central county of the other, then a *Consolidated Urban Region* (CUR) is said to exist. Figure 7.3 shows the result of applying the above criteria to the 1960 journey-to-work data for the United States.

The development of the FEA may prove to be the ultimate step in moving the SMSA concept into a truly viable labor-market concept, or at least an important step in this direction.

---

[4]In New England, the requirements with regard to the central city holds, but the other units comprising the SMSA are towns rather than counties.

[5]The use of this concept was suggested by Professor Karl A. Fox, Iowa State University. See Karl A. Fox, "The Emergence of Multi-County Functional Economic Areas as Labor Markets and Commuting Fields," in Neil A. Palomba and Edward B. Jakubauskas (editors), *An Interdisciplinary Approach to Manpower Research*, Industrial Relations Center, Ames, Iowa (1968).

7.5 STRUCTURED VERSUS UNSTRUCTURED LABOR MARKETS

Up to this point we have been looking at the labor-market concept from the point of view of geography, wage market, job market, etc. However, the labor-market concept can also be viewed according to its structure.[6]

A labor-market structure is a set of established practices which are applied consistently in carrying out the various employment functions—such as recruitment, selection, assignment to jobs, wage payment, and separation. These established practices create a "rule of law" in employment matters, and their main effect is to limit managerial discretion in the solution of employment problems.

Employment problems are a function of plant size. The breaking point which distinguishes the small firm from the medium-sized firm comes when the head of the organization can no longer know all his employees as individuals. For practical purposes of classification, this breaking point is probably 300 employees. As of 1965, firms which accounted for 51% of total U.S. employment had 300 or more employees.

There are two approaches to the solution of employment problems. The employer's approach is a personnel department, while the employee's approach is organization (especially in large firms).

Applying the above to labor markets, we find that a labor market may be either structured or unstructured. The unstructured market contains few, if any, established institutions by means of which people obtain market information or identify with any employer or employee organization. The unstructured market is the market of individual bargaining. It would include most of the employees outside the business population (farm labor, domestic servants, etc.) and a very large proportion of the employees of small business firms. The structured labor markets would be the opposite of the unstructured markets, and consist of the market for public employees, the nonunion labor market in the large firm, and the markets for which the major practices are the rights and privileges established by union work rules and the collective bargaining agreement.

7.5.1 UNSTRUCTURED LABOR MARKETS

The unstructured labor markets in the United States are large and heterogeneous. In 1965 they probably accounted for about 36% of the civilian wage and salary labor force. These unstructured markets fall into two broad categories. The private employees outside the business population (ranging from domestic servants to farm labor to employees of private, nonprofit institutions to office and labor work for self-employed professionals, to miscellaneous service and repair work) form one of the

---

[6]For the pioneering work in this field see Orme W. Phelps, "A Structural Model of the U.S. Labor Market," *Ind. Labor Relations Rev.*, April 1957; and, by the same author, *Introduction to Labor Economics*, McGraw-Hill, New York (1967), Chapter 3.

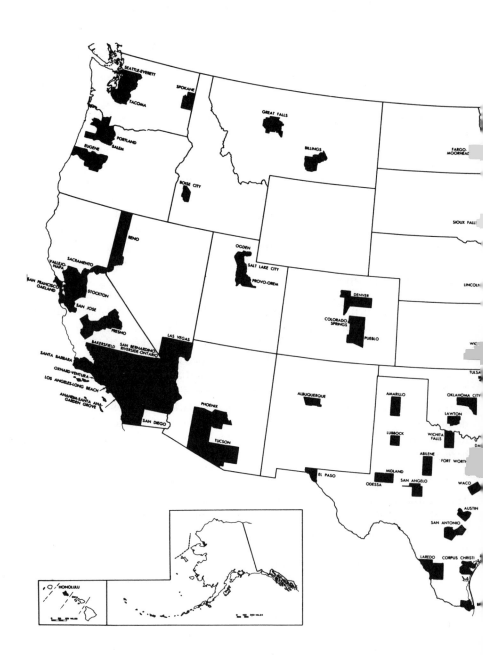

FIG. 7.2 Standard metropolitan statistical areas. Source: U.S. Department of Commerce

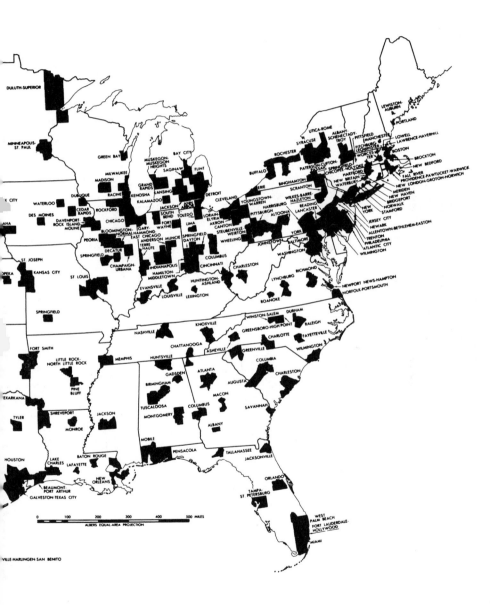

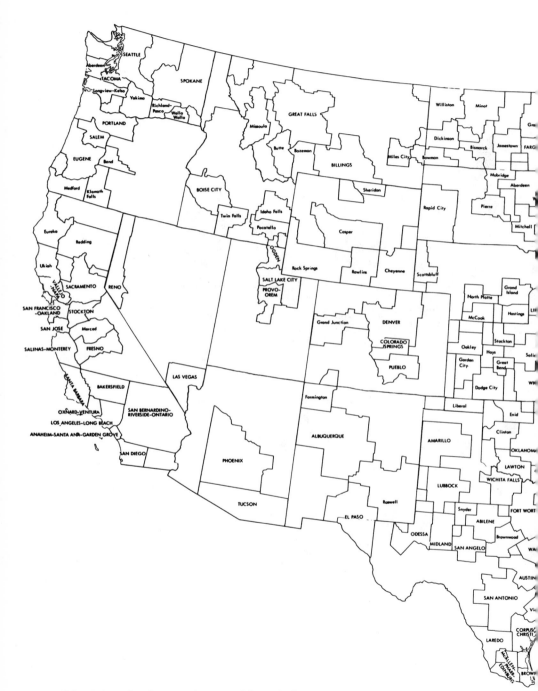

FIG. 7.3 Functional economic areas of the United States

categories. Employment in this category usually involves long hours, low pay, and poor working conditions. Union organization is impractical in these labor markets. With a few exceptions, these employees are strangers to formal personnel management and union contracts. The second broad category of unstructured labor markets consists of nonunion employees of small firms. The majority of small employers have no formal employment policies, but instead rely on the personal approach and *ad hoc* treatment of problems as they arise. Most small employers are engaged in strictly local activities, and therefore do not come under the Federal legislation in the employment area. These employees have their employment relationships determined by individual, face-to-face dealings with their employers. Law, contract, and formal managerial policy play a small role in these unstructured labor markets.

7.5.2 STRUCTURED LABOR MARKETS

The structured labor markets in the United States are composed of three large groups —public employees, employees influenced by formal managerial personnel practices, and employees influenced by union–management agreements. In 1965 the above three groups respectively accounted for about 15%, 19%, and 30% of the civilian wage and salary labor force.

Public employees are a very good example of a labor market structured by law. The prime characteristics of this market are impersonality and technicality. Public-service employment procedures are regulated by statute and administrative agency. Even though many public employees are currently being unionized, the legislatures and agencies involved usually can behave like private, nonunion employers as far as employment procedures are concerned. Most public employees are eligible for civil service status. Civil service status was designed to protect the employee from arbitrary decisions by management. Thus, where employment has become a matter of public policy, the pattern has been to move in the direction of a fully structured labor market with the emphasis on job security, classification, and fringe benefits.

Employees under formal managerial personnel practices fall into two groups— large unorganized firms, and employees outside of bargaining unions in large organized firms. In the many large firms which are still unorganized, the primary labor-market structure is the pattern of formal managerial personnel practices. These practices are instituted unilaterally and usually emanate from the personnel department. Except for custodial personnel, personnel management in these firms typically concerns white-collar employees, including clerical, sales, supervisory, and semi-professional workers. The employees outside of bargaining units subject to formal managerial practices consist mainly of the white-collar and supervisory employees in the large, organized industrial firms. These employees usually find themselves the beneficiaries of union negotiations, and although they cannot themselves affect the terms and conditions of their employment, at the same time their employers do not have a free hand either. They have no security of employment, but it is undeniable that they benefit from the union's presence. Employees in the above two groups work in labor markets structured by the personnel practices of their employers. The essence of this kind of structure is that it is unilateral (binding on the employee only), non-consultative and authoritative (final decisions on all policies are reserved exclusively to the management).

Employees influenced by union—management agreements tend to be manual, hourly rated, blue-collar workers. The market structure in unionized firms is bilateral, consultative, and subject to bipartisan review. No term of employment can be changed in such a labor market without notice, consultation, and agreement between union and management. The unionized market structure provides for bipartisan review of managerial decisions. The grievance procedure is fundamental and the employee's guarantee of due process of law. These employees fall into four categories. First, there are union members outside the business population, but their number is small. Second, there are craft union members in small firms. Here the workers identify with their occupation and union, and not their employer. Third, there are union members in large firms. Here there is true joint management of the work force, and genuine consultation by the two parties during the life of the contract. Fourth, there are non-union employees under union contract. These workers usually lean to management rather than the union, but they enjoy a jointly structured labor market the same as the union members do.

7.5.3 MANAGERIAL, PROFESSIONAL, AND TECHNICAL PERSONNEL IN PRIVATE EMPLOYMENT

This very important labor market in the United States, which should be mentioned separately, is practically unstructured, except for a few occupations whose candidates must meet formal requirements (lawyer, accountant, professor, etc.). The labor market for managerial and professional personnel is usually lightly structured, competitive, has high pay, long hours, and is relatively secure. What structure exists is usually traditional, and there is usually no formal grievance procedure.

7.6 ARE LABOR MARKETS OVERSTRUCTURED?

At this point it should be clear that no matter which labor-market viewpoint one begins with, most labor markets are not the perfectly functioning "structureless" markets that earlier economists talked about. In the real world, most labor markets become structured by worker and employer attachments, personnel policies, law, union agreements, etc. One of the most important causes of the establishment of strong boundaries between labor markets is unionism, and these boundaries make labor markets more specific and harder to cross.[7] Unions establish these boundaries by establishing sovereignty over jobs. The craft unions do this by asserting ownership of occupational and geographical areas, while the industrial unions do it by asserting the central rule of job ownership: "to each man one job." In the former case, the

---

[7]See Clark Kerr, "The Balkanization of Labor Markets," in E. Wight Bakke *et al.* (editors), *Labor Mobility and Economic Opportunity*, Technology Press and John Wiley, New York (1954).

worker gets his security from his skill attachment, whereas in the latter case, the worker is attached to an employer and not an occupation.

A central question at this point is whether or not these labor-market boundaries have become so strong as to make it impossible for workers to quit their jobs and move between labor markets. Many economists have argued that seniority systems, health and welfare plans, and pension plans have chained the worker to his job. However, some recent research has indicated that this is not true, and although labor markets may not function frictionlessly, the worker can indeed change jobs.[8]

Professor Arthur Ross has demonstrated that the recent decline in the quit rate in manufacturing, which has been put forward as proof of the chaining of workers to their jobs, is not due to a growth in seniority systems, health and welfare plans, and pension plans. The workers who usually quit are young in years and low in service, and thus do not have enough seniority to keep them from changing jobs. Moreover, the older worker is kept from changing jobs particularly by the difficulty of securing another job and the probable loss of his settled way of life in general. Mobility has declined with age since before seniority systems and pension plans. Professor Ross finds little evidence that labor resources have become immobilized and that workers can no longer afford to quit their jobs.

Thus, although labor markets are not frictionless and freely operating, at least as of now they are not overstructured and completely noncompeting either.

7.7 WAGE DIFFERENTIALS

If all jobs were equally attractive to workers, if all workers had equal physical and mental abilities, if all workers had equal access to occupations, and if mobility were frictionless, then there would probably be only *one* labor market operating in the economy. However, in the real world, working conditions differ, workers' abilities differ, and mobility is not perfect, which means that significant wage differentials can and do exist as a great many labor markets exist simultaneously in the economy.

7.7.1 EQUALIZING DIFFERENTIALS

In the real world not all occupations are equally attractive to workers, and since rational workers (with free choice) gravitate towards jobs which offer maximum total income, "equalizing wage differentials" develop. Jobs with inferior working conditions have to offer higher wages to offset their disadvantages. These wage differentials tend to equalize the attractiveness of different occupations.

Jobs which offer only irregular employment, jobs which are particularly strenuous or unpleasant, jobs with a long learning time, and jobs with a high risk to life all have to offer higher wages to offset their disadvantages.

---

[8]See Arthur M. Ross, "Do We Have a New Industrial Feudalism?" *Amer. Econ. Rev.* (December 1958).

A classic example of an equalizing wage differential is the traditional night-shift differential. Since most workers prefer to work during the day, a firm which has a day shift and a night shift usually pays a slightly higher wage to night-shift workers.

7.7.2 NONEQUALIZING DIFFERENTIALS

In the real world all workers do not have the same physical and mental abilities, and all workers do not have equal access to certain occupations—usually due to restrictions on the education or training needed for the occupation. Thus "nonequalizing wage differentials" develop which have no relation to the attractiveness of the work involved.

Workers who possess mental or physical abilities which are highly desired by society and which are in short supply are rewarded with higher earnings. Moreover, occupations which are not as easy to enter as others (due to restrictions of school openings, licenses, etc.) develop positive nonequalizing wage differentials.

An example of a nonequalizing wage differential is part of the wage that goes to Joe Namath of the New York Jets. Obviously his football talents are in high demand, but not in abundant supply.

7.7.3 NONCOMPETING GROUPS

Instead of one or a few perfectly operating labor markets, in the real world there are literally hundreds of noncompeting groups (or labor markets). These groups have as their bound a particular skill or industry attachment, and they each operate as a separate, functioning labor market.

Thus for a large number of labor markets there is no interaction, and no matter how high the wage gets in one market there is little or no migration to that market from another labor market. In the real world, no matter how high the wages for a physician go, there is no migration from the labor market for unskilled labor to the physicians' labor market—due to lack of ability *and* lack of financing to undertake the training period necessary for a medical education.

7.7.4 DEMAND AND SUPPLY

One way we can look at wage differentials is to view the demand and supply conditions in each labor market, and study the resultant wage levels. In this viewpoint wage differentials between labor markets arise due to differences in the labor demand and/or supply between labor markets.

Figures 7.4 and 7.5 demonstrate the competitive industry and firm levels' demand and supply in the case of the equalizing wage differential attached to night work.

In Fig. 7.4 we see that the supply of day-shift workers ($S_N{}^1$) is greater than the supply of night-shift workers ($S_N{}^2$). Thus the level of wages is higher for the night shift (W_2) than for the day shift (W_1)—assuming that the marginal revenue product of labor is the same during the day and the night. The industry levels of wages are given to the competitive firm (Fig. 7.5). Of course, if the marginal revenue product of day and night

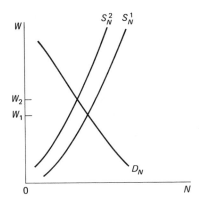

FIG. 7.4 Industry—day and night labor market

workers differed, the labor demands would differ and the wage differential in favor of night work could get larger *or* smaller.

In the real world, most labor markets operate in such a way as to contain equalizing *and* nonequalizing wage differentials simultaneously. Figures 7.6 and 7.7 show the case of comparing a hypothetical labor market for physicians with a hypothetical labor market for unskilled laborers.

The differences in the wages between the physician and the unskilled laborer can be viewed as due to the differences between the physician's and the laborer's demand and supply. In contrasting Fig. 7.6 and 7.7, we see that the physicians are in higher demand than the unskilled laborers (which means that the physicians have a higher marginal revenue product than the laborers); moreover, the physicians are in shorter supply due to the smaller supply of people in the population with the ability to be a doctor, to the limited openings in the medical schools, and to the long period of training. The first two supply factors lead to a nonequalizing differential, whereas the third supply factor leads to an equalizing wage differential. The positive nonequalizing and equalizing wage differentials in favor of the

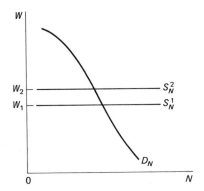

FIG. 7.5 Firm—day and night labor market

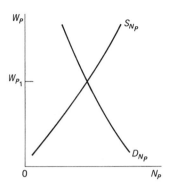

FIG. 7.6 Physicians' labor market

physician occupation outweigh any equalizing wage differential in favor of the unskilled-laborer occupation due to the inferior working conditions of that occupation.

One final point. Fig. 7.6 and 7.7 would probably be a good example of noncompeting groups. No matter how high the wage differential went in favor of physicians, most potential unskilled laborers could not cross from their labor market to the physicians' labor market owing to lack of mental ability and/or lack of money to finance the long training period.

7.8 SOME RECENT TRENDS IN WAGE DIFFERENTIALS

Wage differentials can and do occur between occupations, industries, and geographical locations. For example, in 1966 accountants classified as Class V according to the U.S. Department of Labor earned \$12,336, whereas Class V attorneys were paid \$16,728, and Class V engineering technicians earned \$8,940.[9] The long-term trend has been

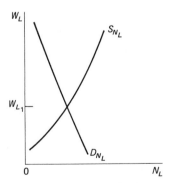

FIG. 7.7 Unskilled laborers' labor market

[9]Data from U.S. Department of Labor, *Handbook of Labor Statistics, 1967*, Bulletin No. 1555, U.S. Government Printing Office, Washington, D.C.

for the wage differential between manual and white-collar workers, which is in favor of white-collar workers (professionals, proprietors, clerical, sales, etc.), to narrow; and for the skilled–unskilled wage differential, which is in favor of skilled workers, to decline. The major economic reason for this seems to be the increase in the supply of white-collar workers and skilled workers relative to manual workers and unskilled workers. Thus, although the demand for unskilled workers has fallen, their supply has fallen even faster—due to the spread of education and training, and the restrictions on new immigration.[10] Moreover, the development of mass production and the declining complexity of skilled work making the skilled category less of a noncompeting group, and the expansion of the equalitarian sentiment reflected in the development and extension of legal minimum wages also help to explain the narrowing skill wage differential.

Since the mid-1950s, the skill differential has seemed to stabilize. It is still too early to tell whether this is a significant economic development. Professor Richard Perlman has put forward one theory about this recent stabilization of the skill differential. It can be argued that during the early stages of economic development the skill differential widens because the increased demand for skilled labor faces a short supply—but what causes the shortage is the inability to transfer skills from the old to the new technology. This argument suggests that since the middle 1950s changing American industrial requirements have created problems in labor supply similar to those facing a developing country. A temporary noncompeting group of skilled labor is created, based on temporary barriers of knowledge and ability. If this is true, then the skill differential narrowing should resume as the economy "develops" and the temporary barriers of inadequate knowledge and capacities are broken.

There have been wage differentials between industries for a very long period of time. The main reason for these differences is the differences in the kinds of labor demanded in each industry.[11] The industrial wage structure in the United States has been *stable* over time. Average wages in an industry change in response to changes in its occupational mix, in rates of pay for different jobs, and in wage movements within job classifications. Under competitive labor market conditions we would expect workers of the same classification to receive the same wage regardless of the product industry they are in. However, the fact that the industry wage differential has not narrowed does not prove that labor markets are not competitive. This is because we do not know very much about the occupational mix by industries, and so we could still have competitive labor markets (with the same pay for the same job regardless of product industry) but stable industry wage differentials.

---

[10]See Harry Ober, "Occupational Wage Differentials, 1907–1947," *Monthly Labor Rev.*, August 1948; and Toivo P. Kanninen, "Wage Differences Among Labor Markets, 1953–54," *Monthly Labor Rev.*, October 1954. For an excellent summary of many wage differential studies, see Richard Perlman, *Labor Theory*, Wiley, New York (1969), Chapters IV, V, and VI.

[11]See Melvin W. Reder, "Wage Differentials: Theory and Measurement" in *Aspects of Labor Economics*, Princeton University Press, Princeton, N.J. (1960).

Geographical wage differentials tend to be highest on the Pacific Coast, lowest in the South, and about midway between these extremes in the Northeast and Midwest. These differentials seem to be due to different industry concentrations in the different regions, different birth rates in the different regions, and different marginal productivity of agricultural labor in the different regions—since agricultural wages usually set the base for nonagricultural wages, as the nonagricultural industries bid workers from agriculture. These differentials have tended to decline slightly over the past few decades.[12]

Looking at the North—South wage differential, the economic data seem to indicate that the greater relative supply of unskilled labor in the South attracted capital to low-wage industries (industries using a relative large amount of unskilled labor) leading to the growth of these industries in the South. The flow of capital southward and the flow of labor out of the South has tended to equalize the wage paid for the same job between regions. However, with investment in the South directed to low-wage industries, the North—South industry-mix wage differential may widen. Recent data indicate that the overall average Southern wage level has stagnated, reflecting the counteraction of the above two effects.

SUMMARY

Professor Clark Kerr puts forward five general labor-market models. They range from the perfect market (the perfect-competition labor market in which the wage market is the job market), to the neoclassical market (the competitive model with some real-world imperfections), to the natural market (the job market sets the limits within which wages are fixed), to the institutional market (the policies of unions, employers and Government are substituted for the traditional action of market forces as the more significant source of wage movements), to the managed market (state control replaces, in whole or in part, private control).

If we try to actually measure labor markets in the real world, we should probably start with the U.S. Bureau of Census concepts. These start with the Metropolitan District, and advance to the Standard Metropolitan Area, and then to the Standard Metropolitan Statistical Area. The best current labor-market concept seems to be the Functional Economic Area (FEA). The FEA attempts to set out the labor-market areas of central cities by defining around them a set of small towns, villages, and farms which comprise the area of active commuting to the central city.

Labor markets can also be viewed according to their structure. Unstructured labor markets contain few, if any, established institutions by means of which people obtain market information or identify with any employer or employee organization. These labor markets consist of most of the employees outside the business population

---

[12]See Victor R. Fuchs and Richard Perlman, "Recent Trends in Southern Wage Differentials," *Rev. Economics Stats.* (August 1960); and Wilfrid H. Crook, "Recent Developments in the North—South Wage Differential," *Ind. Labor Relations Rev.* (October 1952).

(such as farm labor and domestic servants), and a large proportion of employees of small business firms. Structured labor markets would be the opposite of unstructured markets, and they would consist of the market for public employees, the non-union labor market in the large firm, and markets in which the major practices are established by union work rules and the collective bargaining argreement.

In the real world, wage differentials exist in very large numbers. We can discuss equalizing differentials, nonequalizing differentials, and noncompeting groups. Moreover, we can look at all these in terms of the demand-for-labor and supply-of-labor conditions in each labor market. The empirical evidence seems to indicate narrowing skill versus unskilled wage differentials, stable industry wage differentials, and slightly declining geographical wage differentials.

BIBLIOGRAPHY

Brian J. L. Berry, Peter G. Goheen, and Harold Goldstein, *Metropolitan Area Definition: A Re-Evaluation of Concept and Statistical Practice*, U.S. Department of Commerce, Bureau of the Census, Working Paper 28 (June 1968)

Karl A. Fox, "The Emergence of Multi-County Functional Economic Areas as Labor Markets and Commuting Fields" in Neil A. Palomba and Edward B. Jakubauskas (editors), *An Interdisciplinary Approach to Manpower Research*, Industrial Relations Center, Ames, Iowa (1968)

Clark Kerr, "Labor Markets: Their Character and Consequences," *Industrial Relations Research Association Proceedings* (1950)

Richard Perlman, *Labor Theory*, Wiley, New York (1969), Part Two

Orme W. Phelps, *Introduction to Labor Economics*, McGraw-Hill, New York (1967), Chapter 3

LABOR MOBILITY:
CONCEPTS AND MEASUREMENT 8

8.1 PURPOSE OF THE STUDY OF LABOR MOBILITY

Thus far we have been talking about the demand and supply of labor, and their interaction in the labor market to set equilibrium levels of employment and wages. However, we have not had much to say about the major process by which the supply of labor can adjust to changes in the demand for labor, changes in the nation's economy, etc. This process is labor mobility.

Why study mobility? In a growing modern economy, it is mobility which lends flexibility to the nation's productive capacity. Without mobility labor would be frozen into its geographical birthplace, and probably frozen into the occupational and industrial attachments of its parents. This system might work well in a closed, simple economy such as existed in Europe during the Middle Ages (or even to an extent in the United States of the eighteenth century); but in a complex economy such as we have in twentieth-century United States, the lack of mobility would severely interfere with production.

Labor mobility can be looked on as the process by which individual workers decide which job they will accept at a given point in time. The process of selecting a job entails the choice of an employer, an industry, an occupation, and a geographical location. Of course, the workers usually do not have to make any of the above selections only once. Some workers may switch occupations, or employers, etc., many times during their lives.

Figure 8.1 shows a very simple situation, in which the block on the left represents a group of households (or potential workers), and the four smaller blocks on the right represent different jobs.[1] The group of households can represent the millions

---

[1] Of course, in any labor market there are many more than just four jobs available, but this arbitrary number will serve for our simple examples.

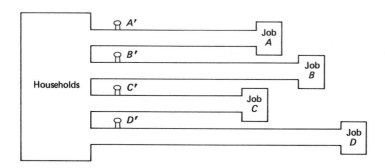

FIG. 8.1 Labor mobility process

of potential workers in an economy, or the hundreds of thousands of workers in a state, or the hundreds of workers in one small town. The four jobs (*A, B, C, D*) can represent the millions of jobs available in a labor market (national, state, or local). Thus job *A* may be a carpenter's job in a construction firm in St. Louis; job *B* may be a bricklayer's job for still another construction firm in St. Louis; and so on. A study of the mobility process helps us understand why and how workers move (or do not move) to certain jobs in their lifetimes.

Any study of the labor flows between households and jobs should also include the study of appropriate institutional factors which affect the mobility of labor. Thus, in Fig. 8.1, the four jobs each have a valve (*A',B',C',D'*) which can increase or decrease the flow of workers to jobs. These valves can be taken to represent minimum wage legislation, pension plans, employers' personnel policies, etc.

In this chapter we will examine labor mobility in the United States both from the conceptual point of view and the measurement point of view. Our purpose is to better understand the flow of workers among jobs and the factors which can increase or decrease certain flows—operate the valves in Fig. 8.1.

8.2 THE CONCEPT OF LABOR MOBILITY

There are at least three different ways we can conceive of the labor mobility process. The first concept is potential mobility—the *ability* of workers to make job moves. The second concept is mobility as propensity to move—the *willingness* of workers to move. The third concept is mobility as movement—the *actual movement* of workers.[2]

8.2.1 POTENTIAL MOBILITY

This first concept of labor mobility involves the *ability* of workers to make job changes of various kinds. That is, it involves research on the transferability of specific skills, and the aptitudes and skills required for particular jobs. For example, is a carpenter

---

[2]The interested reader can get more detailed information about mobility along these lines from Herbert S. Parnes, *Research on Labor Mobility: An Appraisal of Research Findings in the United States*, Bulletin 65, Social Science Research Council, New York (1954).

qualified to take a job as a bricklayer? If not, how much training would be necessary to make this job switch possible?

This concept of mobility would be essential in any attempt to determine the maximum potential flexibility in the distribution of manpower in an economy. We must know the extent to which workers are able to perform alternative jobs in order to make estimates of the levels and distribution of production that could be achieved by shifting workers among jobs. Moreover, we would want to know the skills of potential workers—people not currently in the labor force, but who could be induced into the labor force.

Anyone intending to construct a detailed, realistic model of a real-world economy's labor supply would have to possess detailed knowledge of the alternative kinds of jobs that can be performed by workers in the economy. Thus he would be interested in the potential mobility within the economy.

Despite its importance, relatively little attention has been given to this potential-mobility concept. This is probably due to the great difficulty involved in measuring potential mobility. More research along these lines should be directed at defining families of jobs with common skill and aptitude requirements.

8.2.2 PROPENSITY TO MOVE

Another useful concept of labor mobility is the propensity to move. Some economists have argued that labor mobility really refers to the propensity of workers to make job changes and must be separated from the actual job changes of workers.

This propensity or willingness-to-move concept of mobility is very important for purposes of describing accurately the flexibility of the labor supply in an economy like that of the United States. The ability of workers to shift from one job to another, the potential-mobility concept, is bound to overstate the actual degree of flexibility within an economy, especially a free-enterprise economy. This is true because a worker's ability to change jobs is no guarantee that the worker will make the change at any given time. In a free-enterprise economy, no worker is forced to make a job change just because that worker is *able* to make the change. On the other hand, the actual volume of voluntary job changes in an economy certainly understates the amount of labor flexibility. When flexibility is measured only as actual movement, it leaves out the whole area of movement that would have occurred had the opportunities and the incentives for it been present. Thus propensity to move can be a valuable concept. The willingness of workers to make job changes provides the best indication of the extent of flexibility in a free-enterprise economy's labor supply.

One last point: If mobility is regarded as the propensity to move, there are serious problems in measuring it directly. Conclusions about propensity to move usually have to be drawn from data on actual movement.

8.2.3 MOBILITY AS ACTUAL MOVEMENT

This third concept is by far the most popular. No matter what concept of labor mobility is preferred by various investigators, mobility is almost invariably measured in terms of the actual movement of workers.

By studying the past patterns of labor movement, one can interpret past changes in the distribution of the labor force. These patterns can then serve as the basis of predictions of the potential future flexibility of the labor supply—under assumed conditions.

In the remainder of this chapter, unless otherwise indicated, the term mobility will mean the actual movement of workers. This movement can be into and out of the labor force, or between employment and unemployment, or among different jobs. Mobility under this concept covers all types of changes in the job or labor market status of a worker that alter either his function or his location in the productive process.

At this point we should say something about the differences between labor turnover and labor mobility. Labor turnover is the number of workers separated or hired per 100 workers on the average payroll during the period covered. Thus mobility and turnover are distinguishable on the basis of viewpoint from which the job shifts are seen. A study of mobility requires a comparison of the worker's status before and after a labor-market transaction; turnover is simply a count of accessions or separations.

8.3 LABOR-MOBILITY CLASSIFICATION

Labor mobility can be classified into five categories. Mobility can involve interfirm movement (an employer change); occupational movement (an occupation change); industrial movement (an industry change); geographical movement (an area change); or change in labor-force status (a move into or out of employment, or into or out of the labor force). Obviously the above categories are not mutually exclusive. Thus a single job change can involve a combination of the above; a worker can change jobs and simultaneously change employers, occupations, and geographical location.

In most of the mobility research undertaken, a job is defined as continuous service with a single employer. This definition excludes any study of changes in the work assignments of labor within a given firm. Although this definition understates the occupational mobility of workers, it is used because of data limitations.

Occupational changes are measured as movements from one category to another. Thus measures of occupational mobility are influenced to a large extent by the degree of detail in the occupational classification used. No matter which system of occupational classification is used, two features it should possess are (1) a limited number of classes and (2) homogeneity within each class. However, these two features are in conflict. The fewer the categories in any classification system, the less homogeneity within each class.

In a similar way, the system of industrial classification used in mobility research affects the measurement of industrial mobility just as the occupational classification affects the measurement of occupational mobility. Again the broader the industrial classes, the less the homogeneity within each class. Broad classes cause significant types of shifts to escape analysis.

Measures of geographic mobility are ambiguous, since labor-market areas are overlapping. A worker residing in St. Paul, Minnesota, can easily take a job in Minneapolis or St. Paul. One way that is used to handle this ambiguity is to define geographical shifts as shifts in location in excess of a specified number of miles and not as shifts across the boundaries of political units.

Change in labor-force status can accompany any of the above changes and its classification depends on the definitions used—which in turn depends on the purpose of a particular study. For example, if a worker goes from one job to another with one week of unemployment between, should this be classified as a shift from employment to unemployment, and then a shift from unemployment to employment; or should just the actual job change be recorded? The answer to this question would depend on the purpose of the mobility study.

8.4 COVERAGE AND SOURCES OF DATA

Most empirical studies of mobility have been based on a segment of the labor force in a local labor-market area for a limited number of years. What is needed in this area of research are more studies covering samples of the entire labor force for many labor-market areas over a longer period of time. In fact, the employment records of workers over their lifetime should be explored in these studies.

The three major sources of labor-mobility data in the United States are data obtained from workers, employers' personnel records, and social-insurance records.

Data on mobility obtained directly from the worker have the large advantage of being the only source enabling direct analysis of the motivational factors in labor-market behavior. This source is also much more flexible than the other two.

Employers' personnel records are a useful source of work history information, but this usefulness is reduced by the incompleteness of the data—especially when work records for past years are required. Moreover, there is a great deal of variation in the information contained in the personnel records of different business firms.

The data recorded by the Old-Age, Survivors, and Disability Insurance program probably have a higher degree of validity than mobility data from any other source. These data also permit a researcher to continuously observe any selected sample of workers. However, these social-insurance records data do not cover all employment and they do not have occupational information. This means that occupational shifts cannot be analyzed, and there are no records for workers employed in noncovered industries, and there are gaps in the records of workers who shift between covered and noncovered employment.

8.5 DETERMINANTS OF LABOR MOBILITY

We will now deal with some of the major determinants of labor mobility.

8.5.1 AGE, SEX, AND RACE

The previously cited study by Professor H. S. Parnes found that the variable most clearly associated with mobility is age. The rate of job movement declines with advancing age between the ages of 20 and 65. Even when older workers make job changes, they are less likely than young workers to make a complex job shift—a change of occupational and industrial affiliation.

A recent national study of mobility undertaken by the Survey Research Center of the University of Michigan[3] found that of the family heads interviewed aged 18 to 24, 40% moved to the area in which they were currently living within the past 5 years; however, of those aged 65 or over, only 4% moved to the area in which they were currently living within the past 5 years.

The importance of the relationship between age and mobility has been established in many other studies. United States mobility data consistently shows that workers under 20 are the most mobile groups.[4] However, mobility does exist above 45, as shown by the fact that many older workers make enough employer changes to prevent them from becoming eligible for benefits under private pension plans. One recent study[5] shows that the overall mobility rate for men reaches a peak in the age group 18 to 24, and thereafter the rate falls off rapidly. By the time men reach their late fifties, mobility declines to a small fraction of the level of the early twenties. The decline in the tendency for women to change jobs as they grow older parallels that for men.

The above conclusions have also been supported in studies of specific regions of the United States. A study of mobility in the North Carolina–South Carolina–Georgia area in the 1950s found the young workers to be 45% more mobile than older workers.

Mobility studies undertaken in the United States also agree that there is a definite sex differential in mobility. Males have been generally found to be more mobile than females, with one study estimating that males were 65% more mobile than females. However, Professor H. S. Parnes has pointed out that this male–female mobility difference may be due to differences between the labor-force exposure of men and women, and to the measures of mobility used. When females who have been in the labor force continuously for a decade are compared with a similar group of men, there appears to be little difference in the degree of job movement. But Professor Parnes does point out that females still have a greater tendency to shift into and out of the labor force, and

---

[3]J. B. Lansing, E. Mueller, W. Ladd, and N. Barth, *The Geographic Mobility of Labor: A First Report*, Survey Research Center of University of Michigan, Ann Arbor (1963), especially Chapter III.

[4]The interested reader should examine P. Eldridge and I. Wolkstein, "Incidence of Employer Change," *Ind. Labor Relations Rev.*, October 1956; Robert L. Bunting, "Labor Mobility: Sex, Race, and Age," *Rev. Econ. Stats.*, May 1960; and R. L. Bunting, L. D. Ashby, and P. A. Prosper, Jr., "Labor Mobility in Three Southern States," *Ind. Labor Relations Rev.*, April 1961, for more detailed data on the effects of age, sex, and race on labor mobility.

[5]Gertrude Bancroft and Stuart Garfinkle, "Job Mobility in 1961," *Monthly Labor Rev.*, August 1963.

they probably make fewer occupational and geographical job changes than males.

The previously cited Southern mobility study by Bunting, Ashby, and Prosper (*Ind. Labor Relations Rev.*, April 1961), reveals that Blacks were approximately one-third more mobile than non-Blacks among males, but were actually slightly less mobile than non-Blacks among females.

Table 8.1 reveals the results of one statistical study which support the findings we have been discussing.

TABLE 8.1 Mobility by race, sex and age as measured by arithmetic mean number of employers

Race	Male			Female		
	Less than 30	30−49	49 and over	Less than 30	30−49	49 and over
Black	2.25	1.97	1.64	1.38	1.23	1.11
Non-Black	1.79	1.67	1.48	1.43	1.25	1.20

Source: R. L. Bunting, "Labor Mobility: Sex, Race, and Age," *Rev. Econ. Stats.*, May 1960, page 231.

8.5.2 OTHER WORKER CHARACTERISTICS

One of the worker characteristics—other than sex, age, and race—which has a powerful effect on mobility is education. In the previously cited University of Michigan study (see footnote 3) it was found that for those under 35 with a college degree, 50% have moved within 5 years to the area where they are now living; whereas of those with a grade-school education or less, 23% have moved within 5 years. Moreover, of the people 35 and over who have a college degree, 22% have moved within 5 years; of those with no more than a grade school education, 7% have moved within 5 years.

This study also shows that single people are more mobile than married people. Also, people who own their own homes, or who are receiving public assistance, are less mobile than others. Much more research is needed before generalizations can be accepted about these worker characteristics.

8.5.3 SOME INSTITUTIONAL INFLUENCES

Many labor economists generally agree that unionism has tended to reduce labor mobility by its "system of rules" which appear to strengthen the ties of workers to the jobs they hold. However, this hypothesis has not been empirically established.

The amount of unemployment has an effect upon the amount of labor mobility, since the amount of voluntary job shifting varies directly with changes in employment opportunities. Thus government fiscal and monetary policies can influence mobility by affecting the level of economic activity.

In a study undertaken by Professor Melvin Lurie,[6] the effect of vested and non-vested pension plans on labor mobility in the higher-education industry was studied. He found that for the higher-education industry, mobility was not affected on the whole, by the presence of vested or nonvested pension plans. This agreed with previous findings that industrial workers, in the aggregate, do not seem to let their mobility decisions be influenced by losses in pension-plan equities. However, when the data were disaggregated, some effect on mobility decisions was detected due to the pension plan. This suggests that if aggregate data on industrial workers were subdivided by occupation, similar differential effects would be observed. Thus the full impact of pension, health, and welfare plans on labor mobility cannot be determined without further research.

8.6 CHARACTERISTICS OF LABOR MOBILITY

Let us summarize some of the recent studies dealing with the characteristics of labor mobility in the United States.

8.6.1 OCCUPATIONAL AND INDUSTRIAL MOBILITY

There is a great deal of movement into and out of the labor force, and into and out of jobs in the United States. The major part of the total job shifts, however, are attributable to a minority of workers. In the previously cited study by Professor R. L. Bunting (*Rev. Econ. Stats.*, May 1960) 93.4% of the workers account for only 50.7% of all the recorded moves. In fact, 69.2% of the workers had absolutely no job moves during the period studied.

Professor H. S. Parnes found that when workers move from one employer to another employer they are more likely than not to change both their occupation and their industry. However, if the workers do not change both their occupation and industry affiliation, then they are more likely to change their industry than their occupation.

In the United States there seems to be an approximately inverse relationship between the socioeconomic status of an occupational group and its relative mobility. Professional workers have the lowest job-change rate, and the laborers have the highest rate.[7] Moreover, professional and skilled workers are more likely than other occupational groups to remain in the same occupation when they shift from one employer to another.

A 1966 study by Samuel Saben[8] found that occupational mobility rates, among men, were highest for nonfarm laborers, clerical workers, operatives, and service

[6]Melvin Lurie, "The Effect of Non-Vested Pensions on Mobility: A Study of the Higher Education Industry," *Ind. Labor Relations Rev.*, January 1965.

[7]The interested reader can see Eleanor G. Gilpatrick, *Structural Unemployment and Aggregate Demand*, Johns Hopkins Press, Baltimore, 1966, especially Chapters 6 and 7.

[8]Samuel Saben, "Occupational Mobility of Employed Workers," *Monthly Labor Rev.*, June 1967.

workers. For women, high rates were found in clerical and service occupations, as well as in the sales classifications. Saben's study also revealed that there was comparatively little shifting from blue-collar (craftsmen, operatives, and nonfarm laborers) to white-collar (professional, managerial, clerical, and sales workers) occupations; on the other hand, there was considerable movement among men from blue-collar work to the service field.

Saben found that a change of occupations generally occurs at the same time as a change of employers. Professional, technical, and kindred workers had relatively low rates in both occupational mobility and employer changing. Moreover, in general, white-collar occupation changers made industry shifts less frequently than did their blue-collar or service-worker counterparts.

In the previously cited study by G. Bancroft and S. Garfinkle (*Monthy Labor Rev.*, August 1963), it was found that a worker's attachment to his occupation is somewhat more stable than to the industry in which he works. Professional men and craftsmen had the highest degree of occupational stability. This is to be expected, since these workers have a high investment in their training, and the current demand for these occupations is high.

8.6.2 GEOGRAPHICAL AND FIRM MOBILITY

In the previously cited University of Michigan study (see footnote 3), only 35% of all heads of families were born in the geographical area in which they were living when interviewed. However, job changes that involve a change of residence are much less frequent than changes of occupation or industry. Moreover, geographic mobility is highest among professional workers, probably because the market for these workers is more truly national than for other occupational groups.

Economic theory informs us that geographic mobility should operate away from low wage areas toward high wage areas. Does this happen? In a recent study, Professor R. L. Bunting demonstrates that this seems to occur in the United States.[9]

One further aspect of geographic mobility involves the question of the willingness of long-term unemployed workers, or workers involved in plant relocations, to move to other geographic areas in which jobs exist. On the former question, recent research has revealed that a high percentage (50%–67%) of long-term unemployed workers are willing to move to other geographical areas if assured of steady jobs after moving. On the latter question, recent research indicates that the workers who are very apprehensive about their chances of finding another suitable job tend to transfer when their plant relocates.[10] This means that the transfer rate associated with plant relocations tends to be inversely related to skill and pay levels.

---

[9]See Robert L. Bunting, "A Test of the Theory of Geographic Mobility," *Ind. Labor Relations Rev.*, October 1961.

[10]See Alan B. Batchelder, "Occupational and Geographical Mobility: Two Ohio Area Case Studies," *Ind. Labor Relations Rev.*, July 1965; and Margaret S. Gordon and Ann H. McCorry, "Plant Relocation and Job Security: A Case Study," *Ind. Labor Relations Rev.*, October 1957.

Empirical research has indicated that rural migrants are less highly skilled than the urban population when professional and managerial abilities are considered, but their skills are similar to the nonprofessional portion of the urban male population. On the other hand, interurban migrant groups contain a higher percentage of professional and skilled persons than the urban male population.[11]

In the area of mobility within business firms, there have been practically no empirical studies. One such study indicates that the amount of mobility within firms is high, and that intrafirm mobility is primarily a function of the technology employed, external labor-market conditions, and associated changes in the composition of output.[12]

In a 1962–1963 study of geographic mobility, Samuel Saben[13] found that half of the migrants reported work-related factors (to take a job, look for work, or make a job transfer) as reasons for their moves. The single most important reason (to take a job) accounted for 30% of the geographical moves. Not too surprisingly, the unemployed, more than other groups, gave job factors as the reasons for migration. This survey also indicated that, although some changes in labor-force status and occupation did occur, most migrants who had been employed in March 1962 were also working in March 1963, and that two out of three of these remained in the same major occupational group.

We will conclude this section of our mobility chapter by looking at a recent study on mobility in small towns.[14] Labor mobility in small towns tends to be less complex than in metropolitan areas, because there are fewer opportunities to shift simultaneously between employer, occupation, and industry. Moreover, the workers in small towns tend to consider jobs in a wider geographic area.[15]

8.7 ROLE OF LABOR MOBILITY

The economic role of labor mobility is to shift individual workers from jobs in which the value of their marginal contribution to production is low to jobs in which it is

---

[11]Maurice C. Benewitz, "Migrant and Nonmigrant Occupational Patterns," *Ind. Labor Relations Rev.*, October 1955.

[12]H. M. Gitelman, "Occupational Mobility Within the Firm," *Ind. Labor Relations Rev.*, October 1966.

[13]Samuel Saben, "Geographic Mobility and Employment Status, March 1962–March 1963," *Monthly Labor Rev.*, August 1964.

[14]Irvin Sobel and Richard C. Wilcock, "Labor Market Behavior in Small Towns," *Ind. Labor Relations Rev.*, October 1955.

[15]Within the next few years, a wealth of valuable data will become available from a study being directed by Professor Herbert S. Parnes of Ohio State University's Center for Human Resource Research. It is a five-year study of the labor market experience, characteristics, and work attitudes of four groups of 5000 people each. The Bureau of the Census collects and tabulates the data, and Professor Parnes and his staff analyze and report on the results. Printed reports are beginning to become available, but it will be the end of the 1970s before the final reports are printed.

higher. This can be efficiently accomplished only when workers are informed of job opportunities in the relevant labor markets.

Although many workers seem reasonably well informed about alternative job opportunities, Professor Parnes found that many manual workers seem to have very limited knowledge of job opportunities and even less information regarding the specific characteristics of jobs in business firms other than their own.

Much more research is needed before we have anywhere near complete knowledge about labor mobility, but from what we know now, labor mobility in the United States seems to operate in the correct direction—at least as far as its economic role is concerned.

Although the economic aspects of mobility are of basic importance, labor mobility is by no means an exclusively economic phenomenon. Many people make job changes for personal, family and/or community reasons completely unrelated to economic reasons. These personal (or noneconomic) reasons for changing jobs may be very important when economic factors are not overwhelming. For example, workers who feel assured of employment at what they consider a satisfactory wage may feel free to exercise choice based on noneconomic factors, such as the location in which they want to live.

SUMMARY

In a growing economy it is mobility which lends flexibility to the nation's productive capacity. There are at least three different ways we can conceive of the labor-mobility process. The first concept is potential mobility—the *ability* of workers to make job moves. The second concept is mobility as propensity to move—the *willingness* of workers to move. The third concept is mobility as movement—the *actual movement* of workers. Mobility is usually measured in terms of this third concept.

Labor mobility can be classified in five categories. Mobility can involve inter-firm movement, occupational movement, industrial movement, geographical movement, or change in labor-force status. The major sources of data on labor mobility are workers, employers' personnel records, and social-insurance records.

Most researchers have found that age is the variable most clearly associated with mobility. The rate of job movement declines with advancing age. Mobility rates also seem to differ according to race, sex, and other characteristics. Moreover, in the United States there seems to be an approximately inverse relationship between the socioeconomic status of an occupational group and its relative mobility.

Geographic mobility is highest among professional workers, probably because the market for these workers is more truly national than for other occupational groups. A large percentage of long-term unemployed workers are willing to move to other geographical areas if assured of steady jobs after moving; and workers who are very apprehensive about their chances of finding another suitable job tend to transfer when their plants relocate.

The economic role of labor mobility is to shift individual workers from jobs in which the value of their marginal contribution to production is low to jobs in which it is higher. This can be efficiently accomplished only when workers are informed of job opportunities in the relevant labor markets.

BIBLIOGRAPHY

Gertrude Bancroft and Stuart Garfinkle, "Job Mobility in 1961," *Monthly Labor Rev.*, August 1963

Eleanor G. Gilpatrick, *Structural Unemployment and Aggregate Demand*, Johns Hopkins Press, Baltimore, 1966, especially Chapters 6 and 7

J. B. Lansing, E. Mueller, W. Ladd, and N. Barth, *The Geographic Mobility of Labor: A First Report*, Survey Research Center, University of Michigan, Ann Arbor, 1963, especially Chapter III.

Herbert S. Parnes, *Research on Labor Mobility: An Appraisal of Research Findings in the United States*, Bulletin 65, Social Science Research Council, New York, 1954

LABOR-MARKET IMBALANCES   Part III

Aggregate demand for goods and services often falls short of full employment. Manpower resources are underutilized or not utilized at all. Even when aggregate demand approaches full employment, the allocative feature of the market mechanism—wage—price adjustment—works with varying degrees of effectiveness, time lags, and obstacles to full knowledge of labor-market conditions.

The manpower economist is concerned with the effects of aggregate demand on employment, and with the allocation of manpower resources to alternative activities within the economy. Less-than-optimum operation of the economy at the micro- or macrolevel gives rise to problems of unemployment and poverty.

As indicated in our discussion of the framework of labor-market analysis (Part II) the labor force is a highly flexible resource. It expands and contracts over a wide range depending on the level of aggregative demand and the decision-making patterns of households, firms, and other groups in society. In this chapter we will discuss two types of imbalances in the labor market; unemployment from the point of view of households, and a counterpart measuree of imbalance from the point of view of the firm—the job vacancy concept.

9.1 GENERAL CONCEPTS OF UNEMPLOYMENT

How do we conceptualize unemployment, and how is it measured?

There are various meanings which can be given to the concept of unemployment. First, it can be a condition—a state of "being out of work." Included would be those who are either under age, retired, or not employed for any one of a number of reasons. A second meaning would be related to need: requiring a job to support oneself or dependents. This concept would be concerned with primary family breadwinners who are not currently employed, but from either moral, ethical, or economic points of view should be employed. A third concept is concerned with attitudes of individuals: desiring a job under certain favorable conditions, but not under other conditions. The fourth concept of unemployment, and the one most widely used for policy purposes, attempts to eliminate conceptual ambiguities by measuring unemployment in relation to the activity of individuals in being not only available for work, but in actively seeking work in the labor market. It is the concept of activity which is most often used by manpower economists and by policymakers.

9.2 MEASURING EMPLOYMENT AND UNEMPLOYMENT:
AN HISTORICAL PERSPECTIVE

Practically all members of a nation's population carry on activities that are considered desirable and useful to society. There are those who are too young, and the sick, handicapped, and aged who by the nature of their physical limitations are unable to carry on any economically useful function in society. Most people, however, do carry on work of one type or another that is considered useful. It is often difficult to separate functions which are socially beneficial to society from those which have an economic value. Various labor-force concepts have been developed and used, and only quite recently has a single definition emerged which is acceptable for labor-market analysis.

In the United States attempts have been made to measure the amount of labor as early as the decennial census of 1820. But it was not until the census of 1890 that a successful concept was developed as a working estimate of the labor force. For each decennial census from 1890 to 1930, the labor force was defined to include all "gainful workers." This concept was defined to include all those who were experienced workers whether they were currently in the labor force or not. Various weaknesses were apparent in the use of the "gainful worker" concept. *Current* activity status was not emphasized, since the information obtained related to the *usual* occupation. Data collected did not consider the measurement of the occasional worker, the inexperienced, nor did it develop a workable concept of the unemployed worker. Data from one census to another was not comparable, since different months were used from one decennial census to another. A definite time period of reference was established only with the census of 1930.

It should be emphasized that what is regarded as the "labor force" of a society is *not* the sum of all persons engaged in socially acceptable activities. One can best visualize the labor force as a plastic and flexible portion of the total population whose size and nature varies, and whose characteristics depend on cultural factors and also on the process of economic development. As an economy develops from a subsistence level to an industrial stage, a parallel transformation occurs in the nature of the labor force. Some degree of arbitrariness is always present in any attempt to either develop a labor-force concept, or, once a concept is developed, to accurately estimate the size of the labor force at a particular moment. The "value" of a concept depends on its intended use. Before the 1930s, Governmental policy at the national level was not strongly concerned with employment, unemployment, and the general process of labor-market adjustment to change. The "gainful worker" concept, though limited, was useful for its time.

Beginning with the 1930s, governmental policy at all levels was concerned with manpower and employment problems. High levels of unemployment in the 1930s found policymakers with no accurate measures of either employment or unemployment. In the 1940s, defense and war manpower programs necessitated accurate measures of the labor force to determine the potential size, nature, and characteristics of the nation's labor force for mobilization and production purposes. Then, in the 1950s and 1960s, questions of the employment implications of automation, skill-development programs, and education demanded sharpened tools and concepts in the manpower field. To meet this need, statisticians and economists fashioned and developed a standard concept of the labor force to meet the needs of policy formulation by governmental and private agencies.

9.3 THE LABOR FORCE AND CURRENT-ACTIVITY STATUS

The present-day concept of the labor force was developed by economists of the Works Progress Administration, and utilized by the Bureau of the Census in its decennial census of 1940. The basic emphasis, unlike the "gainful worker" concept, was on *current* activity in the labor market. At the present time, the labor force is the sum of the employed and unemployed during a particular week in a month. A sample survey of households, collected and tabulated by the Bureau of the Census for the U.S. Department of Labor's Bureau of Labor Statistics, provides a comprehensive measure of the total number of persons 16 years of age and over who are employed or unemployed.[1]

The Current Population Survey surveys a sample of households in the United States and this sample is "blown up" to arrive at an estimate of the universe of households in the whole country. In all, some 60,000 housing units in 449 sample areas, comprising 863 counties and independent cities with coverage in every state and the District of Columbia are included.

The sample is rotated each month and a balance is achieved in order to make the sample representative of the whole country. It should be kept in mind that the monthly sample constitutes a measure for the country as a whole, and is inappropriate as an indicator for any of the individual states.

The current attachment to the labor market is measured only for persons 16 years and over who are not inmates of hospitals, prisons, or detention or nursing homes. The use of age 16 as a breaking-point reflects the decreasing importance of child labor. This does not imply, of course, that there are no workers below the age of 16. In fact, two special surveys by the Bureau of Census in 1950 showed that the number of children aged 10–13 employed on farms, as newsboys, baby-sitters, helpers, etc., totaled about 1,000,000 in August and about 700,000 in October.[2]

The employed total from the household survey includes all wage and salary workers and self-employed persons who worked at all during the survey week, or who had jobs or businesses from which they were temporarily absent because of illness,

---

[1]Until very recently, the age 14 years was used as the arbitrary cut-off. Now the age 16 years is used, but separate data are published for 14- and 15-year-olds.

[2]Gertrude Bancroft, *The American Labor Force: Its Growth and Changing Composition,* Wiley, New York, 1958, page 3.

industrial dispute, or various other reasons, *regardless* of whether pay was received.[3] Thus it also includes unpaid workers in family-operated enterprises who worked 15 or more hours during the survey week. Employed persons include those working in agriculture, or in nonagricultural industries. Those holding more than one job—and this category has been growing in recent years—are counted only once and are classified according to the job at which they worked the greatest number of hours during the survey week. This monthly sample gives an unduplicated count of individuals in the labor force at a given point in time, and also provides detailed personal characteristics such as age, sex, color, and marital status. It should be emphasized that the household sample is an adequate measure only for national and aggregative estimates of the labor force. The labor force for smaller regions such as county, state, or labor market would have to be derived from special studies in the interim between decennial censuses.

The unemployed total from the household survey includes all jobless persons who were looking for work, regardless of whether or not they were eligible for unemployment insurance. Also counted as unemployed are persons waiting to be called back to jobs from which they had been laid off; those scheduled to start new wage or salary jobs within 30 days (except students); and those who would have been looking for work except that they were temporarily ill or believed that no work was available in their line of work or in the community. The unemployment *rate* represents the number unemployed as a percentage of the civilian labor force, i.e., the sum of the employed and unemployed. This measure can be computed for groups within the labor force classified by age, marital status, color, etc. When applied to industry and occupational groups, the labor-force base for the unemployment rate also represents the sum of the employed and the unemployed, the latter classified according to industry and occupation of their latest full-time civilian job.

Although time series from the household sample provide the basic information on the number of persons in the labor force at a given time, additional measures are used to explore and present additional aspects of the nature and size of the labor force. These include data from payroll reports of employers and administrative statistics of unemployment insurance systems.

Payroll employment from the employer survey includes nonagricultural wage and salary workers who received pay for any part of the pay period. Data are obtained on hours and earnings, by industry and geographic locality. Persons on paid sick leave, paid holiday, or paid vacation are included, but those on leave without pay for the entire payroll period are excluded, as are self-employed persons, unpaid family workers, and domestics. Persons on the payroll of more than one establishment are, of course, counted more than once. The payroll establishment sample covers about 25 million workers. Because payroll information is based on records of a relatively large

---

[3]For a detailed monthly analysis of the labor force, see: *Employment and Earnings*, published monthly by the U.S. Department of Labor, Washington, D.C.

sample of establishments, considerable detail is obtained which could not be developed from a survey of households. The household survey, however, provides information on personal characteristics of the labor force.

To complete our discussion of labor-force measurement, there are two additional measures of unemployment. These are not directly comparable to the household survey, but rather represent local data developed as a by-product of the operation of public employment services. The first measure represents a count of the insured unemployed reporting a week of unemployment under an unemployment insurance program of one of the 50 states and the District of Columbia. It includes some persons who are working part time who would be counted as employed in the payroll and household surveys. Excluded are those who have exhausted their benefit rights; new workers who have not earned rights to unemployment insurance; and persons not covered by unemployment insurance systems (agriculture, state and local government, domestic service, self-employment, unpaid family work, nonprofit organizations, and firms smaller than a minimum size).

A second measure of unemployment, derived from the operations of employment offices, is the "active file data." When a person seeks a job through a public employment office, his application is placed in an active file. It remains there until a job is found, or the application canceled on the assumption that the person is no longer looking for a job. Changes in the active file list provide a sensitive index of changes in unemployment and employment in local labor markets. Since a significant proportion of the labor force does not usually look to the public employment service for assistance, this measure does not give an accurate picture of the total problem of unemployment. On the other hand, the household sample gives no indication of changes in the level of unemployment within local labor markets.

Table 9.1 summarizes our discussion of current labor-force measurement by presenting the major categories and components of the labor force. The month of December 1970 is used to illustrate the size of the labor force and the dimensions of employment and unemployment.

9.4 PROBLEMS IN MEASURING THE LABOR FORCE

Although it may appear that the concept of "current activity status" may be unambiguous, various problems emerge in conceptualizing the labor force. Basically, labor-force concepts are concerned with "head counts" of people rather than with measures of utilization or nonutilization of labor supply. Some of the workers classified as employed are actually only partially employed. If they worked one hour per week or more and were not looking for work, they are counted as employed. These are more properly designated as "partially employed." Under quite different circumstances, the part-time employed could very well become full-time workers. Included in the category of part-time employed are students, housewives, and retired workers supplementing their retirement incomes. This group constitutes a highly flexible portion of the labor force, and its behavior has been the subject of close study and research. Within the primary labor force, there are those who would prefer to have full-time jobs rather than to be engaged in partial employment. There is a bias in counting these individuals as "employed."

Another problem in measuring the labor force is the arbitrary use of age 16 as a lower limit for those who are considered as "employed" or "unemployed." It might be argued that with rising educational standards and requirements in an economy demanding greater skills, the age should actually be above 16—say, 18 years. In any case, the establishment of age limits is arbitrary. One can either include or exclude thousands of workers by shifting the lower age limit by a few years one way or the other.

A third problem in measurement involves various borderline categories of labor force participation. There is a very cloudy distinction between some workers who are

TABLE 9.1 The United States labor force, by full- or part-time status, December 1970 (in thousands)

Status and/or category	Number
Total labor force	86,165
Civilian labor force	83,152
Employed	78,516
With a job but not at work:	2,781
Bad weather	96
Industrial dispute	65
Vacation	689
Illness	1,234
Other reasons	697
At work:	75,735
Full-time (35 hours or more)	58,403
Part-time (1—34 hours)	17,332
On part-time for economic reasons	2,589
Usually work full-time	1,442
Usually work part-time	1,147
On part-time for noneconomic reasons	14,742
Usually work full-time	4,007
Usually work part-time	10,735
Unemployed	4,636
Looking for full-time work	3,583
Looking for part-time work	1,053
Not in the labor force	55,137
Total noninstitutional population of the United States, age 16 and above	141,301

Source: *Employment and Earnings,* **17** (7), January 1971, U.S. Department of Labor, Washington, D.C.

unemployed and others who are not in the labor force. The definition of "looking for work" becomes crucial in placing individuals in one category or the other. For some, activity in looking for work becomes a difficult activity to measure. Some workers would enter the labor force under favorable conditions, but either remain out of the labor force or look sporadically for the types of jobs which are of interest of them. The area between unemployed, secondary labor force, and "out of the labor force" is often a blurred one which is defined to a great extent by the interviewer's evaluation of what lies in the respondent's mind regarding labor market activity. Currently accepted definitions of labor force classification in the United States involve the following priorities of categories:

1) "In the labor force" over "nonworker"
2) "At work" over "unemployed"
3) "Looking for work" over "with a job but not at work"

Other factors should also be kept in mind in interpreting labor force statistics. First of all, the concept of the labor force is static in nature. It gives the size of the labor force at a given time. The labor force should actually be visualized as a plastic phenomenon which changes from day to day and month to month, depending on entry and exit from the labor market. Many more people take part in the labor market by choosing jobs, and leave the labor market by leaving jobs, than are measured at a given time. The same situation is true for the concept of unemployment. Many more people experience unemployment over the course of a year's time than are indicated in the Government's Monthly Household Survey.

The use of the household interview has the advantage of avoiding much "double-counting" which would result if the data on the employed workers were collected from establishment reports. However, it is often true that the person interviewed is called on to report the labor-market activity of someone who is absent at the time of the interview.

The period of time reference also affects the number and nature of the labor force. The usual reference period is one week, but if it were one day, the labor-force statistics would vary considerably. There would be fewer persons reported at work, and more reported as unemployed if the time reference period were one day. The most appropriate measure depends on the use to which the data will be put. Reference periods vary as to whether researchers are interested in obtaining data on the work histories of persons in the labor force, labor mobility, occupational changes, duration of unemployment, as well as other criteria of labor-market performance and worker adjustment to change. Also, over a long period of time (say, a year), more workers participate in the labor force—employed or unemployed—than are indicated in shorter periods represented by a day, a week, or a month.

9.5 UNEMPLOYMENT AS AN ECONOMIC CONCEPT

As indicated above, unemployment must be conceptualized within the general framework of labor force analysis. There are different degrees of attachment to the labor force, and from primary workers who are strongly attached to the labor force at one extreme, we have varying, and diminishing, degrees of attachment by additional "labor reserves." At the core of the labor force we have the primary labor force: largely males age 25–45 who are employed most of the year. Beyond this group, we have "waves" or groups of workers who would be seeking work, or would be employed under certain conditions. These constitute labor reserves.

The Census concept explained in Fig. 9.1 does not necessarily indicate the degree of hardship of those seeking work, nor does it provide an indicator of potential manpower, since those who are currently "not in the labor force" could, under certain circumstances, enter the labor force and the ranks of the employed.

The particular unemployment measure utilized depends on what we are trying to measure. Unemployment means different things to different people. Depending on circumstances, unemployment could be defined as:

1) Surplus or unused *supply* of labor under current market conditions, including:

    a) Those totally out of work who want work

    b) Part-time workers who usually work full-time

    c) Part-time workers who would like to find full-time work

      Unemployment as "unused labor" could be represented as so many equivalent man-units of unused manpower per capacity of work force.

2) Number of *persons* who "want" work under certain conditions, including:

    a) Secondary workers (students, wives, retired persons)

    b) Those who are employed at lesser-skilled jobs, but could be used in better jobs (underemployed)

    c) New entrants into the labor force, who have had no previous work experience

3) Number of persons who "lost" jobs

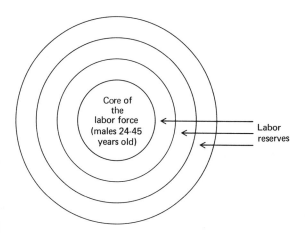

FIG 9.1 Concept of labor reserves

This concept would exclude new entrants, and possibly even secondary workers who are not primary breadwinners in the family. This concept would be a measure of disemployment. Some of these may, however, become discouraged with labor-market conditions and withdraw from the labor force. The concept of disemployment would include those laid off from work who:

a) Are seeking re-employment

b) Are no longer seeking work, are "discouraged" with current labor market conditions

c) Are working part-time, but are seeking full-time work

Unemployment of persons (or man-hours) depends on a complex interplay of forces involving numerous decision-making units. The demand for labor by firms depends on price—wage—output relationships, current and anticipated. The supply of labor by households is determined by leisure-employment preferences, knowledge of job opportunities, propensity for mobility, unionization, etc. Demand and supply is further shaped and conditioned by governmental decision-making in providing rules under which firms hire labor; and households supply labor. Labor-standards legislation, regulation of employment conditions for women, laws pertain-

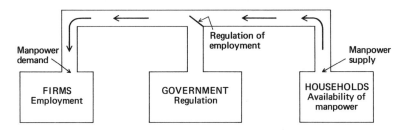

Typical decisions by firms	Typical decisions by Government	Typical decisions by households
Technical relationships in combining factors of production	Protective labor legislation	Leisure versus employment
	Law of unions and labor relations	Employment versus education
Price—wage—output decisions	Fiscal and monetary decisions	Join unions
Occupational mix	Government contract provisions relating to fair employment	Mobility
Work week, work year, etc.		Occupational choice
Production decisions		

FIG. 9.2 Flow chart of decision-making units affecting employment relationship, and typical decisions

ing to unionization, are just a few examples of how government influences the employment relationship.

Figure 9.2 presents a schematic flow chart indicating a model of decision-making units and typical decisions which affect labor demand, supply, and the employment relationship.

An imbalance in the labor market between the demand for and the supply of labor takes place as a result of an imbalance in the decision-making process of the various units in the labor market. The decisions of households to seek work may be out of balance with decisions of firms to hire workers. Superimposed on this is the decision-making process of government which alters the decision-making of firms and households through rules, regulations, and legislation.

9.6 TYPES OF UNEMPLOYMENT

It has been customary in most labor economics textbooks to outline and explain "types" of unemployment. It should be understood that workers can be unemployed for one or a combination of many factors. Definitions abound in the literature, yet all these can be related to the labor-market activities of decision-making units in the economy. Our discussion will be concerned with unemployment as a result of decisions reached by the respective units in the labor market.

9.6.1 DEFICIENCY OF LABOR DEMAND

Firms exist to carry on the production of goods and services. Manpower is one of the factors of production which is managed to meet the goals of firms. A decline in production most often brings about a reduction in the usage of the factors of production. Some resources are relatively fixed and not subject to curtailment in the short run. In the long run (by definition) all factors are variable and can be removed from production or channeled into alternative production activities.

It has been customary to discuss "cyclical" unemployment as a situation in which production peaks and troughs roughly match employment patterns, and unemployment is inversely related to production. There is sometimes an accompanying and often naive assumption that there is a recurring production cycle which is inversely related to an unemployment cycle, as depicted in Fig. 9.3.

A second type of unemployment related to labor demand is seasonal unemployment. As with cyclical unemployment, there is an assumption of a regularity in the recurrence of unemployment on an annual basis which is inversely related to production.

9.6.2 UNEMPLOYMENT RELATED TO STRUCTURAL FACTORS

A third type of unemployment is related to "structural" factors in the labor market. It can result from the decisions of any one or a combination of the decision-making units in the economy. In relation to the firm, a change in the input of labor per unit of output can result in "savings" of man-hours which may result in unemployment.

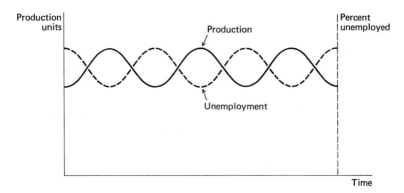

FIG. 9.3 Concept of cyclical unemployment

Or, related to this, there may be a change in the occupational mix of labor require-ments which results in a lesser input of certain types of labor, and unemployment for some workers.

Structural unemployment (often termed technological unemployment) relates in general to differences between the "pool" of unemployed versus the "pool" of job vacancies in the labor market. The workers desired by employers do not match with the workers seeking employment. To redress the imbalance, employers over time may redefine job requirements to make use of existing supplies of labor, or individuals may upgrade their skills to meet employer requirements.

Frictional unemployment (often used to denote structural unemployment) relates to a situation in which job vacancies are about equal to the number of people looking for jobs (see Section 9.8). A certain number of people are in the process of changing jobs, and we have some unemployment even in periods of high employment. Fric-tional unemployment is short-term in nature.

It is important to emphasize that unemployment is the result of a complex process involving many decision-making units in the economy. Decisions of indi-viduals from households to look for work, decisions of governmental units to regulate labor standards, expenditures, etc., and hiring decisions of firms all play a role in determining the level and nature of unemployment.

Types of unemployment can be classified in relation to causes or duration. A summary classification follows.

Types of unemployment

  I. Causes

    A. Deficiency of demand for labor

       1) Cyclical—recurring pattern related to cyclical production and sales pat-terns

       2) Seasonal—recurring pattern on an annual basis

B. Structural factors

    1) Structural—changes in occupational mix, product changes, or labor force composition

    2) Technological—unemployment caused by changes in the production function; redundant skills not readily reabsorbed by the firm in production

C. Normal

    1) Frictional—workers in transit between jobs; mix of job vacancies approximately similar to mix of skills possessed by unemployed workers

II. Duration

  A. Secular—rising levels of unemployment over a number of years, caused by prolonged deficiency of labor demand and/or structural changes in the economy

  B. Long term—unemployment of 15 weeks or more

  C. Short term—unemployment of less than 15 weeks

9.7 WHICH MEASURE OF UNEMPLOYMENT IS APPROPRIATE?

There is no unambiguous definition of unemployment. The appropriate measure depends on the policy questions involved and the changes in behavior which decision-makers seek to alter. For example, in assessing the manpower potential of the economy, we would use as the relevant measure not only the current number of workers seeking employment, but also those who are not currently in the labor force who could be induced to take jobs. The period 1941–1945 during World War II illustrated the flexibility of the supply of manpower. In addition to the number of potential entrants in the labor force, labor supply would also have to be concerned with unemployed man-hours of those partially employed or underemployed.

One of the strongest criticisms of the Current Population Survey concept of unemployment is that an aggregated unemployment estimate for the economy as a whole fails to provide critical information on local labor-market areas or even smaller census tracts or neighborhood communities. Area economic development programs which are designed to reduce unemployment within local labor markets cannot be developed with national unemployment data. Both types of unemployment data—national and local—are needed. Fiscal and monetary policies, designed to raise the level of employment and national output, must be concerned primarily with the national level of unemployment. Particularized programs of vocational training, industrial development, relocation, and mobility would be concerned with local unemployment data.

A question might be raised as to whether the Current Population Survey might be modified to provide local measures throughout the economy. The cost would be great, since the validity of the CPS sample is related to sample size. This would mean that the cost of developing unemployment statistics for each state might be as much as 50 times the cost of the present system. Consequently, local information developed as a by-product of state unemployment insurance programs, though incomplete—covering only a portion of the unemployed—is useful for decision-makers concerned with local and state problems.

It has been suggested by some observers that one way in which comparable state data might be aggregated to national totals or disaggregated to the local community would be to require all unemployed workers to register at public employment offices, whether eligible for UI benefits or not. Only those registering as "unemployed" would appear in a local or national count. A number of European countries follow this system and report only those registered as statistically unemployed. This approach would lose many workers who do not wish to use the services of public employment offices, or who have become discouraged with the job-hunting process.

9.8 THE JOB-VACANCY CONCEPT

We have been discussing one type of labor-market imbalance—unemployment—arising from a decision by an individual to seek work, though unable to find suitable employment during a particular time period. A similar type of imbalance—a job vacancy—takes place on the employer's side of the labor market as he seeks to fill jobs, but is unable to do so at a particular wage level or over a particular time period. A working definition of a job vacancy, analogous to the usual definition of unemployment, can be developed. A *job vacancy* is a position for which an employer is actively seeking a worker. This is comparable with an unemployed person who is actively seeking a job. The number of unemployed persons is a measure of excess supply in the labor market: the number offering services, but not employed, at a point in time. The number of unfilled job vacancies is correspondingly a measure of excess demand in the labor market: the number of persons sought by employers, but not hired, at a point in time.

A simplified model can be generated which will illustrate and compare the concepts of unemployment and job vacancy.[4] Figure 9.4 represents a model in which there are neither frictional nor structural problems, and no hiring costs. The volume of unemployment is measured by ab, while cd measures vacancies. This is a very rough conception, however, since employment at two different wage rates is assumed.

If we were to segment a market by firm, industry, or area, we would obtain a clearer focus of the two concepts. Differentials in the demand and supply of workers in markets A and B with "sticky" wages cause vacancies in one market and unemployment in the other (Fig. 9.5). Conversely, variations in supply which result from entry or withdrawal from the labor market give similar results (Fig. 9.6). The

---

[4]See John G. Myers, "Conceptual and Measurement Problems in Job Vacancies: A Progress Report on the NICB Study," *The Measurement and Interpretation of Job Vacancies*, National Bureau of Economic Research, New York, 1966.

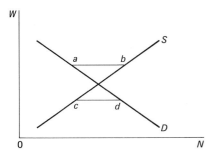

FIG. 9.4 Job vacancy concept: one market

outstanding volume of vacancies and unemployment depends on the nature, extent, and aggregative level of demand in the economy.

   Moving from the above simple job-vacancy concept, the U.S. Department of Labor has conducted a number of experimental job-vacancy surveys to further sharpen this labor-market tool. The Labor Department has defined job vacancies as current, un-filled job openings which are immediately available for occupancy by workers from

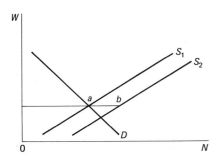
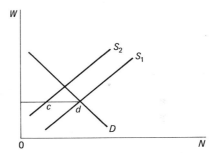

FIG. 9.5 Job vacancy concept: variations in labor demand

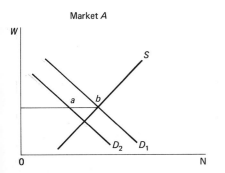
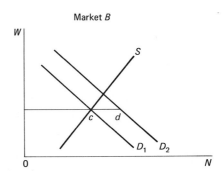

FIG. 9.6 Job vacancy concept: variations in labor supply

outside the firm and for which the firm is actively seeking such workers. Included are full-time, part-time, permanent, temporary, seasonal, and short-term job openings.

"Actively seeking" is defined as a firm's current efforts to fill the job with a worker from outside the firm through the following means.

1) Soliciting assistance of public or private employment agencies, school or college placement offices, labor unions, employment groups, business or professional organizations, business associates, friends, and employees in locating suitable candidates

2) Using help-wanted advertising

3) Conducting recruitment programs

4) Interviewing walk-in applicants

5) Reopening the acceptance of applications from prospective candidates

The Labor Department definition of job vacancy excludes the following.

1) Jobs held for employees who will be recalled

2) Jobs to be filled by transfer, promotion, or demotion

3) Jobs held for workers on paid or unpaid leave

4) Jobs filled by overtime work which are not intended to be filled by new workers

5) Job openings for which new workers are already hired and scheduled to start work at a later date

6) Jobs unoccupied because of labor—management disputes

9.9 JOB VACANCIES AND UNEMPLOYMENT

Although conceptually analogous to the unemployment index the movement of persons in filling job vacancies is a complex process. The decision of an individual to change his labor-force status is affected by a number of conditions, including the following.

1) Knowledge of current and potential earnings in alternative occupations

2) Conditions of work

3) Expense in money and time in searching for an appropriate job

4) Alternative sources of income and support, such as welfare payments, unemployment insurance, and other transfer payments

5) Alternative (nonwage) sources of activity in the home or community, and relationship of this to job preferences.

In the same fashion, employers face a number of alternatives in filling job vacancies. Hard-to-fill jobs may be redesigned, and scarce skills may be utilized more fully through the use of subprofessionals or assistants. Other adjustments may include the substitution of capital for manpower, and also the use of overtime hours for employed workers.

Some writers[5] have equated an equality of unemployment and job vacancies as a sufficient condition for defining full employment. At the most simplistic level, it is assumed that if there are, for example, 3 million unemployed persons and 3 million job vacancies, then unemployment is frictional and we are at relatively full employment. This is incorrect. We would have to have additional information on the relative composition of vacancies and unemployment by occupation, region, and geographical area. Moreover, as Professor Gordon has indicated,[6] the equality of vacancies and unemployment does not give us a unique solution for full employment because we have not specified other conditions in a social-welfare function, such as prices, balance of payments, economic growth, and productivity changes.[7] We must specify a number of variables in a social-welfare function before full employment can be defined in an operational sense. Job vacancies may be equal to unemployment at less-than-full, full, or overfull employment, depending on the magnitude of other variables in the social welfare function.

9.10 THE VALUE OF JOB-VACANCY STATISTICS

Unlike the Census—BLS unemployment series, which has been carefully refined and has been operational for many years, job-vacancy data have been collected either on an experimental basis[8] or as a part of the operation of collecting labor-turnover data (U.S. Bureau of Labor Statistics). Congressional hearings listed the following potential operational uses of job vacancy statistics.

1) Disclose unmet needs for workers in a wide range of occupations, and provide an indication of training requirements for Federal manpower programs

2) Assist in the establishment of vocational training courses for both adults and high school students

3) Counsel workers about opportunities in this labor market

4) Assist the Employment Service in matching workers with job openings and in assisting employers in meeting manpower requirements

5) Assist firms in developing more effective recruiting policies

6) Stimulate firms to improve their efficiency through more conscious manpower planning

---

[5]Remarks of Arthur F. Burns before the Joint Economic Committee on "An Economic Symposium on the Occasion of the Twentieth Anniversary of the Employment Act of 1946," February 23, 1966.

[6]Robert A. Gordon, *The Goal of Full Employment*, Wiley, New York, 1967.

[7]See Chapter 18.

[8]See *Job Vacancy Statistics, A Report of the Subcommittee on Economic Statistics of the Joint Economic Committee*, Washington, D.C., 1966.

7) Assist labor organizations in evaluating the demand for the services of their members and in developing policies for training, apprenticeships, and collective bargaining

8) Assist in the geographic mobility of workers

In addition to operational uses, job vacancy data would also have the following analytical uses:

1) Predict the occupational needs of the country

2) Serve as a leading indicator of the general level of economic activity

3) Prepare regular reports to the President on current manpower shortages

4) Act as an index in determining the tightness of labor markets and possible wage trends

5) Indicate the ability of the economy to undergo the stress of structural changes (defense buildup, or layoffs due to changes in demand or technology)

6) Assist in the determination of how greatly aggregate demand could be increased without wage and price inflation

SUMMARY

The labor force is a highly flexible resource. The determination of who works and who remains unemployed rests on a complex array of factors reflecting an interaction between households, firms, government, and other institutions.

Conceptually, unemployment can have any one of a number of meanings. It can be a condition (being out of work), a need (requiring a job to support oneself), an attitude (wanting a job under certain conditions), or an activity (looking for work and being unable to find it).

The most significant concept of unemployment relates to activity: A person must be out of work and looking for a job. National data are reported monthly from a sample of households to determine work status and activity of all persons age 16 and over. Persons are then classified as employed, unemployed, or not in the labor force.

The labor force can be visualized in terms of both "stocks" and "flows" within the categories of employed, unemployed, and not in the labor force. Levels within each of the categories at any given time represent manpower "stocks," either employed in the production process, unemployed, or not currently in the labor force. Changes in status from one category to another represent "flows." The manpower economist studies the decisions which determine the levels of the "stocks" and the nature of the "flows."

Manpower policy in an overall sense is concerned with optimizing decisions of workers in the labor force to make possible higher resource uses for manpower, to reduce "flows" into the unemployment category, and to permit those out of the labor force to enter (or re-enter) if they desire to do so.

BIBLIOGRAPHY

Concepts and Methods used in Manpower Statistics from the Current Population Survey, BLS Report No. 313, Current Population Reports, Series P-23, No. 22. U.S. Department of Labor, and U.S. Department of Commerce, June 1967

Marvin Adelson, *Manpower, Adjustment, and the System*, Technical Memorandum. System Development Corporation, Santa Monica, California, May 21, 1970

Arthur M. Ross. *Employment Policy and the Labor Market*, University of California Press, Berkeley, 1965

Measuring Employment and Unemployment, U.S. President's Committee to Appraise Employment and Unemployment Statistics, Government Printing Office, Washington, D.C., 1962

Unemployment: Terminology, Measurement, and Analysis, U.S. Congress, Joint Economic Committee, Government Printing Office, Washington, D.C., 1961

The Measure and Interpretation of Job Vacancies, National Bureau of Economic Research, New York, 1966

Job Vacancy Statistics. A Report of the Subcommittee on Economic Statistics, U.S. Government Printing Office, Washington, D.C., 1966

This chapter is concerned with unemployment trends in the United States since World War II. The concept of relative dispersion index will be utilized to examine changing patterns of unemployment by age, sex, color, occupation, industry, etc. The debate on structural transformation versus inadequate aggregate demand of the 1950s and 1960s will also be explored.

10.1 FROM GENERALIZED TO PARTICULARIZED UNEMPLOYMENT

Reliable data on unemployment did not really exist in the United States (except in a fragmentary manner) until about 1940. What data are available indicate that from the end of the nineteenth century until 1929 unemployment fluctuated between 5 and 10%. Unemployment was considered the result of labor pricing itself too high. Thus the proper policy was to keep wages at a level at which labor could be fully employed. Economic progress was also felt to contribute to unemployment. It was believed that the economy developed in spurts that were uneven.

Before the 1930s, there was very little concern by the government with unemployment, which was considered to be an individual problem. A person would have to rely on savings, relatives, or friends when he was unemployed. Alternatively, he could seek agricultural work or return to Europe. It was felt that what unemployment did occur would be short-lived, since the United States had a growth economy in which jobs would reappear in time. All this was to change during the decade of the 1930s.

As Table 10.1 and Fig. 10.1 reveal, the Great Depression brought extremely high unemployment rates. The peak unemployment rate of one in four in 1933 is a conservative estimate. Many economists believe that one in three unemployed is a more accurate figure for 1933. Unemployment at best never went below 14% from 1931 to 1940.

TABLE 10.1 Unemployment in the United States, 1929−1968 (in thousands)

Year	Number	Percent of civilian labor force	Year	Number	Percent of civilian labor force
Persons 14 years of age and over			Persons 16 years of age and over		
1929	1,550	3.2	1947	2,311	3.9
1930	4,340	8.7	1948	2,276	3.8
1931	8,020	15.9	1949	3,637	5.9
1932	12,060	23.6	1950	3,288	5.3
1933	12,830	24.9	1951	2,055	3.3
1934	11,340	21.7	1952	1,883	3.0
1935	10,610	20.1	1953	1,834	2.9
1936	9.030	16.9	1954	3,532	5.5
1937	7,700	14.3	1955	2,852	4.4
1938	10,390	19.0	1956	2,750	4.1
1939	9,480	17.2	1957	2,859	4.3
1940	8,120	14.6	1958	4,602	6.8
1941	5,560	9.9	1959	3,740	5.5
1942	2,660	4.7	1960	3,852	5.5
1943	1,070	1.9	1961	4,714	6.7
1944	670	1.2	1962	3,911	5.5
1945	1,040	1.9	1963	4,070	5.7
1946	2,270	3.9	1964	3,786	5.2
1947	2,356	3.9	1965	3,366	4.5
			1966	2,875	3.8
			1967	2,975	3.8
			1968	2,817	3.6

Source: *Employment and Earnings and Monthly Report on the Labor Force,* April 1969, Table A-I, page 17.

The picture changed dramatically in the 1940s as the economy operated at top capacity due to World War II. By 1944 the unemployment rate had fallen to just over 1% of the civilian labor force. With the end of World War II, unemployment rates began to rise again, but came nowhere near the levels of the Great Depression.

Beginning with 1950, the United States' economy was rarely below a level of 4% unemployment except for the Korean War period (1951−1953) and the last few years of the 1960s. Looking at Fig. 10.1, we see a gradual climb in the U.S. unemployment rate from the end of the Korean War. Each economic upswing left the unemployment rate higher than the previous upswing. At the 1953 peak the unemployment rate was below 3%, while the unemployment rate was over 4% at the 1957 peak, and it was over 5% at the 1960 peak. Between 1960 and 1965 the unemployment rate stayed above 4%. This gradual rise in unemployment finally began to recede in the late 1960s, but not before a long, heated debate over the reasons for the rise in unemployment.

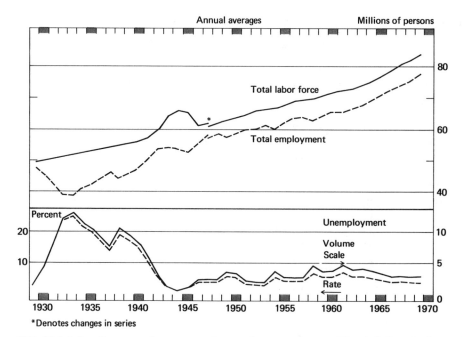

FIG. 10.1 Labor force, employment, and unemployment. Source: *Historical Chart Book*, Board of Governors of the Federal Reserve System, Washington, D.C. (1970), based on statistics data from U.S. Bureau of Census and U.S. Bureau of Labor

It seemed to many economists in the 1960s that the "mass unemployment" of the 1930s had been replaced by "class unemployment" of the late 1950s and early 1960s. Class unemployment entails very high unemployment rates in *specific* groups, such as certain industries (railroads, textiles, mining), certain geographical areas (Appalachia, etc.), certain age groups (over 45 years old), and certain minority groups (Blacks, Indians, etc.) rather than a very high aggregate unemployment rate. Although the low overall unemployment rate of the late 1960s took some of the urgency out of the debate over class unemployment, this debate is still worthy of detailed treatment, which it will receive in the next section of this chapter.

The single unemployment figure for the entire labor force should not be the only figure on which attention is focused. In any year the incidence of unemployment varies by industry, occupation, region, and personal characteristics. The heaviest burden of unemployment usually falls on the least prepared groups: inexperienced young people, Blacks, unskilled workers, etc. Changing patterns of unemployment by specific groups will be examined in the last section of this chapter.

Further evidence that the United States economy has been plagued by particularized unemployment since the late 1950s (as opposed to the generalized unemployment of the 1930s) can be seen by comparing the recent U.S. unemployment record with the recent unemployment record of Europe.

In Table 10.2, the figures in parentheses are unemployment rates revised to correspond to American definitions of unemployment. Examining this table, we see that unemployment of 3% or less has been the rule recently in European countries—less than in the United States. In fact from 1960 to 1964 the United States had the highest unemployment rate of all the countries listed in Table 10.2. In general, European countries seem to define full employment in the 2–3% range, and these countries have much more consistently achieved their goal than the United States has.

In the last years of the 1960s, the United States has shown a growing recognition of and sensitivity to high unemployment rates, especially among Blacks, the young, and the unskilled. Thus there is a strong possibility that, with a proper mix of monetary–fiscal policy and manpower policy, the United States in the 1970s will keep overall unemployment below 4%, and try to reduce the high unemployment

TABLE 10.2 Percentage of civilian labor force unemployed in selected countries, 1950–1964

Year	Belgium	France	Germany* (Fed. Rep.)	Italy	Nether- lands	Sweden	United† Kingdom	United States
1950	5.0		7.2		2.1	2.2	1.2	5.3
1951	4.4		6.4		2.5	1.8	0.9	3.3
1952	5.2		6.1		3.6	2.3	1.5	3.1
1953	5.5		5.5		2.6	2.8	1.3	2.9
1954	5.2	1.7	5.2	8.2	1.9	2.6	1.0	5.6
1955	4.0	1.5	3.9	7.1	1.3	2.5	0.9	4.4
1956	2.9	1.1	3.1	8.9	0.9	1.7	0.9	4.2
1957	2.4	0.9	2.7	7.1	1.2	1.9	1.1	4.3
1958	3.4	0.9	2.7	6.1	2.4	2.5	1.6	6.8
1959	4.0	1.4 (2.8)	1.9 (1.6)	5.3 (5.7)	1.9	2.0**	1.7 (3.1)	5.5
1960‡	3.4	1.3 (2.7)	1.0 (0.7)	4.0 (4.3)	1.1	1.8**	1.3 (2.4)	5.6
1961‡	2.7	1.1 (2.4)	0.7 (0.4)	3.5 (3.7)	0.8	1.5 (1.5)	1.1 (2.3)	6.7
1962‡	2.2	1.3 (2.5)	0.6 (0.4)	3.0 (3.2)	0.7	1.5 (1.5)	1.6 (2.9)	5.6
1963‡	1.9	1.3 (3.1)	0.7 (0.5)	2.4 (2.7)	0.7	1.7 (1.7)	1.9 (3.4)	5.7
1964‡	1.5	1.1 (2.5)	0.6 (0.4)	2.8 (2.9)	0.7	1.6 (1.6)	1.4 (2.5)	5.2

Source: Robert A. Gordon, *The Goal of Full Employment,* Wiley, New York, 1967, page 8. Adapted from *Manpower Statistics, 1950–1962* (Paris: Organization for Economic Cooperation and Development, 1963) and *Manpower Statistics, 1954–1964* (Paris: OECD, 1965) except for the American figures and the Swedish data for 1950 to 1959. The latter are from *International Labor Review,* Statistical Supplement, LXX (November 1954), 98, and *Yearbook of Labour Statistics, 1962* (Geneva: International Labour Office, 1962), Table 10. Minor changes in the method of compiling the Swedish data occurred in 1956 and 1960. American data are from *Manpower Report of the President,* March 1966.

*Includes West Berlin from 1960 on, but not before.

†The figures revised to American definitions for 1959–1964 are for Great Britain only.

**Revised figures not available.

‡The figures in parentheses for these years are unemployment rates revised to correspond to American definitions. They are taken from A. F. Neef, "International Unemployment Rates, 1960–1964," *Monthly Labor Rev.* **88**, 258, March 1965. Figures for 1964 are preliminary.

that has previously been found among certain groups. The real test of this resolve will come after the defense expenditures associated with the Vietnam War are drastically reduced.

10.2 THE GREAT UNEMPLOYMENT DEBATE: STRUCTURAL TRANSFORMATION VERSUS INADEQUATE AGGREGATE DEMAND

As referred to above, a great unemployment debate developed in the 1960s because of the continual updrift in unemployment between 1953 and the early 1960s. Each recession saw the unemployment rate settle at a higher and higher level. Unemployment averaged about $4\frac{1}{4}$% from 1947 to 1957, but it averaged almost 6% from 1958 to 1963. This rise in unemployment occurred even though the whole period was one of general prosperity, and each recession was fairly mild.

In time the debate generated into two schools:[1] structural transformation and inadequate aggregate demand. The structural-transformation school was composed of at least two main arguments. The first argument focused on an increased level of frictional unemployment. The belief was that before 1957 the United States economy had full employment with job vacancies equaling job seekers. Since 1957, however, it was felt that the economy changed in such a way as to create more job seekers and more vacancies, with the length of time it took to find a job increasing. Such a lengthening of the frictional unemployment period would result in an increased overall unemployment rate.

The second major argument in the structural-transformation school was the more important of the two. According to this line of reasoning, the job vacancies and job seekers both increased since about 1957, *but* the jobs called for skills above the level of skill possessed by the unemployed. If the quantity of employees demanded at high levels of skill had become greater than the quantity of employees supplied, while at low levels of skill the quantity of workers demanded had become less than the quantity of workers supplied, the result would be an increased unemployment rate.

This argument is diagrammed in Fig. 10.2.

---

[1]For more detailed expositions of these two positions see: Stanley Lebergott (editor), *Men Without Work*, Prentice-Hall, Englewood Cliffs, N.J., 1964; Eleanor G. Gilpatrick, *Structural Unemployment and Aggregate Demand*, John Hopkins Press, Baltimore, 1966; U.S. Congress, Joint Economic Committee, Subcommittee on Economics Statistics, *Higher Unemployment Rates, 1957—60: Structural Transformation or Inadequate Demand*, 87th Congress, 1st Session, U.S. Government Printing Office, Washington, 1961; Council of Economic Advisers, "The American Economy in 1961: Problems and Policies," *January 1961 Economic Report of the President and the Economic Situation and Outlook: Hearings, Joint Economic Committee*, 87th Congress, 1st Session, U.S. Government Printing Office, Washington, 1961; U.S. Congress, Joint Economic Committee, Subcommittee on Economic Statistics, *Employment and Unemployment: Hearings*, 87th Congress, 1st Session, Dec. 18, 19, 20, 1961, U.S. Government Printing Office, Washington, 1962.

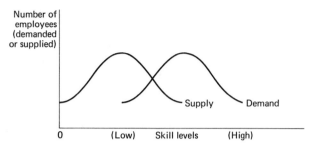

FIG. 10.2 Structuralist argument: demand—supply consequences

The structuralists argued that enough jobs existed in the United States economy, but that people with the proper skills did not exist to fill the jobs. Without proper training for the unemployed low-skilled workers, the structuralists predicted continuing high unemployment rates regardless of how high the demand for high-skilled workers went.

The inadequate aggregate demand *or* expansionist school had a very different diagnosis of the 1957—1964 period. The expansionists believed that the total demand for goods and services had not risen as fast as the capacity of the economy to produce goods and services. The economy was felt to be capable of growing much faster than it had grown, since actual supply was less than potential supply. If the economy were growing less than it could, owing to insufficient aggregate demand, the unemployment rate would have risen as more and more of the labor force could not find jobs.

The expansionist economists would normally consider a 3.5% growth rate in GNP as the potential growth rate of the economy. An actual growth rate below this figure would, therefore, result in a "gap" and unemployment. The 3.5% potential growth rate results from assumptions of a 1% growth in the labor force and a 2.5% growth in productivity. If either or both of these figures were higher, then the potential GNP growth rate would likewise be higher; and the actual GNP growth rate would have further to go to eliminate unemployment.

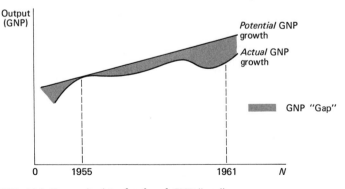

FIG. 10.3 Expansionist school and GNP "gap"

Another important aspect of the expansionist school is the role played by the Federal budget. If the Federal government has a budget which maintains a surplus at full employment, then all the burden of maintaining full employment is on the business sector. The business sector must maintain a deficit (net investment) to balance the consumer sector, which always has a surplus due to consumer savings. A surplus in the Federal budget acts as a "drag" on the economy; and if the business sector does not maintain a high enough deficit (rate of investment), the economy will not achieve full employment. To avoid unemployment the Federal government should strive to run a surplus at full employment which just matches the deficit in the rest of the economy, *or* run a deficit which at full employment just matches the surplus in the rest of the economy.

As the expansionists viewed the United States' economy, the Federal budget had been aimed at too large a full employment surplus and so acted as a fiscal "drag" on the economy. With this drag, the actual GNP growth stayed well below the potential GNP growth rate and unemployment persisted.

As the decade of the 1960s unfolded, the debate on structural transformation versus inadequate aggregate demand took on great significance. If the former school were correct, then aggregate demand was sufficient, but manpower programs were needed to retrain and re-educate the unskilled unemployed to perform the vacant high-level-skill jobs; but if the latter school were correct, aggregate demand had to be increased in order to create jobs and reduce unemployment.

10.2.1 SOME TESTS

In order to shed light on the above debate, a series of tests was conducted in the 1960s. The Council of Economic Advisers examined the unemployment rate of technical people and found it to have risen—contrary to the structuralist argument. The structuralist argument would indicate the same or lower unemployment rates among technical workers when comparing post-1957 to pre-1957.

Another way to test the structuralist argument is to examine the unemployment rates of specific occupations. The structuralists predicted that low-skill jobs would have higher unemployment rates after 1957 than in the pre-1957 period, and the opposite would be true for high-skill jobs. Although the available unemployment data is not as good as economists would like to properly test the above argument, enough data exist to test this argument in the aggregate. Such an aggregate test does not support the structuralist argument. The pre-1957 and post-1957 data revealed the same trend between overall unemployment and unemployment in specific occupations, and not a different trend between the periods, as the structuralist argument predicted.

Another test checked the level of job vacancies in the pre-1957 and post-1957 time period. According to the structuralist argument, the frictional unemployment period had lengthened. The number of unemployed job seekers, now higher, equaled the higher number of job vacancies. Unfortunately good data on job vacancies do not exist, although some proxies do. Two such proxies are the Index of Unfilled Job Orders from the state employment offices and the Index of Help-Wanted Ads from the National Industrial Conference Board. Both these proxies have shown decreases in job vacancies from 1955–1957 to the early 1960s, and not the increases the structuralists would expect.

By 1964 the inadequate-aggregate-demand school had seemingly won the great unemployment debate. Congress passed the largest tax reduction in American history in order to increase demand and create new jobs. At the same time, however, Congress was becoming more concerned with manpower policies aimed at the structurally unemployed.

10.2.2 A SYNTHESIS

As with most great debates, the truth very often lies between the two extreme schools. A recent study[2] of the 1948–1964 period in the United States has revealed strong evidence that inadequate aggregate demand was not the only reason for the persistently high unemployment rates from 1957 to 1964, but that an overall inadequate demand *coupled* with some structural changes (which reinforced these demand inadequacies) caused the high unemployment rates. This study demonstrated the extent to which data limitations hamper any attempt to directly test the structural unemployment argument. This study also reinforces the growing belief among labor economists that low unemployment rates *and* price stability can be achieved only by a strong level of aggregate demand (which will keep the level of new job openings high) *coupled* with an aggressive manpower policy which will ensure that the unemployed will have the proper education and skills for the newly created jobs.

10.3 MEASURING UNEMPLOYMENT PATTERNS

The remainder of this chapter will be concerned with measuring the patterns of unemployment since World War II.[3] We will be particularly interested in identifying any structural aspects of the unemployment problem in the post-World War II United States. Unemployment by age, sex, color, occupation, industry, and education will be examined.

10.3.1 THE DISPERSION INDEX

If every sector of the labor force had the same unemployment rate, then each sector's fraction of total unemployment would equal its relative share of the labor force. If every sector of the labor force had an unemployment rate of 4%, then the overall unemployment rate would be 4%; and if one sector of the labor force represented 50% of the labor force, then that sector would have 50% of total unemployment.

---

[2]Eleanor G. Gilpatrick, *Structural Unemployment and Aggregate Demand*, Johns Hopkins Press, Baltimore (1966).

[3]The rest of this chapter relies heavily on the excellent analysis of Professor Robert Aaron Gordon. See his *The Goal of Full Employment*, Wiley, New York, 1967, especially Chapters 5 and 6.

If a labor force consisted of 1 million people and had an unemployment rate of 4%, then 40,000 people would be unemployed. If *every* sector had a 4% unemployment rate, then each sector's fraction of total unemployment would equal its relative share of the labor force. If one sector of the labor force consisted of $\frac{1}{2}$ million people (50% of the total labor force), then it would have 20,000 people unemployed (50% of 40,000 or 4% of $\frac{1}{2}$ million).

The above suggests that one useful way to study the pattern of unemployment is to compare each sector's share of total unemployment with its share of the labor force. Let U stand for the amount of unemployment, L stand for the absolute size of the labor force, u stand for the unemployment rate (U/L) and the subscript i stand for any specific sector of the labor force. Then the unequal incidence of unemployment among the different sectors of the labor force can be measured as $U_i/U - L_i/L$. If we sum the absolute differences between each sector's relative contribution to total unemployment and its portion of the labor force, we have the result $\sum_{i=1}^{n} |U_i/U - L_i/L|$ (where n is the number of sectors in the labor force). We can call this measure the dispersion index or Du.

If unemployment rates for all sectors are equal, then U_i/U is equal to L_i/L for every sector; and Du sums to zero. However, if the sectoral unemployment rates are unequal, then U_i/U and L_i/L for each sector differ, and Du is positive. Moreover, the wider the discrepancies between the various sectors' contribution to unemployment and to the labor force, the larger Du will become.

Examining Table 10.3, we see that the dispersion index by sex would be 0.666 in 1950 when males comprised two-thirds of the labor force but had a lower unemployment rate than the females.

$$Du(1950) = \sum_{i=1}^{n} |U_i/U - L_i/L|$$

$$Du(1950) = \left| \frac{U \text{ Males}}{U \text{ Total}} - \frac{L \text{ Males}}{L \text{ Total}} \right| + \left| \frac{U \text{ Females}}{U \text{ Total}} - \frac{L \text{ Females}}{L \text{ Total}} \right|$$

$$Du(1950) = \left| \frac{250,000}{750,000} - \frac{10,000,000}{15,000,000} \right| + \left| \frac{500,000}{750,000} - \frac{5,000,000}{15,000,000} \right|$$

$$\therefore Du(1950) = \left| \tfrac{1}{3} - \tfrac{2}{3} \right| + \left| \tfrac{2}{3} - \tfrac{1}{3} \right| = 0.666$$

TABLE 10.3 An illustration of the dispersion index

	1950	1960
Total in labor force	15,000,000	20,000,000
Males	10,000,000	12,000,000
Females	5,000,000	8,000,000
Total unemployed	750,000 (5%)*	800,000 (4%)
Males	250,000 (2$\frac{1}{2}$%)	480,000 (4%)
Females	500,000 (10%)	320,000 (4%)
Dispersion index (Du)	0.666	0.000

*The numbers in parentheses are unemployment rates.

If by 1960 the unemployment rate of males had risen to 4% and the unemployment rate of females had fallen to 4%, then the dispersion of unemployment rates by sex would be equal, and Du in 1960 would be zero.

$$Du(1960) = \Sigma_{i=1}^{n} \left| U_i/U - L_i/L \right|$$

$$Du(1960) = \left| \frac{U \text{ Males}}{U \text{ Total}} - \frac{L \text{ Males}}{L \text{ Total}} \right| + \left| \frac{U \text{ Females}}{U \text{ Total}} - \frac{L \text{ Females}}{L \text{ Total}} \right|$$

$$Du(1960) = \left| \frac{480,000}{800,000} - \frac{12,000,000}{20,000,000} \right| + \left| \frac{320,000}{800,000} - \frac{8,000,000}{20,000,000} \right|$$

$$\therefore Du(1960) = \left| \tfrac{3}{5} - \tfrac{3}{5} \right| + \left| \tfrac{2}{5} - \tfrac{2}{5} \right| = 0.000$$

The dispersion index shows the degree to which the relative contributions to total unemployment of the various sectors of the labor force differ from their relative proportions in the labor force. Some groups (such as the young, the unskilled, etc.) ordinarily account for a larger fraction of the unemployed than of the labor force; however, for other groups, the opposite is true. Both these types of discrepancies increase the size of Du.

It should also be noted that the difference between U_i/U and L_i/L can be used to study the changing incidence of unemployment in one particular segment of the labor force, as well as being added for all groups in the labor force classified along a dimension (such as sex or age). In our example in Table 10.3 the incidence of unemployment for females improved relatively between 1950 and 1960. In 1950 the difference between U_i/U and L_i/L for females was ($\tfrac{2}{3} - \tfrac{1}{3}$) or 0.333, whereas in 1960 it was ($\tfrac{2}{5} - \tfrac{2}{5}$) or 0.000.

10.3.2 THE DISPERSION INDEX AND STRUCTURAL UNEMPLOYMENT

The dispersion index defined above can be very useful in examining the question of structural unemployment. The concept of structural unemployment implies (a) a heterogeneous labor force with unemployment rates at different levels in different sectors when the overall unemployment rate is low enough to be termed aggregative full employment (perhaps 3 or 4%); (b) that these unemployment rate differentials are greater than would be the case if they were due only to sectoral differences in the rate of frictional unemployment; and (c) that wage inflexibility and labor immobility cause these unemployment differentials to persist over a series of years of aggregative full employment. Thus, to show an increase (or worsening) in structural unemployment, one would have to show that for certain ways of classifying the labor force (for example, by age or occupation) there is a growing discrepancy between the patterns of labor demand and labor supply.

In the last section of this chapter we will look at Du over a series of years approximating aggregative full employment. This will enable us to test whether a significant change in the level of structural unemployment has occurred in the United States.[4]

---

[4]For a good discussion of the limitations of Du, see Robert A. Gordon, *The Goal of Full Employment*, Wiley, New York, 1967, pages 109–114.

10.4 UNEMPLOYMENT PATTERNS BY PARTICULAR CATEGORY

We shall now examine the relation between U_i and L_i for the major classifications of the labor force during years in which unemployment was at its cyclical low. We shall also discuss structural changes that seem to have occurred in the United States since World War II.

10.4.1 AGE AND SEX

Looking at Table 10.4, we see that the incidence of unemployment (Du) became less uneven between 1948 and 1959, but that there was a dramatic reversal after 1959 when Du rose by more than 50%. This recent reversal or worsening along the age—sex dimension is due primarily to the deteriorating position of young people, especially teenagers, in the job market. There has also been some relative worsening of the position of women in the labor market.

Between 1959 and 1965 the absolute sum of ($U_i/U - L_i/L$) rose for all age groups of females. The relative unemployment rates U_i/U also rose for all female age groups under 45, but most markedly for teenagers. The relative position of females aged 45—64 improved in contrast to the position of the younger females.

As might be expected, the prime labor force (males aged 25—44 and 45—64) occupied a relatively favorable position. Their employment is below the national average, and their proportion of unemployment is below their proportion of the labor force.

Looking at the unemployment problems of youth, we find that the relative unemployment rate for young men (aged 20—24) fell between 1948 and 1965; however, the situation for young women (aged 20—24) deteriorated over the postwar years. This latter group's relative unemployment rate was higher in 1965 than in the years of lowest unemployment in the 1950s. The teenager's unemployment rate was also extremely high (more than twice the national average). Although there was little worsening of the teenage unemployment problem in the 1950s, by 1965 a significant deterioration in the relative position of teenagers in the labor market had taken place. This deterioration was bad for the male teenagers and worse for the female teenagers.

Since the teenage component of the labor force is expected to expand rapidly, high teenage unemployment rates will continue to be an important structural problem in the United States.

10.4.2 COLOR

The dispersion index (when applied to the color—sex classification of the labor force) doubled between 1948 and 1956, but then rose only slightly between 1956 and 1965. This small rise in Du between 1956 and 1965 is due entirely to the worsened position of women in the labor market. Looking at Table 10.5, we see that the nonwhite males' relative unemployment rate (U_i/U) declined after 1959 and in 1965 was at

TABLE 10.4 Age–sex classifications of the civilian labor force and the unemployed

Age and sex	1948 u_i/u	1948 L_i/L	1948 U_i/U	1953 u_i/u	1953 L_i/L	1953 U_i/U	1956 u_i/u	1956 L_i/L	1956 U_i/U	1959 u_i/u	1959 L_i/L	1959 U_i/U	1965 u_i/u	1965 L_i/L	1965 U_i/U
Males															
14–19	2.37	5.2	12.3	2.52	4.5	11.2	2.43	4.6	11.2	2.51	4.7	11.8	2.85	5.5	15.8
20–24	1.82	7.6	13.9	1.72	4.8	8.1	1.64	5.2	8.5	1.58	5.7	9.0	1.37	6.5	9.0
25–44	0.68	32.4	22.5	0.72	33.2	23.7	0.69	31.6	22.2	0.76	30.6	23.3	0.59	27.8	16.7
45–64	0.74	22.3	16.3	0.86	22.8	19.4	0.76	22.5	17.2	0.78	22.7	17.8	0.61	22.2	13.7
65 and over	0.89	3.9	3.5	0.83	4.0	3.2	0.83	3.9	3.2	0.87	3.3	2.9	0.76	2.8	2.2
Total	0.95	71.4	68.4	0.97	69.3	65.7	0.90	67.8	62.3	0.96	67.1	64.9	0.87	64.8	57.3
Females															
14–19	2.16	3.4	7.3	2.34	3.0	7.1	2.57	3.2	8.4	2.24	3.2	7.2	3.11	3.9	12.2
20–24	1.29	4.4	5.7	1.48	3.8	5.6	1.50	3.6	5.5	1.47	3.6	5.2	1.59	4.4	7.1
25–44	0.95	12.6	12.1	1.00	13.8	13.9	1.02	13.8	14.3	1.00	13.4	13.3	1.09	13.3	14.4
45–64	0.82	7.4	6.0	0.83	9.0	7.2	0.86	10.4	9.0	0.76	11.5	8.7	0.68	12.3	8.2
65 and over	0.61	0.8	0.5	0.48	1.1	0.5	0.55	1.2	0.7	0.51	1.2	0.6	0.61	1.3	0.8
Total	1.11	28.6	31.6	1.14	30.7	34.3	1.17	32.2	37.8	1.07	32.9	35.1	1.20	35.2	42.7
National unemployment rate		3.8			2.9			4.2			5.5			4.6	
Relative dispersion index		0.371			0.321			0.348			0.321			0.497	

Source: Robert A. Gordon, *The Goal of Full Employment*, Wiley, New York, 1967, page 119. Adapted from *Manpower Report of the President*, March 1966, Statistical Appendix. (Reprinted by permission).

u_i/u is the ratio of group's unemployment rate to national unemployment rate.

L_i/L is the percentage of civilian labor force in each group.

U_i/U is the percentage of total unemployment in each group.

approximately the same level as in 1953; however, the relative unemployment rate for nonwhite females rose between 1959 and 1965.

On the whole, the position of nonwhites in the labor force deteriorated markedly up to 1956, but there has been some slight improvement (taking the two sexes together) in the last few years.

Professor Gordon also examined the position in the labor market of nonwhite youth. He found that between 1948 and 1959 unemployment rates for nonwhite teenagers rose more rapidly than did those of white teenagers, and since 1959 the position of nonwhite teenagers in the labor market has deteriorated further, but primarily because the position of all teenagers had deteriorated. The net result is that the unemployment rate for nonwhite teenagers was about twice the rate for white teenagers in 1965.

TABLE 10.5 Color–sex classification of the civilian labor force and the unemployed

Color and sex	1948*	1953*	1956			1959			1965*		
	u_i/u	u_i/u	u_i/u	L_i/L	U_i/U	u_i/u	L_i/L	U_i/U	u_i/u	L_i/L	U_i/U
Total white	0.95	0.93	0.88	89.3	78.5	0.89	89.1	78.8	0.89	88.9	79.7
Male	0.89	0.90	0.81	61.2	49.7	0.84	60.5	51.0	0.78	58.3	46.4
Female	1.03	1.07	1.02	28.1	28.8	0.96	28.6	27.8	1.09	30.6	33.3
Total nonwhite	1.55	1.55	2.00	10.7	21.6	1.95	10.9	21.2	1.80	11.1	20.3
Male	1.50	1.66	1.90	6.6	12.6	2.09	6.6	13.8	1.65	6.5	10.9
Female	1.61	1.41	2.14	4.2	9.0	1.73	4.3	7.4	2.02	4.6	9.4
National unemployment rate	3.8	2.9	4.2			5.5			4.6		
Relative dispersion index	0.111	0.152	0.230			0.206			0.238		

Source: Robert R. A. Gordon, *The Goal of Full Employment*, Wiley, New York, 1967, page 127. Adapted from *Manpower Report of the President*, March 1966, Statistical Appendix. (Reprinted by permission).
*U_i/U and L_i/L data by color and sex was not published for these years, but has been estimated from unpublished data.

10.4.3 OCCUPATION

It is interesting to use the concept of dispersion index to examine the occupational dimension of the labor force, since the structural transformation argument (discussed earlier) implies that certain occupations (blue-collar and unskilled) should be experiencing increased unemployment since 1957.

Examining Table 10.6, we see that Du (including people with no previous work experience) declined from 1948 to 1953, then rose sharply until 1956, showing little change after 1956. Since 1953 there has been a sharp increase in the proportion of the unemployed who have had no previous work experience. However, the fraction of total unemployment accounted for by the blue-collar worker has declined sharply since 1959. This can be shown in the behavior of Du (excluding people with no previous work experience) which stood in 1965 at its lowest level for the entire postwar period.

Looking at the white-collar worker, we see that between 1948 and 1956 their relative position, which was already very favorable, improved. Since 1956 the white-collar unemployment rate worsened moderately, but was still relatively low.

The service group experienced an improvement in their labor market position during the 1950s, but this group's position worsened somewhat between 1959 and 1965. Approximately the same pattern held true for farm workers—improvement from 1953 to 1959, and moderate worsening until 1965.

As the data in Table 10.6 indicate, people looking for their first job experienced a marked increase in unemployment between 1953 and 1965. It appears that the burden of the deteriorating job market between 1953 and 1965 fell fairly heavily on those seeking their first job rather than on experienced workers. Experienced blue-collar workers have *not* been forced into a growing pool of unemployed job seekers, but new entrants into the labor force have had an increasingly difficult time finding their first job.

10.4.4 INDUSTRY

The dispersion index by industry classification of the labor force (for wage and salary workers only) increased between 1948 and 1953, but remained virtually stable in 1956, 1959, and 1965.

Table 10.7 does not reveal any structural worsening of unemployment in industries such as manufacturing, transportation, and public utilities (industries usually singled out by the structural transformation proponents in the early 1960s) since 1956. Thus, as far as structural worsening in the industrial pattern of unemployment is concerned, this worsening took place before 1956 and not after. This finding is confirmed in Tables 10.6 and 10.7. Whatever structural worsening did occur between the middle 1950s and the middle 1960s resulted from supply changes, especially changes in the age—sex composition of the labor force.

10.4.5 EDUCATION

It is clear that the level of unemployment is inversely related to the level of education; however, during the last decade it does *not* seem that unemployment has become more heavily concentrated among people with the least schooling. The Du reported in Table 10.8 rose between 1950 and 1959, but it showed a moderate decline by 1965.

People with eight or fewer years of education experienced a worsening in their relative unemployment between 1950 and 1957, but since 1957 males with no more than four years of education and males with five to eight years of education experienced an improvement or stability in their relative unemployment rates. Also between 1957 and 1965, females with no more than four years of education experienced a rise in their relative unemployment rates, but females with from five to eight years of education experienced a small decline in their relative unemployment rates. Relative unemployment rates rose for high-school dropouts (both sexes, nine

TABLE 10.6 Occupational classification of the civilian labor force and the unemployed

Occupation	1948			1953			1956			1959			1965		
	u_i/u	L_i/L	U_i/U	u_i/u	L_i/L	U_i/U	u_i/u	L_i/L	U_i/U	u_i/u	L_i/L	U_i/U	u_i/u	L_i/L	U_i/U
White collar*	0.60	35.5	21.6	0.56	37.8	20.5	0.45	38.6	17.5	0.47	41.2	19.3	0.50	43.4	21.7
Blue collar†	1.26	40.8	52.0	1.38	40.8	55.8	1.34	39.3	52.6	1.38	37.7	51.9	1.15	36.9	42.5
Service**	1.31	10.3	13.6	1.33	11.4	15.0	1.21	11.8	14.5	1.09	12.3	13.4	1.13	13.0	14.8
Farm‡	0.31	13.0	4.2	0.45	10.0	4.4	0.50	9.8	4.9	0.45	8.3	3.8	0.57	5.8	3.3
No previous work experience	—	0.3	8.8	—	0.1	4.4	—	0.4	10.4	—	0.6	11.6	—	0.8	17.7
National unemployment rate (%)¶		3.8 (3.4)			2.9 (2.5)			4.2 (3.8)			5.5			4.6	
Relative dispersion index															
(excluding NPWE)		0.410			0.415			0.460			0.435			0.378	
(including NPWE)		0.495			0.458			0.560			0.545			0.547	

Source: Robert A. Gordon, *The Goal of Full Employment*, Wiley, New York, 1967, pages 134–135. Adapted from *Manpower Report of the President*, March 1966, Statistical Appendix. (Reprinted by permission).

*White-collar occupations include professional, technical; managers, officials, proprietors; clerical: sales.

†Blue-collar occupations include craftsmen, foremen; operatives; laborers.

**Service occupations include household workers; others.

‡Farm occupations include farmers and farm managers; farm laborers and foremen.

¶The national unemployment rates for 1956 and earlier years shown on this line have been adjusted to reflect changes in definitions adopted subsequently. The figures in parentheses are the unadjusted rates which are consistent with the individual rates for the various groups shown here. The unrevised national rate was used in the calculations for 1956 and prior years.

NPWE stands for those with no previous work experience.

TABLE 10.7 Industrial classification of the civilian labor force and the unemployed

Industry	1948			1953			1956			1959			1965		
	u_i/u	L_i/L	U_i/U	u_i/u	L_i/L	U_i/U	u_i/u	L_i/L	U_i/U	u_i/u	L_i/L	U_i/U	u_i/u	L_i/L	U_i/U
Experienced wage and salary earners	1.09	80.6	87.7	1.08	82.0	88.6	1.03	83.6	85.8	1.02	84.1	85.6	0.91	87.1	79.5
Agriculture	1.38	3.0	4.2	1.88	2.4	4.5	1.71	2.7	4.6	1.58	2.7	4.2	1.59	2.1	3.4
Nonagricultural industries	1.09	76.7	83.5	1.04	80.9	84.1	1.00	81.2	81.2	1.00	81.4	81.4	0.91	83.4	76.1
Mining, forestry, fisheries	0.85	1.6	1.4	1.96	1.4	2.7	1.68	1.2	2.1	1.76	1.0	1.8	1.20	0.8	1.0
Construction	2.24	4.8	10.7	2.44	5.3	12.9	2.18	5.4	11.8	2.18	5.8	12.6	1.96	5.6	10.9
Manufacturing	1.03	27.2	28.0	1.00	27.0	27.0	1.11	26.2	29.0	1.09	25.5	27.8	0.87	25.9	22.5
Durables	1.00	14.3	14.3	0.80	16.4	13.1	1.05	15.3	16.1	1.11	14.5	16.1	0.74	15.0	11.1
Nondurables	1.06	12.8	13.6	1.24	11.2	13.9	1.16	11.1	12.9	1.07	10.8	11.6	1.00	11.4	11.4
Transportation and public utilities	0.88	7.7	6.8	0.72	7.4	5.3	0.63	7.1	4.5	0.76	6.5	5.0	0.59	6.3	3.7
Wholesale and retail	1.26	14.9	18.8	1.20	14.9	17.9	1.08	15.4	16.6	1.05	15.5	16.3	1.09	15.7	17.1
Finance, insurance, real estate	0.47	2.8	1.3	0.64	3.0	1.9	0.37	3.3	1.2	0.47	3.6	1.7	0.50	4.2	2.1
Service industries	1.03	13.5	13.9	0.96	14.7	14.1	0.84	16.9	14.2	0.78	18.3	14.3	0.83	20.3	16.8
Public administration	0.59	4.6	2.7	0.48	4.6	2.2	0.42	4.5	1.9	0.42	4.5	1.9	0.41	5.1	2.1
National unemployment rate (%)*		3.8 (3.4)			2.9 (2.5)			4.2 (3.8)			5.5			4.6	
Relative dispersion index		0.167			0.262			0.230			0.223			0.233	

Source: Robert A. Gordon, *The Goal of Full Employment*, Wiley, New York, 1967, pages 140–141. Adapted from *Manpower Report of the President*, March 1966 Statistical Appendix. (Reprinted by permission)

*The national unemployment rates for 1956 and earlier years shown on this line have been adjusted to reflect changes in definitions adopted subsequently. The figures in parentheses are the unadjusted rates which are consistent with the individual rates for the various groups shown here. The unrevised national rate was used in the calculations for 1956 and prior years.

TABLE 10.8 Educational classification of the civilian labor force and the unemployed by sex (18 years and over)

Educational attainment by sex	April 1950*			March 1957			March 1959			March 1962			March 1965		
	u_i/u	L_i/L	U_i/U	u_i/u	L_i/L	U_i/U	u_i/u	L_i/L	U_i/U	u_i/u	L_i/L	U_i/U	u_i/u	L_i/L	U_i/U
Males															
Total	1.02	71.9	73.6	1.00	67.9	67.6	1.02	67.2	67.9	1.00	66.2	66.2	0.94	65.0	60.7
0–4 years	1.38	6.9	9.7	1.95	4.8	9.5	1.60	4.1	6.6	1.73	3.6	6.2	1.51	2.9	4.3
5–8 years	1.21	25.7	31.0	1.24	19.8	25.0	1.34	18.1	24.3	1.32	16.0	21.3	1.21	13.8	16.6
9–11 years	1.15	13.7	15.8	1.15	13.3	15.4	1.31	13.6	17.7	1.30	13.0	17.0	1.43	12.6	18.0
12 years	0.77	15.3	11.7	0.73	17.8	13.0	0.79	18.3	14.4	0.80	19.0	15.2	0.72	20.8	14.9
13–15 years	0.68	5.3	3.6	0.66	5.6	3.8	0.53	6.1	3.3	0.67	6.9	4.6	0.66	6.8	4.5
16 years or more	0.38	5.1	1.8	0.15	6.5	1.0	0.23	7.0	1.6	0.23	7.7	1.9	0.30	8.1	2.5
Females															
Total	0.94	28.1	26.4	1.00	32.1	32.4	0.98	32.8	32.1	1.00	33.8	33.8	1.13	35.0	39.3
0–4 years	1.47	1.6	2.3	1.63	1.4	2.2	1.66	1.2	1.9	1.25	1.0	1.3	1.89	0.8	1.6
5–8 years	1.21	7.3	8.9	1.34	7.3	10.0	1.26	7.0	8.9	1.15	6.4	7.3	1.15	5.8	6.6
9–11 years	1.26	5.2	6.6	1.44	6.1	8.8	1.50	6.3	9.4	1.53	6.4	9.8	1.83	6.6	11.9
12 years	0.70	8.9	6.3	0.71	11.7	8.4	0.76	12.5	9.4	0.95	13.1	12.5	1.06	14.7	15.5
13–15 years	0.55	2.8	1.6	0.78	3.0	2.4	0.61	3.2	1.9	0.53	3.8	2.0	0.77	3.6	2.7
16 years or more	0.30	2.2	0.7	0.24	2.7	0.7	0.21	2.7	0.5	0.25	3.2	0.8	0.28	3.5	1.0
National unemployment rate (%)		6.1 (4.7)			4.1			6.2			6.0			4.7	
Relative dispersion index		0.278			0.362			0.372			0.332			0.345	

Source: Robert A. Gordon, *The Goal of Full Employment*, Wiley, New York, 1967, pages 144–145. Adapted from U.S. Bureau of Census and U.S. Bureau of Labor Statistics Reports. (Reprinted by permission)

*The 1950 Census and the Current Population Survey of April 2–8, 1950, show important discrepancies with respect to the size of the labor force and the number of unemployed. The latter is generally regarded to be more accurate and more consistent with other estimates. However, it does not provide a breakdown by educational attainment. Charles Killingsworth has made estimates of employment status by educational attainment by taking the proportions obtained from the Census enumeration and applying them to the higher totals found by the CPS. His estimate of total unemployment is 6.1% compared to the 4.7% obtained by the Census enumeration.

The figures shown here are calculated directly from the Census figures. However, except for slight rounding errors, they give the same results as to eleven years of schooling), for female high-school graduates, and for those with four or more years of college (males and females) between 1957 and 1965.

It appears that the level of education has a large effect on one's vulnerability to unemployment, with the association being more pronounced for males than for females. However, the relative position of people with only a grammar-school education improved since 1957, whereas the relative position of high-school dropouts worsened. An increase in the relative unemployment vulnerability of female high-school graduates occurred between 1957 and 1965 and the favorable position of college graduates (which improved between 1950 and 1957) deteriorated slightly after 1957. Thus any increase in structural unemployment among the least-educated occurred *before* 1957, and since 1957 any structural worsening has hit chiefly high-school dropouts and female high-school graduates.

10.4.6 LONG-TERM UNEMPLOYMENT

Professor Gordon examined the question of long-term unemployment[5] and found that people out of work 15 (or 26) weeks or more made up a substantially larger fraction of total unemployment in the 1960s than in the early postwar years. This deterioration occurred chiefly in the 1950s rather than in the 1960s.

Long-term unemployment is concentrated among males aged 45−64, among nonwhite males, and somewhat among semiskilled operatives and unskilled laborers. Table 10.9 shows that between 1957 and 1965 long-term unemployment rose relative to total unemployment chiefly for males aged 25−44, females aged 25−64, and nonwhite females. Long-term unemployment did *not* become increasingly concentrated among unskilled and semiskilled workers.

A decline in the total unemployment rate is the best means to alleviate the problem of long-term unemployment. In addition to needing high aggregate demand, we need specific manpower measures to reduce the burden of long-term unemployment among those over 45, nonwhites, and the less skilled.

10.5 A SUMMATION OF UNEMPLOYMENT PATTERNS

A detailed study of the patterns of unemployment in the post-World War II United States economy seems to yield the following major conclusions.

1) Insufficient aggregate demand was the *major* (but not the only) cause of the high level of unemployment from 1957 to the middle 1960s.

2) Structural shifts since the mid-1950s have *not* caused *growing* structural labor market imbalances among the unskilled, the semiskilled, the nonwhite, the least educated, or manufacturing workers.

---

[5]Robert A. Gordon, *The Goal of Full Employment*, Wiley, New York, 1967, page 149.

TABLE 10.9 Percentage distribution of total and long-term (15 weeks or more)
           unemployment

Classification	1957 Total	1957 Long-term	1959 Total	1959 Long-term	1961 Total	1961 Long-term	1965 Total	1965 Long-term
By age and sex								
Male, total								
18—19	5.4	4.1	5.4	4.4	5.4	4.1	6.7	4.9
25—44	22.3	22.0	23.3	26.4	22.7	25.0	16.7	18.3
45—64	17.8	25.7	17.8	22.9	17.6	22.8	13.7	21.1
Female, total								
18—19	3.6	2.7	3.8	2.3	4.3	2.7	6.7	5.2
25—44	14.3	13.2	13.3	11.1	13.4	12.3	14.4	14.0
45—64	7.7	9.3	8.7	9.8	8.7	9.3	8.2	10.7
By color and sex								
White, total	80.1	77.4	78.8	75.7	79.5	77.5	79.7	77.0
Male	51.8	53.0	51.0	53.4	51.0	53.9	46.4	47.9
Female	28.3	24.4	27.8	22.4	28.5	23.6	33.3	29.2
Nonwhite, total	19.9	22.6	21.2	24.3	20.5	22.5	20.3	22.9
Male	12.7	15.8	13.8	17.9	12.7	15.3	10.9	13.0
Female	7.2	6.8	7.4	6.4	7.8	7.2	9.4	9.9
Selected occupations								
Clerical	9.2	8.2	9.3	9.4	9.9	9.8	10.8	10.3
Operatives	29.4	31.8	25.5	28.7	26.0	29.3	22.4	24.3
Service workers	10.2	10.6	10.5	10.3	10.5	10.6	11.9	12.5
Laborers	13.3	15.5	13.9	15.7	12.2	14.6	10.2	10.5
No previous work experience	10.3	8.4	11.6	8.8	12.2	9.2	17.7	13.8

Source: Robert A. Gordon, *The Goal of Full Employment*, Wiley, New York, 1967, page 150. Adapted from *Manpower Report of the President*, March 1966, pages 172–174. (Reprinted by permission)

3) There was an increase in structural unemployment (resulting from labor-market changes on the demand side) from the late 1940s to the mid-1950s. It was chiefly felt by the least educated, the nonwhites, and the semiskilled.

4) Some structural worsening has occurred since the mid-1950s, but it resulted largely from labor-market changes on the supply side. These supply changes included a rapid increase in the number of young people entering the labor market, and a steady increase in the LFPRs of females.

That a larger proportion of total unemployment is today composed of secondary workers should not lead us to the conclusion that this is not a serious problem. If our economy is to maintain a high growth rate (and thus a growing standard of living), we must make efficient use of our secondary as well as our primary labor force. Each year the secondary labor force becomes a larger part of the total labor force, and thus it must be included in any manpower policy that seriously expects to handle the problem of efficient utilization of all the economy's labor inputs. To allow a large portion of our secondary (or primary) labor force to remain unemployed makes about as much sense as leaving a portion of our manufacturing plants idle.

Although the structural worsening that has occurred in recent years in the United States has not been as serious as some believed, structural unemployment has long been a serious problem in our economy. It is serious at its present level, even if it should not continue to worsen in the future. Our aim must be to *decrease* the problem. We must not be satisfied with just a prevention of its growth.

SUMMARY

Since the 1950s, the United States economy has been plagued by particularized unemployment as opposed to the generalized unemployment of the 1930s. In the 1960s a great unemployment debate developed because of the continual updrift in unemployment between 1953 and the early 1960s. In time the debate generated into two schools: structural transformation and inadequate aggregate demand. The structuralists argued that enough jobs existed in the United States economy, but that people with the proper skills did not exist to fill the jobs. The inadequate aggregate demand (or expansionist) school believed that the total demand for goods and services had not risen as fast as the capacity of the economy to produce goods and services.

A series of tests were conducted in the 1960s and, as with most great debates, the truth lies between the two extreme schools. The persistently high unemployment rates from 1957 to 1964 were due to an overall inadequate demand *coupled* with some structural changes which reinforced these demand inadequacies.

The dispersion index shows the degree to which the relative contribution to total unemployment of the various sectors of the labor force differ from their relative proportions in the labor force. This index can be applied to various categories of the labor force.

A detailed study of the patterns of unemployment seems to reveal that structural shifts since the mid-1950s have not caused *growing* structural labor-market imbalances among the unskilled, semiskilled, nonwhite, least educated, or manufacturing workers; however, there was an increase in structural unemployment (resulting from labor-market changes on the demand side) from the late 1940s to the mid 1950s which was chiefly felt by the least educated, the nonwhites, and the semiskilled. Some structural worsening has occurred since the mid-1950s, but it resulted largely from labor market changes on the supply side. Although the structural worsening that has occurred in recent years in the United States has not been as serious as some believed, structural unemployment has long been a serious problem in our economy.

BIBLIOGRAPHY

Eleanor G. Gilpatrick, *Structural Unemployment and Aggregate Demand*, Johns Hopkins Press, Baltimore, 1966

Robert Aaron Gordon, *The Goal of Full Employment*, Wiley, New York, 1967

Stanley Lebergott (Editor), *Men Without Work*, Prentice-Hall Englewood Cliffs, N.J., 1964

U.S. Congress, Joint Economic Committee, Subcommittee on Economic Statistics, *Higher Unemployment Rates, 1957—60: Structural Transformation or Inadequate Demand*, 87th Congress, 1st Session, U.S. Government Printing Office, Washington, D.C., 1961

U.S. Congress, Joint Economic Committee, Subcommittee on Economic Statistics, *Employment and Unemployment: Hearings*, 87th Congress, 1st Session, U.S. Government Printing Office, Washington, D.C., 1962

U.S. Council of Economic Advisors, "The American Economy in 1961: Problems and Policies," *January 1961 Economic Report of the President and the Economic Situation and Outlook: Hearings*, Joint Economic Committee, 87th Congress, 1st Session, U.S. Government Printing Office, Washington, D.C., 1961

Is poverty a pathological or abnormal condition affecting American society that should be studied and eliminated as are other diseases? Or is poverty the natural punishment for idleness and folly existing in the economy? Where must our attack be aimed—at idleness and folly, or at poverty? An examination of the extent, nature, and causes of poverty reveal the unenlightenedness of the second of these two possible interpretations of poverty.

11.1 UNDEREMPLOYMENT VERSUS POVERTY

At the outset it will be useful to clarify how the concept of poverty relates to the standard labor force classifications. The latter divides the population into three categories—those who are employed, those unemployed, and those not in the labor force. Each of these three categories can and do include persons who are in poverty. One man is employed at a low-paying job, another is available and looking for work but has no job, a third has retired and is no longer in the labor force. But all three *could* be poor. Furthermore, a man could move from one category to another within the labor-force classification and still remain poor. For example, an unemployed person could become employed and nevertheless still receive an income so low that he continues to live in poverty.

A further related concept is that of underemployment. Underemployment occurs when a person is employed, but at less than his full potential. This would occur when a person is employed at a job that does not require the full use of his skill or occupational capacity. A medical doctor employed as an orderly in a hospital would clearly fall into this category. Underemployment would also occur when a person was employed for fewer hours than he wished to be employed. A man who wished to work 40 hours but could only find a 15-hour-a-week job would thus be counted as underemployed. The former has been called *quality underemployment*, while the latter has been called *quantity underemploy-*

ment. Since we have already noted that an employed person can be in poverty, it follows that an underemployed person can also be in poverty.

The essential point to note is that knowing a person's labor-force classification (whether he is fully or underemployed, unemployed, or not in the labor force) does not tell us whether or not that person is poor. As we shall see, it may give us a clue, but it does not give us a definition. We shall see that only 52% of poor families are headed by a person who is not employed. It is to a definition of poverty that we now direct our attention.

11.2 WHAT IS POVERTY?

Poverty exists when families or individuals are not capable of maintaining an adequate standard of living.[1] In order to count the poor, then we would have to define just what constitutes an adequate standard of living, and we would have to have some measure of the resources available to people for comparison with the standard.

Defining an adequate standard of living requires the making of value judgments. The definition differs between societies and at different times, since what constitutes an adequate income depends on the level of income of the society as a whole. In spite of the difficulties, however, attempts to clarify meaningful definitions of an adequate living standard have been defined by various groups, including the Council of Economic Advisors and the Social Security Administration.

The Council of Economic Advisors, in attempting to develop initial standards for purposes of antipoverty program planning, said that any family of two or more with less than $3000 annual income and any single person living alone with less than $1500 would be considered poor. This original standard, however, was not sufficiently sensitive to the size and composition of the family. The poverty line remained the same for families of two, three, four, or more. It remained the same whether the two persons were a husband and wife, a wife and teenager, or a husband and small child.

As more data became available, the Social Security Administration was able to vary the poverty line—the necessary minimum of resources—to reflect the above considerations. They set poverty thresholds for 124 different kinds of families, based on the sex of the head, the number of children under 18, the number of adults, and whether or not the household lived on a farm. The thresholds represent attempts to specify the minimum money income capable of supporting an average family of given composition at the lowest level consistent with the prevailing standards of living in this country. The thresholds are based on the amount needed by each of the given families to purchase a nutritionally adequate diet. The assumption is made that no more than one-third of the family income is used for food. The latter figure was chosen based on the results of food consumption surveys conducted by

[1]This section draws heavily on the five articles on poverty, "Perspectives on Poverty," *Monthly Labor Rev.*, U.S. Department of Labor, Washington, D.C., February 1969.

the Department of Agriculture in 1948 and 1955. These surveys revealed that the average expenditure for food by all families was approximately one-third of income.

The Social Security Administration sets poverty thresholds corresponding to both "poor" and "near-poor" levels. The former was $65 a week, the latter $85 a week for a nonfarm family of four in 1966. It is worthwhile to remember that these income levels are derived solely from the estimated cost of the minimum diet and its presumed relationship to other daily necessities. It should be remembered also that two people spending the same amount on food do not necessarily buy equally nutritious diets. The Agriculture Department, for example, estimates that only 10% of persons spending the estimated cost of the minimum diet on food actually got a nutritionally adequate diet.

The Social Security Administration's index has been criticized on certain grounds. For one thing, the concept relies on income as the sole indication of poverty. Assets other than current income are not allowed for. The exclusion of asset data is practical rather than conceptual. Asset data are just not regularly available. What studies there are, however, indicate that, except among the aged, there are few low-income families with many assets. And, furthermore, asset holdings appear to make little difference in the income position of most aged families.

Others criticize the index for not allowing for income in kind, except for farmers. It appears, however, that nonmonetary income goes mainly to the nonpoor. The cost of all the free medical care and the food stamps received by the poor are more than balanced by the health insurance benefits, expense accounts, vacations, and free tuition received by the nonpoor.

Some critics feel that consumption levels are superior to income levels as indexes of poverty status. But use of consumption as a criterion also involves problems of measurement and definition. For example, how do you value goods received without a direct cash outlay? How do you count the value of an owned home? Should inventories of stocks on hand at home be allowed for? It appears that income, which is a proxy for consumption potential, is a considerably easier concept to define and measure.

Another problem involves changing the poverty thresholds for price changes in the economy. Since 1969, annual adjustments in the poverty levels are based on changes in the Consumer Price Index rather than on changes in the cost of food in the economy food plans.

11.3 THE CHARACTERISTICS OF THE POOR: 1959 to 1968

In 1959, 39.5 million persons[2] in the United States were living below the poverty level. These persons were distributed in 13.2 million households. Families made

[2]This does not include any of the 2 million persons in institutions who usually rank among the poorest of the poor, nor does it include any of the aged persons and parent-child groups who would be on the poverty roll if they had to rely on their own resources instead of on those of the more fortunate relatives whose homes they share.

up 8.3 million of these households, while 4.9 million of the households were comprised of unrelated individuals.[3]

By 1968, the number of persons living below the poverty level had fallen to 25.3 million. Of the 9.7 million households affected, 5 million were families and 4.7 million were unrelated individuals.

The proportion of persons below the poverty level declined from about 22% in 1959 to less than 13% in 1968, but certain groups did not share in this progress as fully as others. Unrelated individuals, for example, increased their share of poverty from 12.5% in 1959 to 18.5% in 1968, and nonwhite persons, in spite of considerable improvement, increased their share of the total number of poor persons from 27.9% in 1959 to 31.5% in 1968. Family members under age 18 still account for more than 40% of poor persons. In order to better understand the extent and nature of poverty as well as the way it is changing, let us compare the characteristics of the poor in 1968 and 1959.

Summary characteristics of poor persons, including those presented above, are displayed in Table 11.1. The table reveals the high incidence of poverty among unrelated individuals, down from 46.1% in 1959 to 34.0% in 1968, among family members under age 18, down from 26.9% to 15.3%, and among Negro and other races, down from 56.2% in 1959 to 33.5% in 1968. Members of these groups share a greater chance of being poor than do others in our economy, the overall incidence of poverty being 12.8%.

For both white and nonwhite groups, the percentage who were poor was greater for unrelated individuals—that is, households made up of single persons—than it was for families of more than one person. The contrast, however, was greater for white persons than for nonwhite. More than 32% of nonwhite persons in families were poor, whereas the figure for nonwhite unrelated individuals was just over 45%. The comparable figures for white persons were 8.4% and 32.2%. The nonwhite person thus has a high likelihood of living in poverty, whether he lives alone or in a family. For white persons, the chances of living in poverty are much greater for a person living alone than for those living in families.

Table 11.2 contains detailed characteristics on *families* living below the poverty line in 1968 and 1959. More than two-thirds of such families were headed by males, but the chances of being poor were much greater if the head of the family was a female. The incidence of poverty was 32% for female-headed households, as compared to just over 7% for those headed by a male.

Likewise, although more than 71% of poor families were headed by a white person, the chances of being poor were much greater if the family head was non-

---

[3]For a detailed description of characteristics of the poor, see *Poverty in the United States, 1959 to 1968*, Bureau of the Census, Current Population Series P-60, Number 68, as well as Mollie Orshansky, *The Shape of Poverty in 1966*, Social Security Bulletin, Social Security Administration, Volume 31, Number 3, March 1968.

TABLE 11.1. Persons below the poverty level in 1968 and 1959, by family status and race (numbers in thousands)

Selected characteristics	1968					1959				
	Total	Percentage distribution of total	White	Negro and other races	Negro and other races as percent of total	Total	Percentage distribution of total	White	Negro and other races	Negro and other races as percent of total
All persons	25,389	100.0	17,395	7,994	31.5	39,490	100.0	28,484	11,006	27.9
In families	20,695	81.5	13,546	7,149	34.5	34,562	87.6	24,443	10,119	29.3
Head	5,047	19.9	3,616	1,431	28.4	8,320	21.1	6,185	2,135	25.7
Family members under 18 years†	10,739	42.3	6,373	4,366	40.7	17,208	43.6	11,386	5,822	33.8
Other family members	4,909	19.3	3,557	1,352	27.5	9,034	22.9	6,872	2,162	23.9
Unrelated individuals 14 years and over	4,694	18.5	3,849	845	18.0	4,928	12.5	4,041	887	18.0
Percentage below poverty level										
All persons	12.8		10.0	33.5	*	22.4		18.1	56.2	*
In families	11.3		8.4	32.4	*	20.8		16.5	56.0	*
Head	10.0		8.0	28.2	*	18.5		15.2	50.4	*
Family members under 18 years†	15.3		10.7	41.6	*	26.9		20.6	66.7	*
Other family members	7.8		6.3	20.9	*	15.9		13.3	42.5	*
Unrelated individuals 14 years and over	34.0		32.2	45.7	*	46.1		44.1	57.4	*

Source: *Poverty in the United States, 1959 to 1968,*, Bureau of the Census, Current Population Series P-60, Number 68, pages 1 and 2.

* Not applicable.

† Other than head and wife.

TABLE 11.2 Selected characteristics of families below the poverty level in 1968 and 1959 (numbers in thousands. Negro data for 1959 from the 1-in-1000 sample of the 1960 Census)

Selected characteristics	1968				1959			
	Number below poverty level	Percentage below poverty level	Percent distribution		Number below poverty level	Percentage below poverty level	Percent distribution	
			Below poverty level	Above poverty level			Below poverty level	Above poverty level
Sex and race of head								
Total	5047	10.0	100.0	100.0	8320	18.5	100.0	100.0
Male head	3292	7.3	65.2	91.9	6404	15.8	77.0	93.0
Female head	1755	32.3	34.8	8.1	1916	42.6	23.0	7.0
White	3616	8.0	71.6	92.0	6185	15.2	74.3	94.3
Male head	2595	6.3	51.4	85.3	4952	13.3	59.5	88.0
Female head	1021	25.2	20.2	6.7	1233	34.8	14.8	6.3
Negro and other races	1431	28.2	28.4	8.0	2135	50.4	25.7	5.7
Male head	697	18.9	13.8	6.6	1452	44.2	17.5	5.0
Female head	734	52.9	14.5	1.4	683	72.0	8.2	0.7
Negro	1366	29.4	27.1	7.2	1860	48.1	22.4	5.5
Male head	660	19.9	13.1	5.8	1309	43.3	15.7	4.7
Female head	706	53.2	14.0	1.4	551	65.4	6.6	0.8
Residence								
Total	5047	10.0	100.0	100.0	8320	18.5	100.0	100.0
Nonfarm	4553	9.5	90.2	95.3	6624	16.1	79.6	94.3
Farm	494	18.8	9.8	4.7	1696	44.6	20.4	5.7

Age of head								
Total	5047	10.0	100.0	100.0	8320	18.5	100.0	100.0
14 to 24 years	437	13.2	8.7	6.3	622	26.9	7.5	4.6
25 to 54 years	2731	8.6	54.1	64.2	4752	16.0	57.1	68.0
55 to 64 years	678	8.2	13.4	16.6	1086	15.9	13.1	15.6
65 years and over	1201	17.0	23.8	12.9	1860	30.0	22.4	11.8
Size of family								
Total	5047	10.0	100.0	100.0	8320	18.5	100.0	100.0
2 persons	1831	10.5	36.3	34.2	2850	19.6	34.2	31.7
3 and 4 persons	1431	7.1	28.4	41.2	2420	12.8	29.1	44.9
5 and 6 persons	991	10.2	19.6	19.3	1793	20.2	21.6	19.3
7 persons or more	794	24.7	15.7	5.3	1257	45.6	15.1	4.1
Number of family members under 18*								
Total	5047	10.0	100.0	100.0	8320	18.5	100.0	100.0
no members	1700	8.0	33.7	42.9	2877	15.9	34.6	41.3
1 and 2 members	1465	8.0	29.0	37.2	2458	14.2	29.5	40.4
3 and 4 members	1119	13.2	22.2	16.1	1854	24.5	22.3	15.6
5 or more members	763	30.7	15.1	3.8	1131	53.0	13.6	2.7
Number of earners								
Total	5047	10.0	100.0	100.0	8320	18.5	100.0	100.0
No earners	1666	40.2	33.0	5.5	1981	59.1	23.8	3.7
1 earner	2096	10.8	41.5	37.9	4030	18.7	48.4	47.6
2 earners	936	4.7	18.6	41.5	1659	10.6	20.0	38.0
3 earners or more	349	4.8	6.9	15.2	650	14.2	7.8	10.7

(continued)

*Other than head or wife.

TABLE 11.2 (continued)

Selected characteristics	1968				1959			
	Number below poverty level	Percentage below poverty level	Percent distribution		Number below poverty level	Percentage below poverty level	Percent distribution	
			Below poverty level	Above poverty level			Below poverty level	Above poverty level
Employment status of head								
Total	5047	10.0	100.0	100.0	8320	18.5	100.0	100.0
Employed	2410	6.0	47.7	83.1	4536	12.8	54.5	84.3
Unemployed	146	19.3	2.9	1.3	559	33.7	6.7	3.0
In Armed Forces or not in labor force	2491	26.0	49.4	15.6	3225	40.8	38.8	12.7
Work experience and occupation group of longest job of head								
Total	5047	10.0	100.0	100.0	8320	18.5	100.0	100.0
Worked	2880	6.7	57.1	87.8	5620	14.6	67.6	89.2
Professional and managerial workers	322	2.6	6.4	26.3	471	5.0	5.7	24.6
Clerical and sales workers	210	3.7	4.1	11.9	284	5.7	3.4	12.7
Craftsmen and foremen	327	3.7	6.5	18.6	558	7.2	6.7	19.6
Operatives and kindred workers	534	6.4	10.6	17.3	1064	14.1	12.8	17.6
Service workers, incl. private household	526	16.5	10.4	5.8	732	25.3	8.8	5.9
Nonfarm laborers	332	15.3	6.6	4.0	701	29.4	8.4	4.6
Farmers and farm laborers	629	26.3	12.5	3.9	1810	54.1	21.8	4.2
Did not work	2107	30.9	41.7	10.4	2538	45.2	30.5	8.4
In Armed Forces	60	6.7	1.2	1.8	162	15.5	1.9	2.4

Source: *Poverty in the United States, 1959 to 1968*, Bureau of the Census, Current Population Series P-60, Number 68, page 4.

white. The incidence of poverty was twice as high for farm families as for nonfarm, even though farm families accounted for less than 10% of all poor families.

Although farm families fell as a percentage of poor families between 1959 and 1968, families with nonwhite heads and families with female heads both increased their share of the total number of poor families. The latter's share increased sharply from 23.0% in 1959 to 34.8% in 1968.

Families whose heads were between the ages 14 to 24, or who were 65 years and over had higher-than-average chances of being poor, even though most poor families, 67.5%, were headed by a person between the ages 25 to 64.

The incidence of poverty was greatest for families with 7 or more persons, even though more than 84% of families living below the poverty line had 6 members or fewer.

More than 40% of families with no earner present were counted as living in poverty in 1968. Likewise, the incidence of poverty was higher for families whose head was an unemployed person, 19.3%, and for those whose head was not in the civilian labor force, 26.0%.

Families with no earner present sharply increased their share of the total number of poor families between 1959 and 1968. They accounted for just under 24% of all poor families in 1959 but almost one-third in 1968. The figure for families with an unemployed head fell from 6.7% to 2.9%, although the figure for families headed by a person not in the labor force jumped from less than 40% to almost 50%. Thus it appears that much of the progress between 1959 and 1968 was enjoyed by those who found themselves able to play a productive role in the economy.

Turning to the occupational data, the incidence of poverty was greatest for family heads who worked as service workers, nonfarm laborers, or as farmers or farm laborers, whereas service workers, farm workers, and operatives accounted for the largest shares of all poor families. Between 1959 and 1968, the incidence of poverty for working heads was reduced for each of the occupational groupings, indicating that underemployment of our labor force declined. In fact, the incidence of poverty among families whose head was working declined from 14.6% in 1959 to 6.7% in 1968.

To summarize, the average poor family is headed by a white male between the ages of 25 and 64. The family most likely has 4 or fewer persons and lives off the farm. The head of the family is most likely unemployed or not in the civilian labor force, although more than 47% were headed by an employed person.

On the other hand, the chances of being poor were much greater if the family head were Negro or a woman, and highest for those headed by a Negro woman. The likelihood of poverty was greater if the family lived on a farm, was made up of 7 or more persons, was headed by a person between the ages of 14 and 24 or 65 or over, or by a head who was unemployed or not in the civilian labor force. Furthermore, the chance of the family living below the poverty line increased for all these groups between 1959 and 1968, except for farm families. With the nonfarm population growing proportionally, however, it is possible that many poor families had merely exchanged a farm address for a city one without substantially improving their ability to maintain an adequate standard of living.

Data on unrelated individuals are presented in Table 11.3 The unrelated individual who is poor is most likely to be female, 65 years or over, and a nonearner. Similar to the case for families, in the case of unrelated individuals the incidence of poverty is greater for those on farms, who are female, nonwhite, for those under 24, and particularly for those age 65 and over, and for nonearners. The incidence of poverty for the latter group is 61.1%.

We have seen that families whose heads did not work were much more likely to be poor than were families whose heads did work. Data on the reasons for not working reveal that illness or disability, keeping house, and other reasons were the major explanatory factors (see Table 11.4). More than three-quarters of the female heads who did not work gave keeping house as the reason, whereas more than 40% of male heads who did not work gave illness or disability as their reason. Both findings have implications for antipoverty programs.

Some data on the geographic location of the poor are also available. Poor persons in 1968 were about equally distributed between metropolitan and nonmetropolitan

TABLE 11.3 Selected characteristics of unrelated
persons below the poverty level, 1968
(Number in thousands)

	Number below poverty line	Percent below poverty line
Sex		
Male	1320	25.4
Female	3374	39.2
Race		
White	3849	32
Nonwhite	845	45
Residence		
Nonfarm	4553	33.8
Farm	141	45.0
Age of head		
14 to 24	608	36.5
65 and over	2584	48.8
Number of earners		
Earner	1500	17.5
Nonearner	3194	61.1

Source: *Poverty in the United States, 1959 to 1968*, Bureau of the Census, Current Population Series P-6, Number 65, pages 21, 34, 47.

TABLE 11.4　Numbers of families below the poverty line in 1968 by work
experience (percentages in parentheses) (Number in thousands)

	Total	Male Head	Female Head
	Number below the poverty line		
Total	5047 (10.0)	3292　(7.3)	1775 (32.3)
Worked	2880　(6.7)	2108　(5.3)	772 (23.9)
Did not work	2107 (30.9)	1124 (24.4)	983 (44.6)
Main reason for not working			
Ill or disabled	635 (37.7)	481 (36.2)	154 (43.2)
Keeping house	775 (47.2)	9　—	766 (47.5)
Going to school	33 (43.2)	15　—	18　—
Unable to find work	37　—	22　—	15　—
Other	627 (18.7)	597 (18.9)	30 (16.0)
In Armed Forces	60　(6.7)	60　(6.6)	

Source: *Poverty in the United States, 1959 to 1958*, Bureau of the Census, Current Population
Series P-60, Volume 65, pages 49, 50, 52.

areas. Within metropolitan areas the majority of poor persons were central-city residents. Thus the latter accounted for 30.5% of all poor persons. In fact, 25.3% of white
poor persons lived in the central cities of metropolitan areas, as did 42.5% of Negro
poor persons. Both these figures increased between 1959 and 1968, as did the share of
poverty found in metropolitan areas as a whole. Thus the decline in the incidence of
poverty which occurred over the period was greater for areas outside metropolitan
areas than it was for metropolitan areas themselves (See Table 11.5).

Regional differences in poverty are also discernible. Data from 1966 reveal that
the percentage of poor households is greater in the South than in other parts of the
country. The contrast is more pronounced for families than for unrelated individuals,
the percentage of Southerners who were poor being almost twice as large as the percentage of those who were poor in other areas. Likewise, when the percentage distribution of poor across all regions is examined, we find that nearly half of all poor
families were in the South and nearly one-third of unrelated individuals who were
poor. The percentage of the poor who were in the West was noticeably lower than in
other areas.

Although the preceding discussion has presented the characteristics of the poor,
it is also useful to have some measure of the degree of impoverishment which these
poor families suffer. This measure is provided by the size of the gap between the
poverty threshold and the amount of money received by the household. In 1968 almost half of all poor families had incomes $1000 or more below the applicable poverty
threshold. This was slightly more than the number with a $1000 or more poverty gap
in 1959.

TABLE 11.5 Persons below the poverty level in 1968 and 1959, by type of residence and
race (numbers in thousands. 1959 data from the 1-in-1000 sample of the
1960 census)

Type of residence	All races		White		Negro	
	1968	1959	1968	1959	1968	1959
Number below poverty level						
United States	25,389	38,766	18,394	28,336	7,616	9,927
Metropolitan areas	12,871	17,019	8,473	11,825	4,144	5,002
Central cities	7,754	10,437	4,394	6,513	3,235	3,816
Suburban rings	5,117	6,582	4,079	5,312	909	1,186
Outside metropolitan areas	12,518	21,747	8,922	16,511	3,472	4,925
Percentage below poverty level						
United States	12.8	22.0	10.0	18.1	34.7	55.1
Metropolitan areas	10.0	15.3	7.6	12.0	26.6	42.8
Central cities	13.4	18.3	9.8	13.8	26.2	40.8
Suburban rings	7.3	12.2	6.2	10.4	28.3	50.9
Outside metropolitan areas	18.0	33.2	14.2	28.2	54.6	77.7
Percentage distribution						
United States	100.0	100.0	100.0	100.0	100.0	100.0
Metropolitan areas	50.7	43.9	48.7	41.7	54.4	50.4
Central cities	30.5	26.9	25.3	23.0	42.5	38.4
Suburban rings	20.2	17.0	23.5	18.7	11.9	12.0
Outside metropolitan areas	49.3	56.1	51.3	58.3	45.6	49.6

Source: *Poverty in the United States, 1959 to 1968*, Bureau of the Census, Current Population Series P-60, Volume 68, page 7.

The poverty gap was greater for families headed by females than for males since almost 60% of female-headed families had incomes $1000 or more below the poverty line and only 19.6% had gaps of less than $500. The comparable figures for male-headed families were 44.4% and 30.7%.

White-headed families appeared to be less impoverished than families headed by Blacks. Less than 20% of the latter had gaps of less than $500, while almost 30% of the former had gaps of that size (see Table 11.6).

For unrelated individuals, as compared to families, there was a smaller proportion of households whose gap was $1000 or greater, only 27.8%. This was a slight improvement over the 32% which had such a gap in 1959. The proportion of males with less than a $500 gap was only slightly greater than the proportion of females, and the proportion of males with a $1000 or greater gap was higher than the proportion for females. Thus the degree of impoverishment of male and female unrelated individuals is approximately equal. Both groups showed some improvement between 1959 and 1968.

Both white and nonwhite unrelated individuals showed some lessening of their poverty gap between 1959 and 1968. The gap, however, remained smaller for white unrelated individuals than for nonwhite (see Table 11.7).

11.4 WHY POVERTY?

In the last sections of this chapter we considered the characteristics of the poor and how these characteristics have changed over time. Now we briefly consider why time has not been sufficient to eliminate poverty, and whether more time will be sufficient to do the job.

At least one observer[4] feels that, with the experience gained in the 1960s, poverty in the American economy could be eliminated in less than a generation. What is needed is a commitment on the part of the American public—a commitment not just to reduce poverty but to eliminate it entirely.

The former commitment has, of course, been made; whether the latter commitment will also be made remains to be seen. Most Americans are sympathetic to the plight of the poor. Very few of us could look at a picture of a starving child and not feel a great deal of sympathy. However, there remain at least a few who do not feel it is the government's responsibility to care for the poor. And many of those who do feel the goverment should take on this responsibility do not place the elimination of poverty high on their list of priorities. Other things appear to be more important. One cannot help but draw this conclusion if they examine the allocation of the resources of the Federal government.[5]

Expenditures earmarked for the needy, such as public assistance, accounted for only 4.7% of the Federal budget in 1968, whereas expenditures on space research accounted for approximately 2.5% and that for farm price stabilization accounted for 2.9%. The large majority of the Federal budget, of course, went for national security, over 48%. Another 5.0% went for commerce, transportation, and housing, and 9% for general government.

A little less than 5% seems an incredibly small amount of the Federal budget to allocate to the very important function of alleviating the poverty of more than 25 million Americans. Other welfare, health, and education programs accounted for an additional 25% of the Federal budget. This includes expenditures for health, including Medicaid, education, veterans' programs, and social insurance, such as unemployment compensation and old age and survivors' insurance.

Some of the latter groups of programs—for example, education programs directed at the disadvantaged—can be considered as poverty programs. Most of the expenditures in the welfare, health, and education group, however, could more properly be regarded as keeping down the number of poor people than actually alleviating the problems of those who are already poor. That is, they help keep those who are not

---

[4]Michael Harrington, "The Will to Abolish Poverty," *Saturday Review*, July 27, 1968.
[5]*The Federal Budget, Its Impact on the Economy*, National Industrial Conference Board (1970).

TABLE 11.6 Size of income deficit for families below the poverty level in 1968 and 1959, by sex and race of head

Size of income deficit and sex of head	All races		White		Negro and other races	
	1968	1959	1968	1959	1968	1959
All families						
Number (thousands)	5047	8320	3616	6185	1431	2135
Percentage	100.0	100.0	100.0	100.0	100.0	100.0
$1 to $499	26.8	27.0	29.7	30.1	19.6	18.4
$500 to $999	23.5	25.3	24.7	26.8	20.5	20.7
$1000 to $1999	28.0	30.7	26.2	29.4	32.7	34.3
$2000 to $2999	13.5	11.6	12.3	9.7	16.9	17.2
$3000 and over	8.1	5.4	7.2	4.0	10.2	9.4
Median income deficit	$993	$956	$907	$868	$1260	$1280
Families with male head						
Number (thousands)	3292	6404	2595	4952	697	1452
Percentage	100.0	100.0	100.0	100.0	100.0	100.0
$1 to $499	30.7	29.5	32.4	32.3	24.2	20.2
$500 to $999	25.0	25.7	26.1	27.2	20.6	20.5
$1000 to $1999	26.7	29.3	25.4	28.5	31.4	32.0
$2000 to $2999	11.1	10.7	10.1	8.8	14.8	17.3
$3000 and over	6.6	4.8	5.9	3.3	9.0	10.0
Median income deficit	$875	$895	$818	$815	$1112	$1259
Families with female head						
Number (thousands)	1755	1916	1021	1233	734	683
Percentage	100.0	100.0	100.0	100.0	100.0	100.0
$1 to $499	19.6	18.9	22.9	21.3	15.2	14.3
$500 to $999	20.6	23.4	20.8	24.7	20.2	20.9
$1000 to $1999	30.5	35.7	27.9	33.5	34.2	39.5
$2000 to $2999	18.2	14.6	17.8	13.3	18.8	16.9
$3000 and over	11.0	7.5	10.7	7.0	11.6	8.5
Median income deficit	$1290	$1165	$1176	$1085	$1445	$1330

Source: *Poverty in the United States, 1959 to 1968*, Bureau of the Census, Current Population Series P-60, Volume 68, p. 5.

poor from becoming poor, but are not specifically designed to eliminate the poverty that already exists in the American economy. That poverty would be a good deal more widespread and in many cases more severe without such programs as social insurance is no doubt true.

TABLE 11.7 Size of income deficit for unrelated individuals below the poverty level in 1968 and 1959, by sex and race of head

	Total		White		Nonwhite		Male Head		Female Head	
	1968	1959	1968	1959	1968	1959	1968	1959	1968	1959
Size of gap	100.0	100.0	100.0	100.0	100.0					
$1 to $499	38.6	31.4	40.3	33.2	30.6	23.3	39.6	34.5	38.2	30.0
$1000 or over	27.8	32.0	25.1	31.5	28.3	34.6	26.4	31.2	25.4	32.4

Source: *Poverty in the United States, 1959 to 1968*, Bureau of the Census, Current Population Series P-60, Volume 68, pages 101–103.

The years ahead, particularly when the Vietnam conflict is ended, will reveal just how committed we are to eliminating poverty. Will we turn over some of the tax dollars we are using to fight a war abroad to fight the war against poverty at home? Just how high on our list of priorities will eliminating poverty be placed?

11.5 THE ROLE OF ECONOMIC GROWTH IN REDUCING POVERTY

One could draw the conclusion that, although the American public is concerned about poverty, it has not committed itself to putting the elimination of poverty at the top of its list of priorities. The point should be stressed that such a commitment must be made if poverty is to be eliminated. Economic growth in the absence of such a commitment will *not* be able to do the job by itself. The reason is simple. Even if economic growth were to provide jobs for large numbers of those who are poor, even if economic growth were to provide jobs for *every* poor person who was readily capable of working, there would still remain a large number of poor people. Many of those who are poor are just not readily capable of working. They are too old, they are disabled, they are mothers with young children and no husbands, they have skills which are unsuited to the labor force. One must remember that nearly three-fourths of poor unrelated individuals and one-half of poor families are headed by a person who is not in the labor force.

Economic growth alone is not going to allow these persons to play a productive role in our society. For some, retraining will be needed; for others new concepts in child care and work scheduling may do the trick. But there are others whom no poverty program will succeed in bringing into the labor force. Removing poverty for this segment of our population will thus entail some kind of remedial income or cash assistance program.

One might repeat a point made at the beginning of this chapter. Being in the labor force does not guarantee that a person will not be poor; nor does having a job. Almost one-half of the heads of poor families were employed in 1968 and 25% of unrelated individuals were employed. Again manpower programs as well as economic growth are needed to raise the productivity and marketability of this category of the poor of our nation.

11.6 PROBLEMS OF DEPRESSED AREAS

Poverty is associated with particular areas as well as with particular groups of people. It seems worthwhile then to at least briefly investigate the particular dimensions of poverty problems in urban neighborhoods as well as those in rural areas.

The Department of Labor's 1969 survey of the employment situation in the poverty areas of six cities[6] reveals that the factors most important in explaining poverty differed from area to area. Low weekly earnings stemming from jobs of low pay and low status were particularly important in Atlanta; in Detroit high unemployment seemed to be of primary importance. The fact that a large proportion of household heads were not in the labor force was also a factor of varying importance in the six cities.

A summary of the employment situation in the urban poverty neighborhoods of the nation's 100 largest cities reveals the extent of the poverty problem in these areas.[7]

Only about 53% of the residents of urban poverty neighborhoods were working in 1968, as compared to 59% in other urban neighborhoods. And those that were employed tended to be more concentrated in low-skilled, low-income occupations. Only 31.4% of those employed in the urban poverty neighborhoods were white-collar workers, although more than 56% of those in other urban neighborhoods were employed in the white-collar group. The figures for service occupations were 20.9% and 10.3%, respectively. A greater proportion of poverty-neighborhood residents worked on part time for economic reasons and a smaller proportion worked overtime.

The unemployment rate in poverty neighborhoods was 6.0% in 1968, compared to 3.2% in other urban neighborhoods, although the LFPR was lower, 56.5% compared to 60.5%. The difference in LFPRs was particularly striking for males age 25 to 54. The rate for this group was 92.0% in the poverty areas compared to 97.3% in other urban neighborhoods. Disability, discouragement, and voluntary idleness thus occur at a higher rate in the poverty neighborhoods. Women age 25 to 54, however, typically have high work rates due to the need for additional family incomes in the poverty neighborhoods.

Thus the urban poverty neighborhoods tend to have a smaller proportion of their population engaged in productive activity as well as a smaller proportion of productive people in the higher-skill, higher-pay occupations. Attacking poverty in urban areas necessarily involves providing more jobs and drawing more people into the labor force as well as upgrading the occupational distribution of those already in the labor force.

Characteristics of the rural poor are described in a report of the U.S. Department

---

[6]See *Employment Situation in Poverty Areas of Six Cities, July 1968–June 1969*, U.S. Department of Labor, Bureau of Labor Statistics, October 1969.

[7]Paul M. Ryscavage, "Employment in Urban Poverty Neighborhoods," *Monthly Labor Rev.*, June 1969.

of Agriculture which was published in 1964.[8] The report refers to data on rural poverty in 1959 and considers as poor those families with incomes of less than $3000 and those unrelated individuals whose incomes are less than $1500. Less than 40% of the 16 million rural poor persons in families in 1959 lived on farms, although 1.4 million of the 1.6 million poor unrelated individuals did.

Much of the poverty existing in rural areas can be attributed to unemployment and underemployment. In 1959 the total number of rural unemployed equivalents for persons 20 to 64 years of age amounted to 18% of the total rural labor force in this age group. Poverty was even more prevalent, however, among families headed by persons 65 years old or older. The educational level of the household head in depressed rural areas was almost always low. Educational facilities were fewer and of poorer quality, as were housing and public utilities. As in urban areas, the nature of the rural poverty problem differed somewhat from area to area.[9] In the Mississippi Delta, the farm-laborer group presented a particular problem. In the Ozarks, older retired persons made up most of the poor, while in South Carolina operators of small farms constituted as great a problem as those not working.

Thus, in rural as in urban poverty areas, programs are needed both to raise the economic status of the individual by providing education, training, and employment opportunities, and to provide welfare programs geared to those not able to play a role in the labor force. Public services such as schools, hospitals, roads, and water supplies also have to be maintained at adequate levels.

Eliminating poverty for those who are capable of participating in the labor force necessarily requires a twofold approach. On the one hand, many of this segment of the population will have to be "educated-up" so that they will be able to hold jobs other than low paying ones, and, on the other hand, employment opportunities need to be provided for those capable of working.

One might at this point briefly consider what it is that makes lucrative employment opportunities readily available in some areas but not in others.[10]

Much of the answer lies in the level of regional development which must be able to maintain an employment base that can support the population of the region. A region's ability to grow and, therefore, to provide such a base is a reflection of demand and supply conditions as well as of its advantages for production. Thus chief among the elements essential for adequate regional development are natural resources, manpower skills, and aggressive entrepreneurship.

---

[8]Alan R. Bird, *Poverty in Rural Areas of the United States*, U.S. Department of Agriculture, Economic Research Service, Washington, D.C. 1964.

[9]*Rural Poverty in Three Southern Regions*, U.S. Department of Agriculture, Economic Research Service, Washington, D.C., March 1970.

[10]For an excellent discussion of regional growth see Brian J. L. Berry, *Strategies, Models, and Economic Theories of Development in Rural Regions*, U.S. Department of Agriculture, Economic Research Service, Washington, D.C., December 1967.

Since regions in a specialized economy must import in order to survive, they must be able to attract industries that produce for export to other regions of the country. They must also maintain substantial internal economic development. Industrial mix, then, is part of the problem. Regions, to develop quickly, must rely on securing one or more rapidly growing industries or greater proportions of slower-growing industries. These are the base for employment. The industrial mix of the continually growing regions is constantly changing. Thus the essence of growth, according to some regional development experts, is continuous innovation. Reliance on one or more declining industries no doubt creates a potentially depressed area rather than an area of growth and opportunity.

SUMMARY

Knowing a person's labor-force classification does not tell us whether or not that person is poor. A poor person is one who is not capable of maintaining an adequate standard of living. The Social Security Administration has defined poverty thresholds for 124 different kinds of families. The thresholds attempt to specify the minimum money income capable of supporting the family at the lowest level consistent with prevailing standards of living in this country. The index has been criticized for relying solely on income as an indication of poverty.

The proportion of persons below the poverty level declined from about 22% in 1959 to less than 13% in 1968. Unrelated individuals and nonwhites increased their shares of poor persons during the period. The incidence of poverty is disproportionately high among these groups, as well as among family members below the age of 18.

Turning to data on families, we see that most poor families are headed by a white male, age 25 to 64, who lives off the farm and is not employed. However, the chances of the family being poor are considerably higher if the family head is a Black, or a woman, or if they live on a farm.

Data on the reasons for not working indicate that keeping house was an important factor for females, whereas illness or disability was important for males.

The poverty gap is measured by the difference between the poverty threshold and the amount of money received by the household. Nearly half of poor families and more than 27% of unrelated individuals had gaps of more than $1000 in 1968.

One must question how high the alleviation of poverty is on our list of national priorities. Something less than 5% of the national budget was earmarked for the needy in 1968. A stronger commitment must be made. Economic growth alone will not do the job. There are too many poor persons that are not capable of playing a productive role in our society.

Some specific data are available on urban as well as rural poor. Residents of urban poverty neighborhoods have a greater incidence of unemployment, and those who were employed tended to be concentrated in lower skilled jobs as compared to those in other urban neighborhoods. Much of the poverty in rural areas can likewise be attributed to unemployment and underemployment.

BIBLIOGRAPHY

Bureau of Census, *Poverty in the United States, 1959 to 1968*, Current Population Series P-60, Number 68

Michael Harrington, "The Will to Abolish Poverty," *Saturday Review*, July 27, 1968

"Perspectives on Poverty," *Monthly Labor Rev.* (February 1969), a collection of five articles on poverty

Mollie Orshansky, *The Shape of Poverty in 1966*, Social Security Bulletin, Social Security Administration (March 1968)

Public Policy in the Manpower Field

Part IV

Manpower policy deals with the process of establishing goals and priorities in the relationship between man and his working environment, seeking to improve his economic status, income, and opportunity in the world of work.

In its broadest terms manpower policy is concerned with the development, maintenance, and utilization of current and potential members of the labor force. A full manpower policy is active, comprehensive, and has a cohesive strategy.

A manpower policy has been evolving in the U.S. economy. Given the operation of the market mechanism which allocates resources through price, wage, and output cues, manpower policy intervenes to provide for alternative social and political goals and priorities.

The period of the 1960s was one of experimentation in manpower programs. The Federal government has developed an active manpower policy in promoting the opportunity of disadvantaged groups. The 1970s appear to be emerging as a period of manpower planning, decentralization of operations to the states, and decategorization of programs.

CONCEPTUALIZING
MANPOWER POLICY 12

12.1 MANPOWER POLICY DEFINED

How do we define "manpower policy," and how is it differentiated from the myriad activities carried out in the public and private sector? Essentially, manpower policy has the implicit or explicit goal of influencing labor-market processes to improve the resource value of a worker either preparing for or already in the labor force. Manpower policy broadly defined deals with the relationship between man and his working environment, seeking to improve his economic status, income, and opportunity in the world of work.

As Professor Harbison has indicated, manpower policy in its broadest terms is concerned with the development, maintenance, and utilization of actual and potential members of the labor force.[1]

The development of manpower is the process of man's acquisition of skills, knowledge, and capacities for work. Included are skill-training programs, such as vocational education, and formal and informal on-the-job experiences which enhance a worker's resource value. To the extent that general education facilitates a worker's acquisition of skill or experience, it is included as a part of manpower policy.

The maintenance of manpower is the process of building the capacity of man's working ability, as well as preventing his work skills and experiences from deteriorating. Maintenance is concerned with the continuous development of manpower. Health, education, and welfare programs all have the effect of maintaining and/or restoring man's capacity for work. In fact, in any developing economy these are

---

[1]Frederick Harbison, "Critical Issues in American Manpower Policy and Practice," *Proceedings of the Seventeenth Annual Meeting of the Industrial Relations Research Association*, edited by Gerald G. Somers, *Chicago, Illinois, December 28, 29*, 1964, pages 216–229.

necessary prerequisites, before manpower development programs can be effectively launched, for the emergence of an industrial labor force.

The third aspect of manpower policy, utilization, is the process of matching men and work with their level of skill attainment and work capability. As indicated in the section on labor-market imbalances, the market mechanism fails to work perfectly even under relatively full employment. Imbalances may exist between regions on the number of unemployed persons in comparison to the number of job vacancies. In addition to this, there are many workers who perform some tasks below the skill level of their training and experience. Whether the causes are related to a lack of knowledge and information, poor mobility, discrimination or lack of motivation, manpower may be used at less than optimum levels. Policies targeting-in on utilization include counseling and placement services, more effective managerial practices, encouragement of mobility, and the enhancement of motivation to attract workers into areas of work having a higher resource value.

Manpower policy, therefore, can be defined as the establishment of a set of programs which are intended to increase the resource value of manpower through more effective development, maintenance, and utilization of an individual's work skills.

Must manpower policy be governmental policy? What is the process by which a society formulates a manpower policy? This will be considered in the next section.

12.2 THE PROCESS OF FORMULATING A MANPOWER POLICY

The central theme throughout this book has been the concept of decision-making by individuals, households, and groups or associations. The manpower economist is concerned with the study of those decisions relating to the preparation and utilization of manpower as an "input" in the process of producing goods and services in an economic system.

In a market system, individuals and firms make decisions as to the types of products produced, prices, plant location, and how manpower and other resources will be combined to carry out production. In like manner, other individuals and their associations make decisions relating to preparation for work, occupational choice, training and education, amount of work offered, and retirement from the labor force.

Where decisions are widely dispersed throughout society and no single individual or group plans the decisions of others, we depend on the market mechanism to allocate resources, produce and price goods, and distribute goods and services produced. The political counterpart of a market system in an economic society where decision-making is widely dispersed is democracy.

It should be noted that production has been carried out in societies where the decision-making process is less widely dispersed, and where one group makes all or most of the essential economic decisions.

Conceptually we can visualize the decision-making process along a continuum,

TABLE 12.1 Continuum of political and economic decision-making

Decentralized economic and political system	Centralized economic and political system
Nature of economic system	Nature of economic system
1 Market mechanism	1 Nonmarket allocation
2 Decisions made by individuals and households	2 Decisions made by one individual or relatively small group
3 Prices and wages allocate economic resources, and goods and services	3 Primary reliance on other than individual decisions
4 Individual choice	4 Small group decision-making
5 Competition	5 Noncompetitive
Nature of political system	Nature of political system
1 Relatively equal individuals and households	1 Compulsion and/or cooperation
2 Power decentralized	2 Power centralized
3 Pluralistic and balanced society	3 Relatively monistic society
4 Decision-making from bottom to top	4 Large role for government
5 Relatively small governmental role	

ranging from the model of pure competition and democracy at one extreme, to the model of nonmarket decisions arrived at by a relatively small group holding power and control over others in a society (see Table 12.1).

Within the two extremes we have mixed economic—political systems, characterized by a considerable range of decision-making by individuals and households, but also by wide areas in which decisions are made by small groups on a more centralized basis.

It is important to recognize the basic structure of decision-making (e.g., whether democratic or centralized) to understand the process by which policies are formulated in a society. In a democratic system, decisions are reached with a minimum of governmental participation. Conversely, in a centralized system, decision-making by individuals is subordinated to that by government, and a mixed system provides for a balance between individual versus group, and private versus public decisions to be made.

The implication of our conceptual framework is that although we shall be discussing government manpower policy in this and the next chapter, we should keep in mind that by far most of the decisions in the manpower field are made by individuals and households and private associations, rather than by governmental units. Government manpower policy operates in a "marginal" sense, e.g., to redress an imbalance between groups, to provide information and services to enable private groups and individuals to reach better decisions, and to initiate manpower programs which will alleviate what major decision-making groups have identified as "problem areas."

Manpower programs will emerge if a sufficient number of groups recognize that a problem exists, and have a sufficient degree of political power to get legislation passed. The nature and diversity of manpower programs is determined by the nature and number of power groups involved in the development of manpower programs, and also the constraints exercised by other groups having political and/or economic power.

Very often questions are raised as to why government does not "eliminate" poverty or unemployment, or why an optimum manpower policy has failed to emerge. An answer to this question can be formulated only if we understand that many individuals and groups do not perceive these problems to be of high priority within their own value systems and decision-making processes, or that the costs of policies are perceived to be greater than the benefits incurred.

Our discussion of the evaluation of a manpower policy will be facilitated if we understand the nature of decision-making in a mixed political—economic system, the goals of the "actors," and the perceptions of the costs and benefits of manpower programs by groups and associations in society. (Table 12.2 presents a schematic descriptive framework.)

TABLE 12.2 Descriptive framework of typical actors and decisions in a mixed political—economic system

Typical actor	Some manpower-related decisions	Typical goals
Individual and household	Work versus leisure	Income
	Occupational, geographical, and industrial choice	Status and prestige
	Education and training	Control over one's destiny
	Migration	Oportunity for self and family
	Association in unions	
Union	Membership criteria	Security of union
	Creation of work rules through contractual agreement	Mutual protection from arbitrary decisions
	Economic versus political action	Control of work environment
Firm	Production of goods	Produce for profit
	Hiring and firing of workers	Survive in a competitive environment
	Train workers	
	Work rules to carry out production	
	Minimize costs of producing goods	
Government	Regulate contractual arrangements between firms and unions	Survive as a society
		Minimize discontent
		Promote general welfare

12.3 THE ROLE OF GOVERNMENT IN THE DEVELOPMENT OF MANPOWER POLICY

We have seen that manpower policy emerges in society as a result of decisions reached by individuals, households, private associations such as unions and business firms, and governmental agencies at all levels. Note that decisions reached may not all be consistent nor be working in the same direction. Conflicts may emerge as various groups and individuals pursue goals.

Note also that governmental manpower policies may develop as a by-product of other goals, such as defense, agriculture, public education, and urban renewal. In fact, the by-products related to manpower policy may be quite significant even though not directly intended by policymakers. In addition to this, the degree of governmental involvement and explicit formulation of a manpower policy may be quite minimal. In fact, in a political—economic system characterized by a pattern of widely dispersed decision-making, the role of government may be solely that of an intervenor to promote the interests of a particular group, or to intervene in a "crisis" situation.

Like an iceberg, in which only a small portion is visible above the surface, governmental manpower policy is only the visible portion above a vast and intricate network of decisions relating to manpower which are made by individuals, households, and private groups (see Table 12.3).

As shown in Table 12.3, the identification of a society's "manpower policy" involves an analysis of the structure of the pyramid of decisions which are made in society. Governmental policies are perhaps the most visible, and occasionally exert leverage at the margin on decisions at the organizational, and household and individual levels. In a totally free-enterprise, market-oriented economy, the governmental "tip of the iceberg" would be barely visible. Decisions relating to the formulation of manpower policy would be concentrated at the private organizational and household/individual levels. Conversely, growth of the role of government and

TABLE 12.3 Pyramid of governmental, organizational, and individual decisions in the formulation of manpower policy

GOVERN-

MENTAL

Local, State,
Federal

ORGANIZATIONAL

(e.g., unions, firms, educational
institutions, associations, etc.)

HOUSEHOLD AND INDIVIDUAL

Decisions relating to manpower

movement away from private decision-making would show a more visible govern-mental manpower policy.

12.4 THE DYNAMICS OF MANPOWER POLICY

Our discussion in this chapter will be limited to governmental manpower policy, since this is the area in which we can provide for major changes in the direction of programs. Is governmental policy, as determined by legislation and executive ad-ministration, a conscious, coordinated, and planned activity? Does government have an explicit "plan" to raise the resource value of workers?

In a political—economic system which is characterized by decentralized decision-making, the development of governmental manpower policy at the national level would be a difficult task. It would require the coordination and integration of thousands of policymakers—private employers, local school boards, community action groups, state education, labor and welfare departments, a wide-ranging group of Federal government agencies and institutions, as well as the Federal, state, and local governments as direct employers of manpower.

Although it would be possible to design and administer such a system, it might be inconsistent with a society's preferences toward a large role for the private sector, and maximum individual decision-making. Also, it is important to note that many programs which are designed for other purposes have important manpower implica-tions, whereas some manpower programs may have very minimal implications for manpower.

In theory one could conceive of manpower policy as being active, comprehen-sive, and/or cohesive.[2] An active policy is a conscious attempt to intervene in the labor market to raise the resource value of manpower. Conversely, an inactive policy is a situation in which it is not the primary intent of government to influence the resource value of manpower. For example, the training of military personnel (pilots, craftsmen, truck drivers, etc.) may eventually have significant effects on the skill level of civilian manpower, although the primary goal is defense.

A comprehensive manpower policy encompasses all programs or activities related to the development, maintenance, and utilization of the labor force. Programs are in existence for all segments of the labor force, covering pre-employment preparation, training, and services for optimum utilization of workers. Characteristic of a compre-hensive manpower policy is coverage of most or all of the segments of the labor force with a wide array of programs.

Although governmental manpower programs may in effect be comprehensive, there may be no overall consciously developed plan to coordinate programs in man-power. A cohesive manpower policy is one in which there is a logical and consistent strategy in guiding activities in such a way as to maximize the resource value of

---

[2] Frederick Harbison, "Critical Issues in American Manpower Policy and Practice," *Proceed-ing of the Seventeenth Annual Meeting of the Industrial Relations Research Association*, Chicago, Illinois, December 28, 29 (1964). Edited by Gerald G. Somers.

individuals and groups. In theory a cohesive strategy would require the coordination of thousands of policymakers, firms, households, and other public and private organizations.

12.5 FROM MANPOWER POLICY TO HIGHER RESOURCE VALUE

Having discussed the nature of manpower policy, we are now left with the question of precisely how manpower policy transforms itself into higher resource values of manpower. We are interested in the process by which manpower policy changes manpower as an economic resource.

Manpower programs which develop or provide for more effective utilization and development amount to "investments" in which it is anticipated that outcomes generated will exceed inputs of resources into the programs. Conceptually one can conceive of inputs of resources into alternative programs, each of which generates a particular stream of income returns. Investments for each of the programs continues to the point at which the internal rate of return is equalized among the program.

Where i = manpower program, r = rate of return, I = investment input, and R = income returns, we have

$$I_i = \Sigma \left[\frac{R_1}{(1 + r_i)} + \frac{R_2}{(1 + r_i)^2} + \cdots + \frac{R_n}{(1 + r_i)^n} \right].$$

TABLE 12.4 Summary of conceptual framework of manpower development

Decision-making units	Nature of manpower policy	Means to reach goal	End goal of manpower policy
Individuals	Active	Conservation	Higher resource value of manpower resources
Households Private associations	Comprehensive Cohesive	Development Utilization	Income Work satisfaction
Firms			Individual and society's well-being
Educational institutions			
Public groups Local State National			Widening of individual choice Production of goods and services

Investments continue in programs i_1 to i_n until the rates of return r_{i_1} to r_{i_n} are equalized. In utilizing this approach one would have to include other investment outlets besides manpower. All forms of public and private investment would have to be opened up. For our discussion here we have eliminated nonmanpower program investments.

It is important to emphasize that the investments in manpower need not emerge solely from the public sector. These could be individual, household, or private group investments.

A fourth point needs to be mentioned. We have indicated investments in utilization and development programs. Investments in conservation also have income returns and an internal rate of return, but the difference is that investment in manpower conservation *prevents* a deterioration of quality. It is an attempt to minimize losses which would be incurred without these investments. Without manpower conservation, the health of individuals would be impaired, skill level and potential for future development or utilization impaired.

SUMMARY

Conceptually manpower policy has the goal of influencing the operation of the labor market for the purpose of improving the current and future economic status of an individual. Manpower policy in its broadest sense is concerned with the development, maintenance, and utilization of current and potential members of the labor force.

Manpower development is concerned with the process of acquisition of skills, knowledge, and capacities for work. Manpower maintenance is the process of building the capacity of man's working ability as well as the prevention of deterioration of his work skills and experiences. Utilization is concerned with matching men and jobs in terms of skill attainment and work capability.

Manpower policy is, therefore, defined as the establishment of a set of programs which are intended to increase the resource value of workers through more effective development, maintenance, and utilization of an individual's work skills.

A society's manpower policy emerges as a result of decisions reached by individuals, households, and numerous associational groups. Government intervenes in the decision-making process to effect changes which are not readily brought about by the operation of private decision-making processes.

Government manpower policy may have elements of being active, comprehensive, and cohesive. An active policy is a conscious attempt to intervene in the labor market to raise the resource value of particular manpower groups. A comprehensive manpower policy encompasses all programs or activities which have an influence on the development, maintenance, and utilization of the labor force. A cohesive manpower policy is one in which there is a logical and consistent strategy in guiding programs toward preconceived goals.

BIBLIOGRAPHY

Eli Ginzberg, Dale L. Hiestand, and Beatrice G. Reubens, *The Pluralistic Society*, McGraw-Hill, New York, 1965

Henry David (ed.), *Education and Manpower*, Columbia University Press, New York, 1960

Henry David, *Manpower Policies for a Democratic Society*, Columbia University Press, New York, 1965

Human Resources for Industrial Development: Some Aspects of Policy and Planning. International Labor Office, Geneva, Switzerland, 1967

EARLY DEVELOPMENT OF
MANPOWER POLICY 13

13.1 KEY THREADS IN MANPOWER-POLICY FORMULATION

In Chapter 12 we indicated that manpower policy is concerned with the development, maintenance, and utilization of the labor force. We have also specified that the full emergence of manpower policy would be active, cohesive, and comprehensive. We are, of course, far from attaining all of the six elements of completeness in manpower policy formulation. Moreover, policymakers are concerned with pragmatic solutions to immediate problems, rather than grandiose and visionary planning horizons. Yet there is a discernible pattern which emerges over time from individual programs. New programs build on past accomplishments, and successful programs set the stage for new approaches in dealing with problems facing society. Taken together, and added over time, a manpower policy begins to focus into shape as more ingredients are added and as separate threads of development are woven into a meaningful fabric of national policy.

It is important to keep in mind that many programs which may appear to be irrelevant to our study have, in fact, a very profound impact on manpower policy. We must note indirect effects as well as the by-products of programs. If one were to list only those programs which are directly identifiable as manpower oriented, one would get an incomplete picture of how policy develops over time.

Rather than to list in catalog fashion all programs that have had an influence on manpower policy, our approach will be to suggest a number of separate threads of development, which, taken together, have formed the main outline of our national manpower policy. If an explicit policy should ever be articulated, it would have to include discussion of the influence of at least the following development streams:[1]

1. Basic education and universal literacy

2. Science and technology

3. Immigration and labor supply

4. The New Deal and the Great Depression

5. Military manpower and veterans' readjustment policies

6. Racial policy

We shall discuss each of these areas in this chapter and suggest relevant factors in the development of manpower policy.

13.2 BASIC EDUCATION AND UNIVERSAL LITERACY

Egalitarian pressures in colonial and post-revolutionary America placed a high value on basic elementary education both as a vehicle for opening up social and economic opportunities for members of the working class and as a means for the Americanization and assimilation of a polyglot of culturally and linguistically diverse masses of immigrants. Proponents of public education feared that private education would either fail to reach the masses comprising American society or would be splintered along religious and ethnic lines. The former would be inconsistent with emerging pressures for an egalitarian-type society which offered opportunities to all, and the latter would threaten the development of an "American" society. Also, proponents of public education argued that a democratic society could function only if citizens were literate and could exercise free and independent judgment in making political decisions.

Proponents of private education argued in favor of individual and family choice, and emphasized that private gains achieved in education should be accrued as a private gain consistent with the belief that individual choice and costs should be determined by the operation of the market mechanism.

As so often happens in conflicts of this nature, a compromise was reached and a "mixed" educational system was established. On the one hand the value of educational diversity and market allocation of resources was recognized as private education was permitted to coexist within a basic structure of near-universal, and heavily subsidized, public education. The compromise between private and public education was an uneasy one, as newer conflicts raged in areas such as government control of standards in private schools, and also the use of public funds in supporting private educational efforts. Also, in early days, education was far from universal, as large segments of the population—Blacks, children from poor states, etc.—failed to receive the benefits of public education.

---

[1]Professor Ginzberg identifies 7 key elements in the development of manpower policy: the free market, immigration, racial policy, basic education, higher education, science policy, and military manpower policy. See Eli Ginzberg, *Manpower Agenda for America*, McGraw-Hill, New York, 1968. This chapter depends heavily on Professor Ginzberg's analysis.

Superimposed on the public/private conflicts was the problem of determining the sphere of government control in public education. Local decision-making was retained by states and local communities, with the Federal government acting in the role of catalyst for change and financial supporter through Federal legislative action. The pattern established by the passage of the Northwest Ordinance in 1787, in which the Federal government set aside a given ratio of land tracts for schools in newly acquired territories, became a model for Federal—state relations in public education. From then on, primary responsibility for public education was to rest with local and state governments, though the Federal government would give significant financial support and would be involved in promoting changes to meet new national needs.

Although there have been some exceptions and shortcomings in public educational policy, the following pattern has emerged:

1. Access to public education is available to all, and is subsidized by government

2. Education is compulsory for all youth

3. Diversity in education is acknowledged, as private and public education coexist

4. Major control of public education is at State and Local levels

5. The Federal government is involved only in major efforts to redirect educational goals, and not as a primary dispensor of educational services

13.3 SCIENCE AND TECHNOLOGY

There has always been a strong national interest shown in the development of science and technology, particularly in the applied aspects which tend to promote industrial development. Efforts to develop the economy through the application of science and technology led to the passage of the Morrill Act in 1862, which created our great system of land-grant colleges. This landmark legislation was inaugurated to develop a system of higher education in the states which would conduct basic and applied research in agriculture and related areas, and train a supply of professional and technical workers who would, over the years, have a profound impact on agricultural output and productivity. Through experiment stations in all states, researchers were involved in developing new products, improving older methods, and in training skilled researchers and technicians in agriculture.

Moreover, through the cooperative extension program, land-grant colleges demonstrated that the substance of higher education could be transmitted to all segments of a community's population. In a three-way cooperative effort between the Federal government, state college, and local community, technical assistance was provided in management of farm enterprises and eventually expanded to cover a wide range of subjects. For many land-grant colleges, the motto of "the boundaries of the campus are the boundaries of the state" became a very real accomplishment. Over the 108-year period since the enactment of the Morrill Act, land-grant colleges have educated thousands of skilled scientists, technicians, and professionals who have transformed agriculture into a highly productive industry. Even more importantly, land-grant colleges have demonstrated that higher education could serve a broad base of population in a vast number of fields heretofore ignored by institutions of higher education.

Supplementing and reenforcing the development of land-grant colleges was the emergence of vocational education at the secondary and post-secondary educational levels. Like the land-grant system, vocational education was viewed, initially, as a means by which the manpower needs of industry could be met. Vocational education was launched on a formal basis in the early 1900s, when a small group of men formed the National Society for the Promotion of Industrial Education in order to bring the need for industrial education to the attention of the American people. As a result of efforts of this and similar groups, Congress passed the Smith–Hughes Act in 1917 and provided a grant of about $7.2 million annually to the states for the purpose of promoting vocational education in agriculture, trade and industrial education, and home economics. Supplemental legislation (George–Reed Act, 1930–34; George–Barden Act 1946) widened the scope of vocational education and provided additional funds.

From the beginning of the century, and accelerating rapidly during and after World War II, the heavy emphasis has been on science. During World War II, the Federal government promoted vast research expenditures in atomic energy, electronics, aeronautics, and numerous other fields. After 1957, as a result of the Soviet Union's achievement in orbiting "sputnik," expenditures accelerated on science research, fellowships for training future scientists through the National Defense Education Act of 1958, and even the establishment of the National Science Foundation to promote basic research.

All of the above developments demonstrated that national policy would be strongly concerned with the promotion of science and technology to further national goals such as industrial and agricultural development, and military and defense preparedness. Resources would be made available to train high-level manpower in promoting science and technology.

13.4 IMMIGRATION AND LABOR SUPPLY

The vastness of the country and the existence of untapped natural resources has always provided an attraction for new migrations, and has led to positive efforts to increase the supply of labor. In colonial days indentured servitude and slavery were promoted as sources of cheap labor supply. Under the former system, workers would contract themselves into virtual bondage for a period of years in return for passage to the colonies. Also, the colonies had served as a convenient receiving point for convicts and prisoners from jails in Great Britain. Slavery had been in existence from the earliest days of the colonial period, and though the importation of slaves was made illegal in the early 1800s, this practice continued until the end of the Civil War.

Although slavery, indentured servitude, and convicts constituted a large proportion of the labor supply in the colonial period, immigration became the prime source of new manpower in the mid-1800s and thereafter. Famine in Ireland and unsuccessful revolutions on the continent in the 1840s brought waves of immigrants to the United States. Population movements were even greater in the period from 1870 to 1914 and brought in newer ethnic groups from Southern and Eastern Europe. A prime force in permitting large numbers of immigrants to enter the country was the desire to tap a large and relatively cheap source of labor supply for the nation's rapidly growing industries. Though opposed by important segments of the labor union movement, immigration on a large scale continued up to the 1920s. After World War I immigration policy was structured in favor of West European nationals, with severely restricted quotas for other groups. Immigration had always been highly restrictive against Africans and Orientals.

13.5 THE NEW DEAL AND THE GREAT DEPRESSION

A major development in the formation of a manpower policy was the Great Depression of the 1930s and the experimentation of the Federal government in attempting to deal with the crisis of widespread unemployment. Beginning with the stock-market crash of 1929, unemployment rose to record highs and ranged from 10 to 25% for most of the decade of the 1930s.

Government was caught in the middle of a serious crisis without any semblance of an economic policy, and the market system seemed to be incapable of coping with difficulties which threatened the continuation of the free-enterprise system. Caught without a policy or strategy for dealing with the Depression, President Roosevelt inaugurated a New Deal policy which was characterized by its experimentation, a wide variety of programs touching on all areas of economic activity. Probably the most significant aspect of the New Deal was the lowered status of the market mechanism in bringing forth full employment and an efficient allocation and utilization of resources.

For the study of manpower, significant alterations were made in limiting discretionary areas of employers in worker—management relations. Collective bargaining was legalized, minimum wage and hour standards were established, and the hiring of children restricted and regulated. Social Security (retirement, survivors' insurance) became a federal program operated on a national basis, implemented through taxes on employers and employees. An unemployment insurance program was established as a state-operated system through Federal enabling legislation, and through a uniform Federal tax on payrolls, a large part of which could be diverted to state treasuries, in which an unemployment insurance system was in operation. All these measures implied that the operation of the market mechanism was no longer to be completely "free." Its operation would have to bear the test of whether results were optimizing social welfare. If not, government would intervene at various points of decision-making to alter glaring injustices or imbalances. Yet, in all of this, the Federal government did not discard the free-enterprise system, but merely "polished up" or altered limited areas in which the market mechanism seemed to be falling short of meeting social-welfare criteria.

The New Deal period also noted the establishment of a Federal—state employment service system. The passage of the Wagner—Peyser Act in 1933 developed a network of offices throughout the country which served as a labor exchange for workers seeking jobs and employers seeking suitable workers. In addition to the labor-exchange function, the employment service provided a checkpoint for unemployment-insurance eligibility. Operated as a state agency, but with heavy regulation and funding by the Federal government, the employment service provided a useful means by which less-skilled workers were matched with employer needs. Private agencies continued to "cream" the placement of professional and highly skilled workers on a fee basis, and craft unions often placed their own members under a "hiring-hall" system. Though one would hardly characterize the public employment office as the cornerstone of an active manpower policy, developments in the 1960s were to lead to the expectation that whatever manpower policy emerged in the future it would have to consider the Federal—state public employment structure as the single most significant governmental institution in this area.

13.6 MILITARY MANPOWER AND VETERANS' READJUSTMENT POLICIES

The growing role of the military during and after World War II has significantly affected the development of manpower policy. We have already noted that military needs spawned heavy investments in science and technology, which in turn accelerated the development of large numbers and categories of professional and technical manpower. Military activities affected manpower policy in many other ways.

Over the past 30 years (except for a brief interlude from late 1946 to early 1948) we have had a Selective Service System in operation. A peacetime conscription system was established after considerable conflict and debate in 1940, and was narrowly renewed on the eve of our entry into World War II. Postwar conflicts in Korea and Indo-China and the continuation of the Soviet—U.S. cold war made what was initially a marked departure from our free-enterprise system into virtually a permanent institution.

The conscription of more than 20 million persons into the armed forces over the last 30 years led to the emergence of the military as a large educational institution—both in the training role of imparting military skills, and also in training recruits for civilian-type jobs which were in demand. Military service also highlighted the manpower problem in the country by identifying many thousands of individuals who were rejected for failing to meet educational levels needed by the military, and also made clear the need for basic remedial education for many others who were accepted for service, but were substandard for many military needs.

The interruption of civilian education for many recruits during World War II led to pressure for passage of legislation which would reward past service through veterans' readjustment programs. After World War II thousands of veterans entered colleges and universities, and vocational programs, through the "G.I. bill." This program was continued for veterans of the Korean and Indo-China conflicts. Various evaluation studies have shown the significant impact made by the G.I. bill in raising the social—economic level of recipients who might otherwise have had no opportunity of obtaining professional and skilled-worker status without this assistance.

13.7 RACIAL POLICY

Our sixth factor in the development of a national manpower policy, and one which is still in the process of being formulated, relates to policy toward race. From the end of the Civil War to the 1930s, public policy was largely unconcerned with questions of racial discrimination. It was presumed that the 13th and 14th amendments to the Constitution had assured racial equality in a legal sense, and that what remained was to be solved by people on a private basis. The bare beginnings of a positive racial policy began to emerge under the New Deal with the establishment of a Committee on Fair Employment Practices (FEPC) created by President Roosevelt in 1941, as well as numerous government contract provisions established by every President since the New Deal. In addition, FEP laws were passed in many states and municipalities seeking to provide equal employment rights for nonwhites. Also, during the Truman Administration, racial segregation was abolished in the military forces by edict.

It is fair to say, however, that up to the 1950s little real progress had been made in relation to the growing seriousness of racial problems and the expanding political consciousness and power of Blacks. Up to 1954 "separate but equal" had been accepted by all levels of government in educational policy toward Blacks. Brown versus Board of Education (1954) changed this view so far as the Supreme Court was concerned, and this momentous decision ushered in a more positive policy on racial policy.

In 1964 national racial policy was further strengthened by the passage of the Civil Rights Act. Title VII of this law outlawed discrimination against any individual because of his race, color, religion, sex, or national origin. Together with the Supreme Court decision of 1954, the Civil Right Act of 1964, and numerous state laws which outlawed discrimination, racial policy was firmly on the side of equality.

Yet a recognition emerged that *de jure* equality did not translate itself into *de facto* employment, opportunity, and equality. No matter how strong the statutory exhortation against racial discrimination was, the mere outlawing of discrimination was insufficient to the task at hand. More positive efforts were needed if any semblance of change was to be achieved. By the mid-1960s Federal policy began to move in the direction of preferential treatment for Blacks in job training and employment on Federal contracts. The theme became "outreach" as attempts were made to seek out and assist Blacks in getting jobs.

By the end of the 1960s, racial policy had still not been clearly defined and wavered between positive preferential treatment and nondiscrimination between equally qualified though racially different persons. But Federal racial policy on employment had moved far away from allowing the free-enterprise system to determine economic and job opportunity. The Federal government was moving rapidly in the direction of a more clearly defined manpower policy which was to be more active than it had been in the past.

13.8 KEY FACTORS IN THE DEVELOPMENT OF A MANPOWER POLICY

The foundation for decisions in manpower has been strong reliance on the marketplace to bring about an adjustment between people who want to work and those who want to hire workers. The market mechanism has provided the basic structure in establishing a balance between the demand for and the supply of manpower. Individuals, households, and firms—guided and regulated by price, wage, and output forces (the market mechanism)—have shaped and molded manpower decisions.

A national manpower policy has been emerging over time through governmental programs which have modified private decisions made in the marketplace. Political decisions heavily oriented toward concepts of equality, justice, and opportunity have modified economic processes when these have failed to provide optimum social-welfare results. Basic elementary education, vocational training, and land-grant colleges have been sponsored by government legislation to promote economic and social opportunity.

Government has also been an active participant in promoting industrial development, and as a by-product of this, manpower resource development and utilization. Immigration was fostered to assure an adequate labor supply for an expanding industrial economy. Land-grant colleges and vocational–technical programs were developed to train and educate a professional and technical source of skilled manpower.

The promotion of science and technology, and international developments leading to a growing military sector, have as a matter of course necessitated strong deviations from the market system and growing governmental intervention.

Lastly, domestic crises such as the Great Depression of the 1930s, the labor movement of the 30s and 40s, and Civil Rights issues in the 50s and 60s have forced the government into a more active decision-making position. Considerable modification of the market system has taken place to redress imbalances, or to promote the welfare of certain groups. Taken together, domestic problems have moved government away from being just another minor decision-making unit to being a major governor of change, though still operating as an intervenor and change agent within the structure of private decisions (Fig. 13.1).

In the years that followed the end of World War II the seeds of a national manpower policy—which would include manpower development, conservation, and utilization, and which, moreover, would be comprehensive, cohesive, and active in nature—had been planted and awaited further nourishment and suitable conditions for growth. No one as yet had consciously mapped out a manpower policy as such. In fact, clearly defined goals had not appeared, and much more information and knowledge were required before an appropriate path could be charted. A national commitment did appear immediately after World War II and a wide variety of

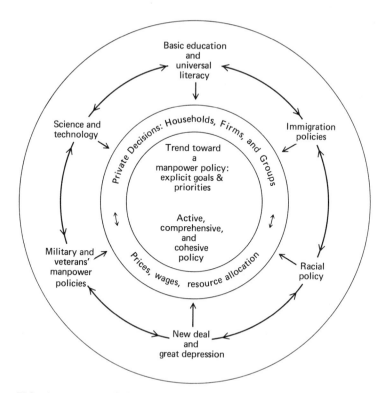

FIG. 13.1 Conceptual framework: key threads in manpower policy formulation, private decisions, and the trend toward an explicit national manpower policy

experimental programs proliferated in the early 1960s in search of a national manpower policy.

SUMMARY

Manpower policy is concerned with the development, maintenance, and utilization of the labor force. The full emergence of a manpower policy must also consider whether it is active, cohesive, and comprehensive.

The development of manpower policy has emerged gradually as new programs have built on past accomplishments, and problems and solutions have interacted in a continuous process of change.

National manpower policy has been influenced by contributions from six major developments:

1. Basic education and universal literacy

2. Science and technology

3. Immigration and labor supply

4. The New Deal and the Great Depression

5. Military manpower and veterans' readjustment policies

6. Racial policy

These six developments have modified private decisions reached through the operation of the market mechanism. These modifications have taken place when economic processes have failed to provide optimum social-welfare results. Basic education and universal literacy, and later, expansion of education by vocational training schools and land-grant colleges have been sponsored by government to promote economic and social opportunity. Science and technology and immigration were sponsored to promote economic development, and the New Deal and racial policy to redress economic and social distress. Military manpower was promoted for defense purposes during and after World War II in an increasingly unstable world environment.

Taken together these six factors form the necessary primary ingredients for a national manpower policy. These are the raw materials for a national policy, but are insufficient for a conscious commitment. This emerges in the 1960s as conscious manpower goals are formulated by the Federal government and a national consensus begins to take shape.

BIBLIOGRAPHY

Eli Ginzberg, *Manpower Agenda for America*, McGraw-Hill, New York, 1968

Garth L. Mangum, *The Emergence of Manpower Policy*, Holt, Rinehart and Winston, New York, 1969

Eli Ginzberg, *The Development of Human Resources*, McGraw-Hill, New York, 1966

Edward B. Jakubauskas and C. Phillip Baumel, *Human Resources Development*, Iowa State University Press, Ames, Iowa, 1967

Frederick Harbison, "Critical Issues in American Manpower Policy and Practice," *Proceedings of the Seventeenth Annual Meeting of the Industrial Relations Research Association*, Chicago, Illinois, December 28, 29, 1964. Edited by Gerald G. Somers

THE EMERGENCE OF A MANPOWER POLICY

14.1 A LANDMARK IN GOVERNMENT MANPOWER POLICY: THE EMPLOYMENT ACT OF 1946

Earlier legislation and governmental programs were developed to meet specific problems and priorities facing the country at a particular moment in time. It had never been the policy of government to concern itself with preventive or futuristic programs which were designed either to ensure full employment or to develop manpower resources as such. The Employment Act of 1946 was a landmark piece of legislation, in that for the first time in the history of the country it became the explicit responsibility of government to provide opportunities for those able, willing, and seeking to work, and in addition, to promote maximum employment in the economy. Operational definitions of "useful employment opportunities" and "maximum employment" were left to be shaped by future statutes and administrative actions, but in specifying government's responsibility, Congress implicitly recognized that the billions of independent decisions made in the market could very well yield results which would be less than optimum for certain individuals and groups and possibly even for the general welfare of the whole economy.

The Act was a product of the experiences of the Great Depression and World War II. The Depression had shaken the foundations of the automaticity of the market mechanism as an optional regulating device, and the temporary departure from orthodox principles was made with regret and a hope for a return to "normalcy" after extraordinary problems had returned to a manageable level.

Memories of the Depression of the 1930s loomed very much in the mind of Congress and the executive branch, and fears were expressed that depressed conditions would return once military spending ended. Opponents of the Act feared that, in addition to unwise public spending, a massive redistribution of income would take place from higher- to lower-income groups, and that the free-enterprise system would be threatened. Advocates of the Act argued that a more optimal setting would be established in which the market mechanism could operate more effectively, and that governmental intervention would take place only at the margin and in areas which could not be better handled by private decision-makers. Emerging from the debate, the Employment Act of 1946 established the principle of reviewing economic and employment problems on a continuing basis and of developing appropriate programs before problems emerged on a large scale. It is essential to emphasize that:

1. The market mechanism (individual choice, prices, wages, etc.) would still be the mainstay of economic and manpower policy.

2. The Federal government would be concerned with the effectiveness of the market mechanism in attaining welfare goals.

3. Changes would be made in the operation of the market mechanism if needed, and this would be done as a matter of national policy.

14.2 AN INTERLUDE IN MANPOWER POLICY: 1946 to 1961

Although the Employment Act of 1946 marked an important policy statement in regard to the role of government in economics and manpower, little was done to implement lofty policy statements by actual programs. Rather than experiencing the expected deflation and unemployment, inflation became the immediate concern in the late 1940s as price controls were removed. Economic orthodoxy prevailed as government economists and Congress concerned themselves with price stability, budget balance, and foreign balance of payments.

The 15-year gap between the passage of the Employment Act of 1946 and the emergence of manpower programs was due to a lack of a significant consensus in Congress as to the most appropriate remedy for pockets of unemployment which were beginning to develop in the 1950s. It was much simpler to get consensus when general unemployment ranged from 10 to 25% in the 1930s, but a creeping unemployment rate which was particularized in nature did not seem to carry enough strength in Congress to generate manpower programs. A number of Congressmen whose areas were experiencing heavy and prolonged unemployment introduced several New Deal public-works bills, and special short-run assistance which would benefit their areas. A notable development in this period was the coalescence of individual efforts under the leadership of Senator Paul H. Douglas of Illinois. An economic development assistance bill was passed in the Senate in 1956, and after numerous amendments and Presidential vetoes in 1958 and 1960, a pallid and half-hearted Area Redevelopment Act was finally passed under the Kennedy Administration in 1961.

Another significant development in the Senate was the establishment in 1959 of a Special Committee on Unemployment Problems, headed by Senator Eugene McCarthy of Minnesota. This committee played a significant role in shaping manpower legislation in the years that followed. Recommended were the area redevelopment program, Youth Conservation Corps, and broadening of vocational education and retraining. All of these, however, were separate threads without an operational mandate and certainly without a plan of responsibility, authority, and priority setting. These were to emerge as needs of groups affected were sharpened, and as a consensus began to emerge in Congress and the executive branch in the early 1960s.

14.3 THE AREA REDEVELOPMENT ACT OF 1961

In meeting rising levels of unemployment in the 1950s, manpower programs were limited to stopgap measures which would enable experienced workers to bridge temporary distress during job layoffs. In 1958 Congress passed the Temporary Unemployment Compensation Act which provided Federal funds to those who had exhausted unemployment compensation benefits. Extension under this Act was equal to 50% of individual benefit entitlement. In 1961 benefits were continued under supplementary legislation passed by Congress.

The first appearance of a "modern" manpower program came with the passage of the Area Redevelopment Act in 1961. The philosophy of ARA was to deal with particularized unemployment. Federal aid was provided to local depressed areas, and new employment opportunities were to be created through development of new industries. Loans of up to $200 million were provided for industrial development, and $175 for creation of public facilities. Occupational training and retraining subsistence payments were authorized for $14.1 million.

The criterion for aid under the ARA was determined by the severity and duration of unemployment. Areas were approved for assistance if the unemployment rate was at least 6% and had averaged above the national rate for specified periods of time. For rural areas eligibility was determined by the degree of underemployment measured by low income levels. An area was also required to develop a blueprint for its economic recovery—an Overall Economic Development Program.

In 1962 the Public Works Acceleration Act was passed, modeled on New Deal construction of public facilities, which was intended to buttress the efforts of the ARA.

ARA's philosophy was basically to support industrial development. The unemployed and the poor were to be the indirect beneficiaries of direct aid to private enterprise. The expenditure of $322 million over the period 1961–1965 was far too meager to have an impact either on local or national unemployment. Funds provided and government incentives were also inadequate in attracting good industries to relocate in areas which had little to offer to business enterprise. The problems of encouraging economic growth and manpower development in depressed areas were far too complex for the ARA, and the resources available were too niggardly to reach the ambitious goals outlined in the legislation.

The philosophy and approach of the ARA has continued in two successor programs: the Economic Development Act and the Appalachian Act, both passed in 1965. These have yet to be evaluated, but appear to face problems similar to those which confronted the ARA.

If one conceives of the ARA as a pilot program, designed to shed light on new approaches heretofore untried, then its major contribution was the experience gained which helped shape the present mainstay of manpower—the Manpower Development and Training Act of 1962.[1]

14.4 THE MANPOWER DEVELOPMENT AND TRAINING ACT

A primary goal of the ARA was to attract jobs to depressed areas. To further this goal a small allocation of funds ($14.5 million) was earmarked for job training. Committee hearings for the ARA established the need for manpower training as a means for dealing with anticipated dire consequences of automation which had attracted the public's imagination by the late 1950s. Some states, such as Pennsylvania, experienced sharp and concentrated job losses in the steel industry, coal, and railroads, and as a result Congressmen from that state began to agitate for a job-training law which would cover a larger segment of the labor force than had been covered under ARA, and would involve greater expenditures of funds. Senator Joseph S. Clark and Congressman Elmer Holland, both of Pennsylvania, provided leadership which led to the passage of the Manpower Development and Training Act (MDTA) of March 1962.

MDTA was not simply another short-run program designed as a temporary stopgap measure to deal with unemployment, but rather a mandate for manpower development on a broad scale. Although reference was made to displacement effects of automation and technological change, foreign competition, relocation of industry, shifts in market demand, and other structural changes, great emphasis was also placed on filling shortages with qualified personnel and in identifying future occupational needs and problem areas. The "statement of findings and purpose" was broad enough to provide the foundation for virtually any programs which had an effect on improving the employment status of workers or in meeting manpower shortages for employers. Not only was the Federal government to appraise manpower needs and resources and to develop methods of dealing with problems of unemployment, but it was also the goal of MDTA to increase the nation's productivity and its capacity to meet the requirements of the space age. Although the Employment Act of 1946 indicated the Federal government's commitment to full employment, MDTA in 1962 began to specify an active manpower policy with specific goals and target groups. Though the manpower policy was still implicit, one could begin to discern at least the beginnings of a national manpower policy.

14.5 PROVISIONS OF MDTA

Title I provides a key provision for eventual planning in the manpower field by specifying that research be carried out on a broad range of manpower subjects, including

---

[1]For an excellent evaluation of the ARA see Sar A. Levitan, *Federal Aid to Depressed Areas*, Johns Hopkins University Press, Baltimore, 1964.

skill requirements, occupational outlook, job opportunities, labor supply in various skills, and employment trends on a national, state, and area basis. The information accumulated would be used in the educational, training, counseling, and placement activities which were to be performed under MDTA.

Title II constitutes the core of MDTA, and provides for a broad range of manpower services—testing, counseling, selection for occupational training, actual classroom or on-the-job training, and job placement. Under MDTA a step-by-step process in supplying manpower services is specified in roughly the following sequence.

1. The U.S. Department of Labor, and delegated state agencies, are responsible for screening workers into training programs. Priorities for referral in training are specified (unemployed, underemployed, labor shortage occupations, etc.). Counseling, testing, and selection services are provided at the intake level, and placement on completion of training.

2. The U.S. Department of Labor, and delegated agencies, determine whether there are appropriate job opportunities in a labor market before occupational training is authorized.

3. Institutional classroom training under MDTA is the responsibility of the U.S. Department of Health, Education, and Welfare, and related state agencies. After certification of trainees and availability of jobs has been completed by Labor, education agencies determine curriculum, instruction, as well as teachers. On-the-job training is contracted out directly by the Department of Labor.

Training allowances were authorized for unemployed persons who had at least three years of experience in the labor force or were heads of households. A smaller allowance was permitted for youths whose ages were in the range 19–22, but in general, MDTA in 1962 did not address itself fully to the problems of youth which began to emerge by the mid 1960s.

In contrast to ARA which provided funds for only certain designated areas, Title III provided for the allocation of funds to all states based on a formula which would give consideration to five factors.

1. The proportion which the labor force of a state bears to the total labor force of the country

2. The proportion which the unemployed in a state bears to the total number of unemployed in the country in a preceding calendar year

3. The lack of appropriate full-time employment in the state

4. The proportion which the insured unemployed within a state bears to the total number of insured employed within such state

5. The average weekly unemployment compensation benefits paid by the state

14.6 AMENDMENTS TO MDTA

In 1962 primary emphasis had been on experienced workers who were "heads of households." It became apparent that employment problems of youth were becoming serious in 1963, and a special amendment was added to provide a program for testing, counseling, selecting, and referral of young people 16 or older for occupational training and further schooling.

In addition, part-time workers employed for 20 hours per week or less were permitted to collect full training allowances, with pro rata reductions for those working in excess of 20 hours.

Of greatest importance to MDTA was section 208, which provided for pilot demonstration projects to assess labor mobility. The purpose of this section was to gain knowledge and experience of the effectiveness of manpower-relocation programs in reducing unemployment through increased job mobility. Loans and/or grants were authorized to workers who were unemployed and had no reasonable chance of gaining meaningful employment in their home communities.

In 1965 a friendly Congress broadened the scope of MDTA by creating new provisions and amending others to convert what was essentially a pioneering program into a continuing measure of active manpower development. The major 1965 amendments provided for the following.

1. Transfer to the Title I research program authorization of experimental and demonstration projects to test new methods for rehabilitation of disadvantaged groups in the labor force

2. Basic research funding and authorization for the awarding of grants in addition to entering into contracts for manpower research

3. Authorization for active job development as a part of a comprehensive manpower program in service and related occupations

4. Extension of studies into labor-mobility relocation and incorporation of this program into Title I of MDTA

5. Encouragement of the use of private facilities for institutional training as well as expansion of the individual referral method

Further refinement of MDTA took place in 1966 as experimental programs for part-time workers were carried out to meet problems of critical skill shortages. Also, vocational training of inmates in correctional institutions was included as a part of MDTA's training package. There was also recognition given to the need for supportive services to trainees; this recognition took the form of an amendment allowing up to $100 for medical services which were deemed necessary for trainees as pretraining assistance.

14.7 HIGHLIGHTS OF MDTA PROGRAM ADMINISTRATION

The types of persons served by MDTA has changed over time. Initially the program was designed to assist family heads who had a strong attachment to the labor force and had been unemployed for a long time. Later, emphasis began to shift in the direction of serving the growing number of unemployed youths, particularly those from disadvantaged families. By the late 1960s, as economic conditions improved for experienced workers, the focus of MDTA shifted toward serving those with multiple handicaps, such as low educational attainment, age, color, long-term unemployment, welfare status, or physical, mental, or emotional handicaps. In addition to serving those with multiple handicaps, MDTA also began to serve nonwhites more intensively. For example, between 1963 and 1966 the training of nonwhites increased from 27 to 40% of total trainees.

Statutory language does not convey the full flavor of innovation under MDTA. One significant development was the emergence of "institutional multioccupational projects" which emphasized techniques which would prepare trainees for total preparation for work. Under this program various types of prevocational preparation were given to trainees, to lay the groundwork for effective occupational training. Services such as special testing and counseling, along with basic education, were given to trainees either before training or concurrently with it. Also a system was designed which provided for "work tryout," in which trainees were given orientation in several fields or types of work to determine their interest and aptitude before they were assigned or referred to training in a particular skill. In 1965 about one-third of all trainees were in projects of this type, while in the following year the proportion rose to 39%.

Another major development under MDTA was the initiation in 1967–68 of a framework for coordinating diverse manpower programs sponsored under MDTA and other statutes. The Cooperative Area Manpower Planning System (CAMPS) provided for coordination, planning, and implementation of manpower programs by selected major metropolitan areas within states, and by all the states. A wide range of programs was brought in under CAMPS, including skill training and related services such as counseling, remedial education, attitudinal and health problems, and job development and placement assistance. Federal departments included under CAMPS are:

Health, Education and Welfare
Commerce
Housing and Urban Development
Labor
The Office of Economic Opportunity

Planning at local, state, and regional levels was to take place, with coordination so that there would be no duplication of layers of control. Although it was the most significant planning mechanism designed up to that date, a lack of enforcement provisions weakened the overall structure. CAMPS remained essentially a "paper treaty" among autonomous and powerful agencies. Its major importance was to serve as an early and experimental venture in more ambitious proposals for planning and coordination which began to emerge in the early 1970s.

14.8 VOCATIONAL EDUCATION ACT OF 1963

The second major manpower statute on the national scene in the 1960s was the Vocational Education Act of 1963. This represented the first reconsideration of vocational education since 1917. A panel of consultants on vocational education established by President Kennedy in 1961 reported that existing vocational education had been insensitive to changing occupational needs of the labor market and also had neglected to serve certain segments of the population.

The Vocational Education Act of 1963 focused upon the employment problems of four groups of people. This act included: those in high school, those who had completed or discontinued their formal education and who were preparing to enter the labor market, and those who had already entered the job market but needed to upgrade their skills or learn new ones, and lastly, workers with special educational handicaps.

Unlike MDTA, the Vocational Education Act provided direct grants to states, with little or no control over types of training or groups served. State vocational plans were reviewed by the U.S. Commissioner of Education, but this was essentially a routine procedure without real provisions for enforcement.

One very real impact of the Vocational Education Act of 1963 was the construction of area vocational schools, offering training in a wide variety of subjects and occupational categories. About one-third of the funds under the 1963 act were earmarked for post-secondary training or vocational schools. A large proportion of these funds were expended for construction of facilities, often providing access to training with greater economies of large-scale operation to smaller communities unable to afford facilities or training with their own resources. In the late 1960s the area vocational school (and community college) began to emerge as the focal point for training under MDTA and the Vocational Education Act. Enrollments in community colleges began to rise rapidly and became the growth area for post-secondary education.

14.9 MANPOWER PROGRAMS UNDER THE ECONOMIC OPPORTUNITY ACT OF 1964

As previously indicated, the main object of the MDTA initially was to help experienced, but temporarily unemployed, workers in the labor force to develop job skills which would give them some insulation against insecurity in the labor market.

Another strong argument for MDTA was the employer's need to fill job-shortage areas with skilled and trained workers. The concept of serving youth and the disadvantaged developed much later in the life of MDTA.

A growing uneasiness about the inadequacy of Federal legislation to meet the needs of the poor and disadvantaged led to the passage of the Economic Opportunity Act (EOA) in 1964. Under the EOA, local community action agencies were able to design manpower and other programs with little limitation so long as these had the effect of promising to reduce poverty.

Placement centers, job development, and even training programs designed under the auspices of the EOA began to compete with old-line agencies for action in the manpower field. Aside from a wide variety of programs generated by the Community Action Agencies, there were three manpower programs explicitly provided for under the EOA. These were:

Job Corps
Neighborhood Youth Corps
Work Experience and Training

The purpose of the Job Corps was to increase the employability of disadvantaged youths aged 16 to 21 by providing residential training and basic education. This program was focused on the special needs of a relatively small group of youths whose family environment was not conducive to normal training programs. Residential urban and rural training centers were established away from family influences, and training and education intervened to change motivation, values, and attitudes toward learning and work. The Job Corps was deemed very expensive by its critics, and though some successes were scored, the Nixon Administration transferred this program to the U.S. Department of Labor, which transformed Job Corps centers into smaller residential training centers in home communities. This virtually eliminated the "away-from-home" concept of the original Job Corps centers, as well as the attempt to intervene in the lives of trainees in ways other than the immediate development of jobs skills. Various evaluations of Job Corps were conducted from a cost/benefit point of view. A mixed picture has emerged, showing some successes as well as shortcomings. In the final analysis, President Nixon's campaign promises in the election campaign of 1968 determined the demise of Job Corps as it had been conceived under EOA, although Nixon did not disavow the social and economic goals of the Job Corps.

The Neighborhood Youth Corps (NYC), established under the EOA but operated by the U.S. Department of Labor, had two functions:

1. To provide a part-time job creation program for youths attending school

2. To provide a separate full-time work program for idle 16–20-year-olds who were mainly school dropouts.

In a strict sense NYC was not a manpower program. Work opportunities under NYC were not designed for careers or "ladders" to higher-skilled-job opportunities. It has been observed by Levitan and Mangum that NYC performed a useful function as an "aging vat" for youth by providing income and work during early years in the labor force when public policy was unable to absorb the large number of young people into meaningful jobs in the economy.[2]

A major gap in manpower programs was the failure to assist the long-term unemployed and those who were unable to reenter the labor force and had become discouraged with the job-search process. The 1962 amendments to the Social Security Act encouraged states to establish community work and training programs to offer more meaningful work relief. In 1964 Title V of EOA provided for "work experience and training" for welfare recipients and others experiencing extreme hardship, but capable of working at some tasks. In late 1967 the work-experience program was phased out and a work-incentive program (WIN) adopted as part of congressional amendments to the Social Security Act. Under WIN, relief recipients were allowed to keep a part of public-assistance payments if they agreed to accept employment (also provided under a concept of "government as an employer of last resort"). As with NYC, the work-incentive program is a stopgap measure designed to alleviate economic distress and to at least make an attempt to provide jobs to those not readily absorbed into the labor market under "normal" circumstances. It is presumed that these workers are "reclaimable" if given an incentive to work and receive income from work. Critics have argued that a simple income-maintenance program would be more realistic than an attempt to provide jobs with a dubious future and limited opportunity for adequate income without continued public support.

14.10 VOCATIONAL REHABILITATION AND MANPOWER DEVELOPMENT

Predating the manpower legislation initiated during the 1960s was the vocational rehabilitation program. It was established to supplement vocational education by assisting disabled veterans in the first World War, and over the years has been expanded to provide a wide range of services to most anyone who has an employment handicap.

The vocational rehabilitation program has been carefully shaped over time, and in a real sense it appears to be directly in the mainstream of manpower programs offered with respect to the following characteristics:

1. Persons served include almost anyone with an employment handicap—physical, mental, social, etc.

2. Almost any service can be provided which will assist in the removal of handicaps and permit individuals to be employable

3. Block grants are made directly to states, which avoids the cumbersomeness and administrative inefficiency of the project proposal process of other manpower programs

[2] Sar A. Levitan and Garth L. Mangum, *Federal Training and Work Programs in the Sixties,* Institute of Labor and Industrial Relations, University of Michigan, Ann Arbor, 1969, page 230.

4. Relationship with universities through research, fellowship, and training grants have developed an on-going source of talent for operation of vocational rehabilitation programs

5. Cost-benefit analyses have been used long before other agencies and programs have grasped the usefulness of this tool to focus on the human resource benefits of resource investments

6. Federal financing was provided for planning grants for the development of state-wide comprehensive plans

7. Broad Federal guidelines are laid down and the details of program administration are provided by state agencies. Each state, therefore, has considerable freedom in tailoring its program to fit specific community needs

The most important aspect of the vocational rehabilitation program for our study is its comprehensive approach to manpower and poverty problems. MDTA and EOA programs have been heavily impeded by many limitations on the services they can provide and the clients they can serve. Vocational rehabilitation is solely concerned with a person's handicap in being employable (regardless of age, previous work experience, etc.) and offers no limitations on what can be done in providing services to make one employable. A personalized and comprehensive rehabilitation service is offered without the weaknesses of MDTA and EOA, which sometimes amounted to "filling slots with people" to meet program needs in specific categories.

14.11 THE DIRECTION OF MANPOWER PROGRAMS IN THE 1970s

If the 1960s can be characterized as a period of development, experimentation, and "trial-and-error" in the manpower field, the 1970s appear to be emerging as a period of consolidation, unification, and coordination. By the end of the 1960s it became apparent to many observers that a proliferation of programs had led to some confusion, overlap, and adverse competition among agencies. Moreover, the Federal government's attempts at controlling services had led to an overcentralization of administration of programs in Washington and at Federal regional offices.

To redress the ingrown shortcomings of the manpower program, and yet at the same time to continue the successes which had been achieved, program administrators and legislators drafted bills in Congress which would provide permanence and at the same time unify, decategorize, and decentralize programs. Not all the bills were in agreement in all details, and in fact, some were at variance with one another on basic philosophy. Three major bills were introduced in Congress in 1970: (1) Ayres (Administration-sponsored); (2) Steiger (Republican); and (3) O'Hara (Democratic).

Ayres Bill The Administration's bill, prepared largely by the staff of the U.S. Department of Labor, sought to implement a policy of greater action by the states with only general supervision by the Federal government. Block grants were to be made if a state had prepared a workable state plan, and a bonus would be paid to states with a co-ordinating manpower agency. Individualized services would be provided on a personalized basis without restriction as to categories or service groups. Also, a computerized job bank was included in the Ayres Bill, as well as a provision to broaden manpower training as the overall unemployment rate increased.

Steiger Bill Like the Ayres Bill, the Steiger proposal attempts to coordinate all manpower programs through state plans administered by the state's governor. Also, the Steiger Bill proposes to utilize existing institutions (schools, employment service) with states fully responsible for program administration in accordance with approved state plans. The Ayres Bill, in contrast, provides for a three-step process of decentralizing programs from the Federal to the state level.

O'Hara Bill Unlike either the Ayres or Steiger bills, the O'Hara Bill does not provide for any uniform decentralized planning system. It allows the Secretary of Labor to select the mode of operation that he thinks best and most efficient in each community. All funds would remain under Federal control, as at present. A major contribution of the O'Hara Bill is the provision of funds for mandatory employment of workers in the public sector if they are unable to locate jobs with private employers.

At this stage it is difficult to determine which of the bills will be adopted. Most likely compromises will be reached, depending on current political power forces. Yet the main outline appears to be shaping up along the lines of the vocational-rehabilitation approach. A concern for manpower will be the main thrust of future legislation; this concern will not be simply a by-product of other programs. There will be a decategorization of programs as services are personalized to the individual in need. A decentralization of operations to the states is inevitable. The Federal hierarchy is simply too cumbersome to handle all programs efficiently. A system of "creative federalism" will emerge in which states will develop and implement manpower plans, while the Federal government will monitor operations through evaluation and general policy compliance.

Although the main outline of manpower programs appears to be clear—planning and coordination, decentralization, decategorization, and consolidation of independent and duplicating programs—the details remain hazy because of serious problems which must be overcome. Many states operate under a "weak-governor" system, in which departments are virtually autonomous in policy and operations. Constitutional and legislative changes would have to take place at the state level in many cases before the Ayres Bill could be operative. If this problem is overcome, rural versus urban and suburban versus inner-city problems present themselves. Who is to have control, the mayor or the governor? Another facet is the question of whether the level of competence of state employees would be sufficient to carry out a state plan. Low salaries and the attraction of poor-quality workers into state government continues to be a problem. Another question raised by some observers relates to the incentive structure for good state plans. Can the Federal government provide an adequate incentive structure for good work? Will the Secretary of Labor be prepared in some cases to reject inadequate state plans?

Manpower programs in the 1970s will continue to be remedial in nature—to pick up where the educational system and the industrial world have failed to provide adequate skills or jobs. The main thrust of government should be to maintain a high level of employment through economic measures which sustain a high aggregate demand in the economy. Given this, an educational system is needed which not only provides skills but permits people to adapt to changing work conditions. Economic, educational, and manpower policies are, therefore, the warp and woof of the fabric of society. Taken together, they give hope of providing a better quality of life for all members of society.

14.12 "CRYSTAL-BALL GAZING" INTO THE FUTURE: A MANPOWER POLICY YET TO BE

It is hazardous to try to chart the future course of manpower policy. Social and political changes may occur very rapidly, and priorities may shift abruptly in response to new crises or community goals. By its very nature, American society is pragmatic, and loath to develop policies beyond the solution of immediate short-run problems. Yet certain outlines appear to be moving into focus. Much has been learned by trial-and-error from manpower programs preceding the 1970s.

Future manpower policy appears to be moving toward the inclusion of at least the following characteristics.

1. An attempt to widen the spectrum of choice available to the individual by permitting him to select a future course of action which will optimize his "well-being."

2. Information will be provided to the individual to enable him to recognize the costs and benefits of alternative courses of action.

3. An individual's choice of programs in meeting goals will be "custom-designed," and will not necessarily be limited to training or any other single program. In government jargon, there will be a "decategorization" of programs.

4. Education will be career-oriented rather than designed for a particular occupation. An individual will "learn" to become adaptive to change, and will have the capability of "retooling" his work skills periodically during his work career.

5. The present untenable gap between school and work will be bridged by more effective career counseling, and a closer working relationship between employment offices and schools. Entry into the labor force will become a smoother process than it has been in the past.

6. Local public employment offices will be linked up through a computerized job-vacancy/unemployment-reporting system, and possibly closed-circuit television for interviews between employers and applicants.

7. The "right-to-a-job" concept will become a reality for disadvantaged and hard-core unemployed. Government will serve as an "employer of last resort" for those unable to secure positions in the private sector.

8. Organizationally, states and local communities will play a greater role in carrying

out programs, with the Federal government setting national priorities, evaluating state plans, and providing funds on a block or revenue-sharing basis.

9. National economic policy (fiscal, monetary, and growth) will be linked up with manpower policy in optimizing social and economic welfare (see Chapter 18).

10. Those unable to work, those who are retired, or those who are handicapped beyond rehabilitation will be provided economic security through an income-supplement plan.

SUMMARY

The Employment Act of 1946 was the beginning of the "shaping process" of a national manpower policy. The Federal government now had an explicit concern for manpower development in its own right. This was a landmark piece of legislation, and yet little was done in this area from 1946 to 1961.

Growing levels of unemployment in the late 1950s led to the enactment of the Area Redevelopment Act in 1961. The ARA's philosophy was to support industrial development in depressed areas in the hope of eliciting secondary manpower effects. Expenditures were too meager in the aggregate and too diluted over a wide number of labor markets to have an appreciable effect.

The Manpower Development and Training Act (MDTA) of 1962 is the mainstay of manpower programs. Early emphasis was on the unemployed experienced worker, and on skill shortages facing employers. Later emphasis shifted toward youth and disadvantaged persons. MDTA was administered jointly by the U.S. Department of Labor and the U.S. Office of Education.

The Vocational Act of 1963 provided for a redirection away from outdated vocational occupation toward a modern industrial training program. Also, new segments of the population were served, most notably those in the nonagricultural sector. Area vocational schools and community colleges developed through the impetus of this legislation.

The Economic Opportunity Act of 1964 attempted to serve the hard-core disadvantaged, particularly youth, through the Job Corps, the Neighborhood Youth Corps, and Work Experience and Training. Job Corps attempted to change adverse influences of family and community by conducting training in facilities located some distance away from the homes of the Job Core participants. Neighborhood Youth Corps was an incomes program providing temporary financial assistance to youth. Work Experience (later, work incentive) attempted to provide jobs to able-bodied welfare recipients.

The vocational-rehabilitation program, under the aegis of the U.S. Department of Health, Education, and Welfare, is designed to assist those who have physical, mental, or social handicaps which impede employability. Vocational rehabilitation is able to provide any type of assistance to a needy individual. Programs are custom-designed. Vocational rehabilitation offers a "model" for the design of future manpower programs.

After a period of experimentation in the 1960s, national manpower efforts appear to be moving in the direction of decentralization of authority and operations to the states, elimination of detailed program categories, and a comprehensive, planned system for delivery of services at the state and local level. Proposed Administration legislation before Congress at the present time is designed to encourage states to develop comprehensive manpower plans and to receive block grants from the Federal government. Bonus funds would be provided to states with exemplary plans, and the Federal role would be phased out to one of evaluation of state plans. Categorization of programs would be eliminated and states would have discretionary power to develop programs which meet the needs of their own population groups.

An Appendix to Chapter 14 follows, giving a summary of Federally assisted manpower training and support programs.

BIBLIOGRAPHY

Sar A. Levitan and Garth L. Mangum, *Federal Training and Work Programs in the Sixties*, Institute of Labor and Industrial Relations, Ann Arbor, Michigan, 1969

Garth L. Mangum, *MDTA: Foundation of Federal Manpower Policy*, Johns Hopkins University Press, Baltimore, 1968

Robert A. Gordon (Editor), *Toward a Manpower Policy*, Wiley, New York, 1967

U.S. Department of Labor, *Manpower Report of the President*, U.S. Government Printing Office, Washington, D.C., March 1970

Sar A. Levitan, *Federal Aid to Depressed Areas*, Johns Hopkins University Press, Baltimore, 1964

APPENDIX TO CHAPTER 14   A Guide to Federally Assisted Manpower Training and Support Programs[1]

Program title and date started	Legislative authorization (source of funds)	Administering agencies	Services provided and groups served[2]	Persons served in fiscal 1969[3]
Adult Basic Education (ABE), 1964	Adult Basic Education Act of 1966. (Initially, Economic Opportunity Act of 1964)	Department of Health, Education, and Welfare, Office of Education (through grants to State and local educational systems)	Provides basic education in classroom setting for persons 16 years of age and older, with less than eighth-grade achievement.	Estimated 523,000 enrollments
Apprenticeship, 1937	National Apprenticeship Act of 1937	Department of Labor, Bureau of Apprenticeship and Training	Encourages and assists employers and unions in developing apprenticeship programs for youth, including the unemployed and disadvantaged and inmates of correctional institutions.	Estimated 250,000 registered apprentices, June 1969
Community Action Program (CAP), late 1964	Economic Opportunity Act of 1964 (Title II)	Office of Economic Opportunity	Provides human resource development services, including manpower and related services and adult basic education, for persons below the poverty level (18 years of age and over for basic education).	108,000 enrollments in training and job placements; estimated 350,000 additional persons furnished manpower-related services
Concentrated Employment Program (CEP), May 1967	Economic Opportunity Act of 1964 and Manpower Development and Training Act of 1962	Department of Labor. (Local prime sponsors are usually Community Action Agencies)	Provides a coordinated program of manpower and supportive services for hardcore unemployed youth and adults in selected areas where they are concentrated.	127,000 first-time enrollments

Employment Assistance for Indians, 1952	Adult Vocational Training Act for Indians of 1956 and appropriations legislation of 1921	Department of Interior, Bureau of Indian Affairs	Provides vocational, apprenticeship, and on-the-job training and job placement assistance for Indians 18 years of age and over residing on or near reservations.	11,300 family units
Federal–state employment service system, 1933	Wagner-Peyser Act of 1933 and Social Security Act of 1935	Department of Labor	Recruits, tests, refers to training, and places job applicants; enhances the employability of disadvantaged persons; provides job market information. Serves entire labor force but focuses on the unemployed.	9,963,000 job applications
Job Corps, January 1965	Economic Opportunity Act of 1964 (Title IA)	Office of Economic Opportunity until delegated to Department of Labor, July 1, 1969	Assists low-income disadvantaged youth 16 to 21 years of age, who require a change of environment, training, to become more responsible, employable, and productive citizens through a residential program of intensive education, skill training, and related services	53,000 first-time enrollments
Job Opportunities in the Business Sector (JOBS), March 1968	Manpower Development and Training Act of 1962 (Title II) and Economic Opportunity Act of 1964 (Title IB)	Cooperative arrangement between Department of Labor and National Alliance of Businessmen (NAB)	Encourages private industry to hire, train, retain, and upgrade hard-core unemployed and underemployed 18 years of age and over. Initially limited to major metropolitan areas but expanding to nationwide basis in fiscal 1970	51,200 hired under contract with the Department of Labor; 119,200 noncontract hires
MDTA institutional training, August 1962	Manpower Development and Training Act of 1962 (Title II)	Department of Labor; Department of Health, Education, and Welfare	Provides occupational training or retraining in a classroom setting for unemployed and underemployed persons 16 years of age and over, at least two-thirds of them disadvantaged. Eligible persons receive training, subsistence, and transportation allowances	135,000 first-time enrollments

(continued on next page)

Appendix to Chapter 14 (*continued,*

Program title and date started	Legislative authorization (source of funds)	Administering agencies	Services provided and groups served[2]	Persons served in fiscal 1969[3]
MDTA on-the-job training (OJT), August 1962	Manpower Development and Training Act of 1962 (Title II)	Department of Labor; Department of Health, Education, Welfare, when projects include related classroom instruction	Provides instruction combined with supervised work at the jobsite, under contracts with public and private employers, for unemployed and underemployed persons 16 years of age and over, at least two-thirds of them disadvantaged. Preference given to persons at least 18 years of age	85,000 first-time enrollments
MDTA part-time and other-than-skill training, last half of 1967	Manpower Development and Training Act (Title II) as amended in 1966	Department of Labor; Department of Health, Education, and Welfare	Provides upgrade training and training in job-related requirements, such as communication skills, work habits, and interpersonal relations for underemployed persons 16 years of age and over	Included in MDTA institutional enrollments
MDTA training for inmates of correctional institutions (pilot program), August 1968	Manpower Development and Training Act (Title II) as amended in 1966	Department of Labor; Department of Health, Education, and Welfare	Provides training, related supportive services, job placement assistance (including bonding), and followup for inmates of local, state, and Federal correctional institutions whose scheduled release follows completion of training by no more than 6 months. Some projects provide incentive and dependents' allowances	Included in MDTA institutional enrollments (approximately 3,000)

MDTA training in redevelopment areas, 1961	Manpower Development and Training Act (Title II) as amended in 1965. (Initially, Area Redevelopment Act of 1961)	Department of Labor; Department of Health, Education, and Welfare; Department of Commerce	Provides classroom and on-the-job training, associated with area economic development, for unemployed and underemployed residents of redevelopment areas designated by the Economic Development Administration	Included in MDTA institutional and OJT enrollments (approximately 17,000)
Model Cities, 1966	Demonstration Cities and Metropolitan Development Act of 1966 (Title I)	Department of Housing and Urban Development. (Services also supplied by other agencies, principally Department of Health, Education, and Welfare; Office of Economic Opportunity; and Department of Labor.)	Improves the environment and general welfare of residents of designated urban poverty areas having a high incidence of disadvantaged persons. Usually includes manpower services	Program largely in planning phase in fiscal 1969
Neighborhood Youth Corps (NYC): in-school, summer, and out-of-school programs, January 1965	Economic Opportunity Act of 1964 (Title IB)	Department of Labor	Encourages disadvantaged youth of high school age (14 to 21) to continue in or return to school by providing paid work experience. Emphasis shifting to job preparation, especially in out-of-school program. New design for out-of-school program limited to 16- and 17-year-old dropouts	504,100 total first-time enrollments: 84,300 in-school; 345,300 summer; 74,500 out-of-school
New Careers, first half of 1967. (To be absorbed by Public Service Careers Program during fiscal 1970)	Economic Opportunity Act of 1964 (Title IB) as amended in 1966	Department of Labor	Prepares disadvantaged adults and out-of-school youth for careers in human service fields (e.g., health and education) through work experience, education, and training	3,800 first-time enrollments

(continued on next page)

Appendix to Chapter 14 (*continued*)

Program title and date started	Legislative authorization (source of funds)	Administering agencies	Services provided and groups served[2]	Persons served in fiscal 1969[3]
Operation Mainstream, December 1965	Economic Opportunity Act of 1964 (Title IB) as amended in 1965	Department of Labor	Provides counseling, basic education, and work experience for chronically unemployed adults in newly created jobs in community betterment and beautification, mainly in rural areas	11,300 first-time enrollments
Project 100,000, October 1966	Military Service Acts	Department of Defense	Qualifies for military service men with low academic achievement or remediable physical defects, who would not have been accepted except for lowering of entrance requirements	103,000 served
Public Service Careers (PSC), early in 1970	Economic Opportunity Act of 1964 (Title IB) as amended in 1966 and Manpower Development and Training Act of 1962 (Title II)	Department of Labor	Secures, within merit principles, permanent employment in public service agencies of disadvantaged, unemployed youth and adults and stimulates upgrading of current employees, thereby meeting public sector manpower needs	New program in fiscal 1970; 27,800 training opportunities budgeted
Special Impact, first half of 1968	Economic Opportunity Act of 1964 (Title ID) as amended in 1966 and 1967	Office of Economic Opportunity (delegated to Department of Labor prior to July 1969)	Provides manpower training as a component of economic and community development for poor and unemployed persons in selected urban poverty areas	2,700 first-time enrollments

Program	Legislation	Administering agency	Description	Enrollment/results
Transition, January 1968	National Defense Act of 1916	Department of Defense with co-operating agencies: Department of Labor (MDTA); Department of Commerce; Department of Justice; Civil Service Commission; Post Office Department; Veterans Administration	Provides counseling, basic education, skill training, and placement assistance in civilian employment for enlisted personnel with approximately 6 months of active duty remaining. Priority given those with job handicaps. Participation voluntary.	66,600 trained; 302,000 counseled
Vocational Education, 1917	Smith-Hughes Act of 1917 (substantially amended in 1946) and Vocational Education Act of 1963 (substantially amended in 1968)	Department of Health, Education, and Welfare, Office of Education (through grants to state school systems)	Provides vocational training, primarily in a classroom setting, full or part time, for youth and adults, in or out of regular public schools. New emphasis on the poor and disadvantaged.	Estimated 8,034,000 enrollments: secondary schools, 4,344,000; post-secondary schools, 693,000; adults, 2,997,000
Vocational Rehabilitation, 1920	Vocational Rehabilitation Act of 1920 (substantially amended in 1943, 1954, 1965, and 1968)	Department of Health, Education, and Welfare	Provides intensive rehabilitation services to enable youth and adults who are physically or mentally handicapped to obtain jobs commensurate with their maximum capabilities	781,000 persons served; 241,400 persons rehabilitated

(continued on next page)

Appendix to Chapter 14 (*continued*)

Program title and date started	Legislative author-ization (source of funds)	Administering agencies	Services provided and groups served[2]	Persons served in fiscal 1969[3]
Work Incentive (WIN), first half of 1968. (Replaced Work Experience and Training Program under the EOA, Title V, which operated from 1965 into fiscal 1969)	Social Security Act of 1935 (Title IVC) as amended in 1967	Department of Labor. (Department of Health, Education, and Welfare is respon-sible for referral of enrollees and for furnishing social services during enroll-ment)	Provides work, training, child care, and related services designed to move into productive employment employable persons on rolls of the Aid to Families with Dependent Children (AFDC) and AFDC–Unemployed Parents programs.	80,600 first-time en-rollments

[1]Includes primarily those Federal programs aimed at assisting the unemployed and the poor to obtain satisfactory employment. Some programs have additional objectives such as community betterment or meeting manpower demands in shortage occupations. Omits income maintenance programs such as unemployment insurance and workmen's compensation.

[2]"Disadvantaged" means poor, not having suitable employment, and either (1) a school dropout, (2) a member of a minority, (3) under 22 years of age, (4) 45 years of age or over, or (5) handicapped.

[3]The intent of this column is to show the general magnitudes of programs. Some entries are based on enrollment records; others are estimates.

Source: *Manpower Report of the President*, U.S. Government Printing Office, Washington, D.C. 1970, pages 193–197.

If manpower programs are to be improved and become more efficient and more effective, then evaluation of these programs is essential. In this chapter we will discuss the importance of evaluation and some current research approaches to it. A large, and growing group of literature on evaluation has developed in the United States over the past decade, and this literature will be our main focus.

15.1 A DEFINITION OF MANPOWER-PROGRAM EVALUATION

An underlying premise of the evaluation of programs is its importance in providing evidence about the relative merits of manpower programs so that administrators of these programs can make rational decisions. From the viewpoints of the trainees (the target population), the government, and society, we are obligated to evaluate and improve manpower programs. The trainees deserve the best possible program, and so evaluation must show how and to what extent one particular program is superior to some other program for the individuals. The government has a large but limited amount of resources available for manpower programs, and so evaluation must show what each program will cost the government in tax revenues and what these programs will bring into the government by way of increased tax receipts as individuals are retrained and receive better-paying jobs. Society has a large and growing investment in manpower programs, and so evaluation must indicate how society can spend its resources to achieve the greatest efficiency for society's maximum welfare.

At the outset of new programs, most public agencies are under pressure to show immediate results, and so the need for a good show often overwhelms scientific objectivity. Thus it is not too surprising that there is little time for evaluation during the first few years of new programs. Moreover, it is only recently that our statistical and computational tools have enabled us to undertake the complex and demanding activity known as program evaluation.

We can look on the evaluation of manpower programs as the process of attributing differences between actual and comparative outcomes to program characteristics, under different conditions of trainee characteristics and other intervening influences, and of making judgments about the value of the program characteristics.[1] The system of evaluation starts with the trainees, each of whom differs in aptitudes, motivation, health, etc. The program the trainees enter has characteristics, and it is these characteristics which are to be evaluated. Moreover, the trainees are inevitably affected by other experiences and conditions in the environment, which are not due to the program but whose effects might be mistaken for outcomes of the program. It is the interaction of trainee, program, and other influences that produces actual outcomes. The evaluation system concludes with one or more sets of comparative outcomes. These outcomes are the anticipated, expected results of the program, or they can be the actual outcomes of a different program, or the outcomes of the same program at different points in time. They provide the standard by which the value of a given manpower program is judged.

The above definition has two very prominent points. The evaluation must be comparative; a comparison has to be made between actual outcomes and some other set of expected or actual outcomes. Moreover, evaluation requires that any differences in the outcomes compared must be attributable to the characteristics of the program (or to the interaction of characteristics of trainee and program).

In performing an evaluation study of any manpower program, it is well to keep in mind that the expected outcomes can be stated at several levels. One level is the time dimension, or the elapsed time since the program was provided. This level is needed to indicate when it is feasible to measure each expected outcome. As the elapsed time increases, so does the difficulty of data collection, and the number of intervening influences make it much harder to correctly attribute outcomes to the program. A second level is the target dimension, or the trainee and "other" (or secondary) expected outcomes. The "other" category would include any people, agencies or institutions, other than the trainees, affected by the manpower program. A third level is needed to distinguish among types of expected outcomes. For example, we can talk of economic, educational, psychological, etc., expected outcomes.

It is essential in the evaluation process that the costs of providing each program be measured, and that wherever possible the outcomes of the programs be measured in monetary terms. Once these costs and benefits are compared, the evaluation system can play its two main roles of (1) improving manpower programs, and (2) providing a basis for choosing among programs based on their respective effectiveness.

---

[1] For a very good discussion along these lines see Jerome Moss, Jr., *The Evaluation of Occupational Education Programs*, University of Minnesota Technical Report, Research Coordination Unit in Occupational Education (September 1968).

15.2 GOVERNMENTAL EVALUATION

There is a growing need for analysis in the Federal government simply because of the growing size and complexity of Federal programs. Our needs are continually growing faster than the resources available to meet these needs, and so the government faces the ever-present problem of efficiently allocating its limited resources. This is even more important since the government lacks the private-sector mechanisms for encouraging greater efficiency, such as the price system and the threat of bankruptcy. In recent years, the Department of Defense has applied systems analysis to the choice of complex weapons systems to satisfy national defense objectives. These techniques were put into an integrated management system called Planning—Programming—Budgeting (PPB), and recently PPB has been extended by Presidential directive to the major civilian agencies of the Federal government.

15.2.1 PLANNING—PROGRAMMING—BUDGETING

PPB is a systematic method of obtaining the maximum effectiveness from related programs through the efficient application of the available program resources.[2] By 1965, the government had recognized several shortcomings in the then existing budgeting practices of the executive branch. Program reviews had been frequently concentrated into too short a period; objectives of agency programs and activities had too often not been specified with enough clarity; accomplishments had not always been concretely specified; alternatives had been insufficiently presented; in many cases the future costs of present decisions had not been laid out systematically enough; and formalized planning and systems analysis had had too little an effect on budget decisions. To improve this situation, the Bureau of the Budget, at the direction of the President, introduced an integrated PPB system.

PPB places its priority on developing and providing the information required for management decision-making. It does this by encouraging and facilitating a clear identification of objectives, and the appropriate analyses for determining the increased costs and benefits associated with various programs. The purposes of PPB can be clearly stated as permitting rational choice between objectives; permitting rational choice between programs; facilitating selecting rational levels of programs; facilitating review and evaluation of programs and accomplishments; and providing adequate historical records.

There are three principles on which the PPB system is based. First, each agency must have the analytic capability to undertake continuing in-depth analyses of the agency's objectives and its various programs to meet these objectives. Second, there must exist a multiyear planning and programming process which incorporates and uses an information system to present all the meaningful data essential to the making

---

[2]For an excellent discussion of PPB, see *Program Analysis Manual to Support a Planning—Programming—Budgeting System*, prepared for U.S. Department of Labor Manpower Administration, Washington, D.C. (October 1966).

of major decisions by agency heads and by the President. Third, there must exist a budgeting process which can take fairly broad program decisions, translate them into more refined budget decisions, and present the appropriate data for Presidential and Congressional action.

The PPB system has four points which are essential to its operation. The program structure must be objectives-oriented; that is, it must present data on all the operations and activities of the agency in categories which reflect the agency's objectives. The agency must undertake analyses of possible alternative objectives of the agency and of alternative programs for meeting these objectives. The agency must also adhere to a time cycle within which data and recommendations are produced at the times needed for decision-making and for the development of the President's budget and legislative program. Finally, the line officials, with the appropriate staff support, must accept the responsibility for the establishment and effective use of the PPB system.

Once the system is fully operative it will have two main products. First, PPB will yield a comprehensive multiyear program and financial plan which is systematically updated. Second, analyses will be prepared annually, along with special studies in depth from time to time which will contribute to the annual setting-up of the budget.

A basic concept of PPB is systems analysis. A "system" is a group of resources directed toward achieving a single objective; and systems analysis entails taking a comprehensive view of all relevant factors. This technique requires the quantification of major variables as much as possible. A basic requirement for this analysis is a high degree of familiarity with the operational components of the system and their interrelationships. Systems analysis can significantly increase the quantity and quality of information available to the decision-maker.

The use of PPB involves specifying objectives and criteria. Objectives are the ultimate ends to be achieved by the operation of any program, and criteria are the tests by which one program alternative is selected rather than another. Since the criteria must be measurable, it is often necessary to use a proxy criterion (one which indicates changes in the ideal criterion). The major manpower objective is to give every worker the opportunity for employment in a job in which he can utilize his full productive potential for both his own and society's benefit. Earnings is usually a good proxy criterion for testing this manpower objective.

A program structure, which is a series of output-oriented categories which encompass all the activities of an agency, is the framework for PPB. The most practical way to evaluate manpower programs is to split (for evaluation purposes) established programs that serve multiple objectives into simpler components directed toward achieving individual objectives.

15.2.2 ANALYTICAL TECHNIQUES APPLICABLE TO MANPOWER PROGRAMS

In evaluating manpower programs, it is usually useful to distinguish between costs incurred by the Manpower Administration and those incurred outside the Administration. Furthermore, the costs within the Manpower Administration should be separated by major categories, such as research and development, investment, and annual operating costs.

As in the case of costs, it is useful to distinguish between direct and indirect program benefits. Direct benefits are the positive effects directly related to the manpower program, whereas indirect benefits are the reduction in the costs of other activities (either in or out of the Manpower Administration) resulting from the manpower programs. These indirect benefits are usually best treated as negative program costs.

Systems analysis can help the decision-maker make three types of decisions within the PPB system. These three approaches are called cost/goal analysis, cost/effectiveness analysis, and cost/constraint analysis.

Cost/goal analysis is useful in establishing the program goals or levels by determining the slope of the program cost curve. That is, cost/goal analysis reveals the rate of change in program costs if program goals are raised or lowered.

Figure 15.1 presents an example of cost/goal analysis. At program level G_1 the program cost curve reveals that the costs will be C_1. If the analysis correctly determines the shape of the cost curve, then the decision-maker knows how high costs can be expected to go if the program levels are increased (or decreased). With resources being limited, the government can make more efficient allocations of resources if it knows the various costs associated with different program levels.

Cost/effectiveness analysis begins with identified goals and tries to determine the most efficient program to achieve the identified goals. There is usually more than one way to achieve a particular goal (or set of goals), and an analysis of the cost curves of alternative programs can help reveal the optimal program for any particular goal.

We have a simplified example of cost/effectiveness analysis shown in Fig. 15.2. If the program goal to be achieved in G_1 and two alternative programs are available (program 1 and program 2), then the decision-maker uses cost/effectiveness analysis to determine the most efficient program. At goal level G_1, program 1 is the most efficient program, since it could achieve G_1 with costs of $C_{1.1}$ which are less than the

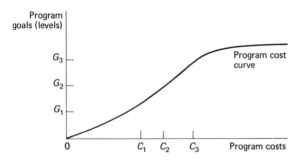

FIG. 15.1 Example of cost/goal analysis

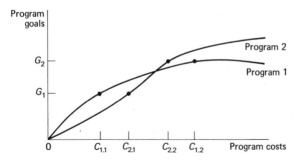

FIG. 15.2 Example of cost/effectiveness analysis

costs associated with program 2 ($C_{2.1}$) in achieving G_1. However, Fig. 15.2 shows that for the particular example we have presented the decision-maker would find program 2 more efficient than program 1 if the goal level to be achieved were G_2 instead of G_1. At level G_2, program 2 has costs of $C_{2.2}$, which is less than the costs associated with program 1 ($C_{1.2}$).

The purpose of cost/constraint analysis is to determine the costs of various constraints on a manpower program. The constraints can be legislative in nature, or they can involve union rules, employer rights, community attitudes, intergovernmental relationships, etc. Cost/constraint analysis proceeds by comparing the cost of a manpower program that could be adopted if no constraint were present and the cost of the program that must be adopted due to system constraints. Figure 15.3 graphically shows an example of cost/constraint analysis.

Examining Fig. 15.3, we see that in this particular example the goal is G_1, and we have two possible programs illustrated: a constrained program and a program without constraints. These constraints may be political, legal, etc. The cost of the constraints is the difference between the costs on the program constrained curve and the costs on the program not constrained curve, or C_2 minus C_1. Once the costs of these constraints have been identified, a rational decision can be made concerning the costs of removing the constraints. Of course, the value of the constraints may

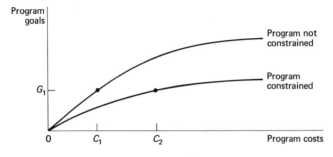

FIG. 15.3 Example of cost/constraint analysis

outweigh the cost savings to this particular manpower program, and the decision may be made to keep the constraints. Thus one possible manpower-program constraint is the local prerogative to determine eligibility standards. Although this constraint may make a particular program less efficient (more costly), the value of this constraint for different objectives may be large enough to justify its existence.

15.2.3 THREE PILOT STUDIES

The U.S. Department of Labor has recently prepared (with the help of private researchers) three pilot studies utilizing the above-mentioned analytic techniques. The cost/effectiveness analysis of the alternative programs technique was applied to two training programs. The cost/goal analysis technique was applied to the activities of the Federal–State Employment Service system. The cost-constraint analysis technique was applied to the unemployment-insurance system.

The first of the pilot studies was a comparison of the costs and benefits of institutional and on-the-job training under the Manpower Development and Training Act. This study indicated the value of both training programs as Federal investments. The average net Federal benefit-cost ratio, defined as the direct and indirect benefits to society compared to the Federal investment per trainee, was found to be 3.28 to 1 for on-the-job training and 1.78 to 1 for institutional training—after only one year of training. When the corresponding benefit-cost ratios are computed only for those trainees who completed the program, they fall somewhat, because the total costs are spread over a smaller number of trainees. But even here, the ratios are favorable. They are 2.13 to 1 for on-the-job training, 1.09 to 1 for institutional training.

The second pilot study concerned itself with a cost/goal analysis in the U.S. Employment Service. It tried to estimate the benefits to the GNP that would result from an additional dollar of expenditure on Employment Service activities. The main conclusion of the study is that GNP would benefit by 14 dollars a year for each additional dollar of resources invested in the U.S. Employment Service nonfarm activities. This study was undertaken with fiscal year 1965 data, and so these findings are based on the economic situation of that year.

The third illustrative pilot study was an attempt to measure the costs of failure (as related to the anticyclical objectives of unemployment insurance) to enact the proposed 1966 amendments to the unemployment-insurance legislation. Available data indicate that those who would have been affected by the amendments would have longer durations of unemployment, fewer assets, and higher current indebtedness than current unemployment-insurance recipients; and all these factors strongly affect their marginal propensities to consume.

The U.S. Department of Labor is currently working on a whole range of program-evaluation studies to be done by Department of Labor staff and outside contractors, which hopefully will cover all significant new manpower programs, and the essential elements of manpower development and delivery systems operated within the Department of Labor.

15.3 BENEFIT/COST RATIOS AS A TOOL OF ANALYSIS

Of all the techniques that have been developed to measure the effectiveness of man-power programs, the so-called benefit/cost ratios approach (or cost/benefit or cost/effectiveness analysis) has been the best developed. In this section we will be concerned with this benefit/cost analysis of manpower programs. Thus, we will be concerned with discussing how to find the most efficient program to achieve a given goal once that goal has been set.

15.3.1 SPECIFYING PROGRAM OBJECTIVES

The first rule for the evaluation of a manpower program is to specify the objectives of the program to be evaluated. The analyst should direct his attention to all the disadvantages as well as the advantages of the program. The principal objectives of manpower-training programs can usually be stated in such terms as increased rates of pay, decreased average unemployment, and increased employment stability for the trainees.

Since few programs have a single, clearly defined objective, it is usually necessary to assign weights to the different objectives and to guard against double-counting or under-counting. The ultimate objectives of most programs usually have to be measured by using intermediate objectives; and these intermediate objectives are the usual ones of income change, employment gain, and educational attainment. The less tangible measures of self images, community images, and opinion polls are usually given lower priority in an evaluation study. This is due to the difficulty of accurately measuring the less-tangible objectives; moreover, the degree of correlation between the tangible and less-tangible changes in any program is probably very high.

We should mention here that there are many studies in which it is first necessary to find out what a program is doing, and in this process of observation the analyst identifies what the objectives are. This can be termed a "search evaluation." The first stage of such an evaluation is to discover what the nature of the program actually is, and the cost/benefit evaluation goes on at the same time as the search for the objectives of the program.

The problem of objectives which are difficult to measure is also related to a search type of evaluation. Here a part of the study is a search for adequate measures.

15.3.2 MEASURING BENEFITS

One of the critical elements in benefit/cost analysis is to accurately measure the benefits that accrue due to a particular program. If a program affected no one except trainees, then its evaluation would involve something similar to comparing the individual's income and employment experience with and without the program—other things being equal. However, no program affects only the participants, and so we are usually interested in the benefits that accrue to the individual participants, the government (which is usually financing the program), and society.

If we are looking at a simple retraining program, then the individual's benefits would consist of any increase in his disposable income and any decrease in his unemployment which results from the retraining. However, in measuring how a program affects an individual, one must estimate how that individual would have fared in the labor market had he not been enrolled in the program. A simple before-and-after comparison of the experience of the trainees is not very useful, since the earnings and employment experience of a particular group of persons normally changes over time, due to cyclical and seasonal variation. Therefore it becomes necessary to construct, for each program, a control group of nontrainees who are as nearly similar to the trainees in their characteristics as it is possible to find. Then the analyst can compare the earnings and employment experience of the participants and controls for the same period. Such a control group can consist of people who have been considered for enrollment in the manpower program, who have shown an interest in the program, and who have the qualifications for enrolling, but who in fact have not enrolled.

In addition to the above, the evaluator can use personal background data from the time period before the program in regression analysis in order to try to eliminate statistically the major remaining differences between the participants and controls as to initial skills, motivation, work habits, and other marketability factors. Moreover, the analyst can make distinctions between controls who never enrolled in the program because of jobs or job promises and controls who didn't enroll for other reasons. In this way the analyst can try to construct upper and lower bounds to the estimates of the benefits due to a particular program.[3]

In evaluating a program with the use of a control group there is usually the choice between a small-group study or a large-group study. The best compromise probably involves using a small-group study in which there is a design concept to be evaluated which is very different from existing designs or in which there is a very narrow hypothesis which requires detailed examination; and using a large-group study in those situations in which the underlying program concept is quite broad and in which large-scale resource allocation decisions are involved.

Once the analyst has estimated the gross individual benefits due to a particular program, he should also take into account the factors which reduce these benefits. Thus, if a particular program raises an individual's earnings, some account should be taken of the increased taxes the individual may have to pay on these earnings. Moreover, if a manpower program reduces an individual's unemployment experience, then reduced transfer payments (such as welfare or unemployment benefits) must be taken into account. Another example of a factor which could reduce an individual's gross benefits is the fact that the benefits of a program could "wear away" after a

---

[3] For a detailed discussion of the problems associated with measuring benefits and costs, see Michael E. Borus, "A Benefit-Cost Analysis of the Economic Effectiveness of Retraining the Unemployed," *Yale Economic Essays*, Fall 1964; and Einar Hardin and Michael E. Borus, "An Economic Evaluation of the Retraining Program in Michigan: Methodological Problems of Research," *Proceedings of the Social Statistics Section*, American Statistical Association, August 1966.

number of years. Thus, after a few years, a certain percentage of the program trainees may change their occupation and cease to use the benefits of the program. If this is true, then it should also be accounted for by the evaluator.

At this point we should mention that most evaluations depend on interview data to get at changes in earnings, etc. Interview data unfortunately are expensive and not completely reliable. Wherever possible, the analyst should try to use data sources such as the records of the Social Security Administration. Of course, the limit on taxable reported earnings reduces the usefulness of Social Security records.

Once the individual benefits have been estimated, it is then desirable to estimate the social or economy-wide benefits of the program. For example, it we are interested in the social—economic benefits of a manpower program, then we are looking for the contribution this program makes to aggregate national output over and above the direct effect of increased government expenditures on the program.

Using a simple retraining program as our example again, the social benefits can be estimated from individual benefits by assuming that the change in aggregate output equals the difference between the trainee's earnings before and after the program. Thus one can infer that the gains in aggregate output attributable to a program are roughly equal to the sum of the gains in earnings of the trainees. Moreover, any reduction in crime, unemployment, deliquency, etc., due to the program lowers the demands placed on the public employment, welfare, and social-service agencies. These social benefits are not reflected in the wages the trainee receives; however, an attempt should be made to quantify them and include them in the estimate of social benefits.

In estimating social benefits, the evaluator must be careful to include only actual benefits. Thus, if a program merely enables an unemployed person to get a job which otherwise would have been filled by someone else, then there would be no addition to social product. On the other hand, the program may enable a person to fill a vacancy which would otherwise have remained unfilled, and the program participant may have been recruited from an occupation easily filled from among the unemployed. In such a case, the social benefits would then equal the total earnings of the participant after the program. This latter case is usually known as the *vacuum effect*.

The social (or economy) benefits are usually considerably larger than the individual benefits. This is due to the vacuum effect, and the nonmarket benefits (such as reduced crime, etc.).

Finally, the evaluator is usually interested in the benefits of the program going to the government. These benefits would consist of two main categories. First, the manpower program may cause savings in unemployment compensation, welfare payments, etc. Second, the manpower program may increase tax revenues to the extent that it increases the economy's output (by putting previously unemployed people to work, etc.). Thus the analyst would approach the measurement of the government's benefits problem by estimating the increase in tax revenues and the decrease in transfer payments due to the particular manpower program.

We should emphasize at this point that the benefits (individual, social, and government) are measured only for those participants who actually utilize the program. If some trainees should drop out of a program and *not* benefit from that program, then while the costs incurred for these participants should be counted, the benefits are zero for these participants.

15.3.3 MEASURING COSTS

The second critical element in benefit/cost analysis is to accurately measure the costs of a particular program. As in the case of benefits, we are usually interested in the costs of the program from the individual, society, and government levels.

From an individual point of view, the main costs of manpower programs are the loss of income (if any) during the program and the out-of-pocket expenses (if any) that the participant in the program must absorb due to the program. For manpower programs, it is usually best to have a control group in order to measure the opportunity costs (loss of income) of the time spent by the participants in the program. As for the out-of-pocket expenses (such as transportation to and from the program), these can usually be derived from the program's records or interview data.

The evaluator will also be interested in society's (or the economy's) costs of any particular program. These costs are composed essentially of two categories, as in the case of the individual's costs. First, there is the output foregone by society while the participants are in the program. Second, there is the output foregone by society due to the diversion of resources to the program. The second category consists of any instructional costs, the costs of recruiting and selecting the program participants, the costs of placing and following up the participants, the costs of developing the program, and the costs of administering the program.

There will be many problems in estimating the true value of the resources devoted to any manpower program. The analyst should be careful to include the costs of all facilities used in the program. At the same time, the analyst may have to point out where costs are higher than "normal" due to the fact that equipment had to be purchased, and this equipment may have a life expectancy much longer than the initial program.

The costs of a program to the economy are usually lower than the costs of that program to the government sector. This is due to the fact that many programs are run with unemployed participants, making the production lost during the program very small or zero. Moreover, the living allowances provided by most manpower programs are transfer payments which are not costs from the economy's point of view. Transfer payments are costs for the government, but they represent no real cost of resources to the economy—or they can be considered a cost which is immediately offset by the benefit it yields to the recipient.

Finally, the costs of the program to the government consist of all the monetary outlays for the program, and any tax revenues lost to the government during the duration of the program. These costs range from recruiting and selection of trainees, to living allowances, to salaries of program personnel, to administrative costs, etc.

15.3.4 DISCOUNT RATE

Since the costs of practically all manpower programs are concentrated in a short time period, but the benefits are realized over a long period after the program, the program evaluator must utilize some discount factor for the purpose of measuring the importance of additional income received in future years.[4]

There are many discount rates which can be used, depending on the relevant analysis level (individual, society, or government). The rates used in empirical work usually vary from 5% (for the society and government levels) to 15% (for the individual level). Probably the best procedure is to make the evaluation computations with high and low discount rates, thereby demonstrating the sensitivity of the results to the discount rate chosen.

15.3.5 THIRD-PARTY AND DISTRIBUTIONAL EFFECTS

Manpower programs are usually evaluated from the point of view of the participants—both individually and as they affect the government and society. However, in the ideal situation the benefits and disbenefits to nonparticipants should be more carefully measured from the individual, governmental, and society levels. For example, a training program which takes unskilled or low-skilled people and gives them relatively scarce skills could break resource bottlenecks, thereby expanding employment and income among nonparticipants far in excess of any increase which is detected by looking only at the participants.[5]

Moreover, in addition to computing the benefit/cost ratios of various programs in order to determine program efficiency, the analyst can look at the distributional effects of these programs. The analyst can present information about the specific groups which receive benefits and bear costs. These groups can be listed by minority status, age, region of the country, etc.

15.3.6 ORGANIZATIONAL PROBLEMS AND ACCEPTABILITY OF EVALUATION RESULTS

Right at the beginning of any manpower program, there are timing or organizational problems to be faced. It can be argued that a fair evaluation of a program cannot be undertaken until a couple of years after it has begun. However, this reasoning should not delay the formation of the process which will generate the final evaluation. A failure to recognize the information-generating problems can mean information that is inadequate for a meaningful evaluation. Moreover, the evaluator must be careful that in postponing his evaluation until after the "settling-down" period (the initial

---

[4] A dollar of income 10 years from today is not worth as much as a dollar of income today. For some people, in fact, the difference over a 10-year period would be quite large.

[5] For a discussion of this and other sections of this chapter, see Burton A. Weisbrod, "Conceptual Issues in Evaluating Training Programs," *Monthly Labor Rev.*, **89**, October 1966.

two years or so) of the program he does not run into the beginning of fundamental shifts in the program process.[6]

The analyst should always be careful to supplement the internal data system of any program with other types of information sources, such as a small sample interview or an outside source such as Social Security data.

It can be argued that even before we know everything we would like to know about various program concepts, we can still undertake social action programs to cure social problems, but we should undertake a varied approach and carefully evaluate each approach as to its respective costs and benefits. A program can be large and action oriented and still be designed as a series of intentional experiments which must be evaluated.

Most manpower programs are so complex (on both the input and output sides) that simple positive or negative verdicts are rarely possible. Instead, the evaluator must provide the evidence which suggests useful modifications in the program. And over time, the various evaluations should improve manpower programs so that they can achieve their goals in a more efficient manner.

Another point we would like to emphasize is that whenever an evaluation shows a program to be "successful," it should also deal with the question of replication. Unless a "success" is replicable in other areas, the success of the individual project is not very valuable. We would like to allocate resources on the basis of evidence that certain concepts are successful in theory, in individual experiments, *and* in large-scale implementation.

15.4 SOME EMPIRICAL RESULTS

In this section we will examine some of the empirical studies that have been done recently evaluating different manpower programs. Although not enough research has been done to reach final conclusions about any of the programs, the current research does indicate in approximate terms the benefits and costs associated with many manpower programs.

15.4.1 MDTA EVALUATION

Many studies have attempted to evaluate the Manpower Development and Training Act (MDTA) program; their results have been broadly consistent and the margins of benefits over costs sufficiently large to leave little doubt that the program has been a good economic investment.

One study of a state-sponsored retraining program in Massachusetts found that

---

[6] For a discussion of this and other sections of this chapter, see Glen G. Cain and Robinson G. Hollister, "The Methodology of Evaluating Social Action Programs" in *Public-Private Manpower Policies* edited by Arnold A. Weber, Frank H. Casseil, and Woodrow L. Ginsburg. Industrial Relations Research Association, Madison, Wisconsin, 1969.

the savings in unemployment compensation alone from the reemployment of the trainees would repay the program costs in a little more than five years.[7] Another study of a MDTA program, in the same state estimated that the government investment of $600,000 would return more than $3,000,000 in benefits over the working lifetime of the trainees.

A study of a training program sponsored by the Area Redevelopment Administration in West Virginia found that an average investment of $800 per trainee brought a social return of $4300 and $16,800 (depending on the assumptions made about the discount rate). Moreover, a study of some Connecticut MDTA programs revealed a benefit/cost ratio of between three and six for the average trainee and a ratio of eleven for the government.

A recent study by the U.S. Department of Labor[8] reveals that the MDTA trainee increased his earnings by 20%, and that the family head and nonwhite family head trainees showed a greater advance in earnings than other categories. Moreover, Professors Cain and Somers looked at two retraining programs for the disadvantaged worker[9] and found that the nonwhite trainees fared at least as well as the white trainees, and both groups fared substantially better than the nontrainees.

Professor Borus undertook a study[10] of the benefits of one retraining program over a five-year period and found evidence that the program yielded substantial benefits over all five years. This indicates that manpower programs can have a beneficial effect for more than just the first or second year after the retraining takes place.

---

[7] This section leans heavily on the publication Garth L. Mangum, *Contributions and Costs of Manpower Development and Training*, Policy Paper No. 5 in Human Resources and Industrial Relations, The Institute of Labor and Industrial Relations, University of Michigan and Wayne State University (December 1967). Professor Mangum's publication in turn surveys a few MDTA program evaluations including David A. Page, "Retraining Under the Manpower Development Act: A Cost-Benefit Analysis," *Studies of Government Finance, Reprint 86*, Brookings Institution, Washington, D.C. (1964); Gerald G. Sommers and Ernst Stromsdorfer, "A Benefit-Cost Analysis of Manpower Retraining," *Proceedings of the Industrial Relations Research Association* (December 1964); Glen G. Cain and Ernst Stromsdorfer, *An Economic Evaluation of the Government Retraining of the Unemployed in West Virginia, 1965* (mimeographed); Michael E. Borus, "The Economic Effectiveness of Retraining the Unemployed," *Yale Economic Essays* (Fall 1964); and *Cost Effectiveness Analysis of On-the-Job and Institutional Training Courses*, A report to the Office of Manpower Policy, Evaluation and Research of the U.S. Department of Labor by Planning Research Corporation, Washington, D.C. (June 1967). This last study is the first pilot study we discussed (institutional and on-the-job training under MDTA) in an earlier section of this chapter.

[8] U.S. Department of Labor, Manpower Administration, *The Influence of MDTA Training on Earnings*, Manpower Evaluation Report No. 8 (December 1968).

[9] Glen Cain and Gerald Somers, "Retraining the Disadvantaged Worker," *Proceedings of a Conference on Research in Vocational and Technical Education*, University of Wisconsin (1966).

[10] Michael E. Borus, "Time Trends in the Benefits From Retraining in Connecticut," *Proc. Ind. Relations Res. Ass.* (1967).

15.4.2 JOB CORPS EVALUATION

Professor Glen Cain has examined the Job Corps and found some favorable social benefit/cost ratios.[11] He believes that a set of conservative and realistic assumptions yields ratios between 1.02 and 1.70, with the sole measure of benefits being the improvement of labor market earnings of the Corpsmen. The estimated social cost of the Job Corps program varied between $3500 and $7490 per Corpsman. The smaller figure was associated with a five-month stay in the Job Corps and the larger figure with a twelve-month stay. The benefits were fairly consistently greater than the costs (depending on assumptions made about the discount rate, months in the Job Corps, etc.).

He also compares the benefit/cost ratios of the Job Corps to the ratios for several water-resource projects advanced by the Army Corps of Engineers, and he finds that the Job Corps ratios are consistently greater.

15.4.3 TECHNICAL EDUCATION EVALUATION

A pilot study was recently undertaken to measure the costs and returns created by two years of post-high-school technical education.[12] The estimated average total cost to society for the two years of technical education was $7425 per student. The average total private cost per student amounted to $4920.

The technical-education graduates began to accrue monetary returns the first year after graduation, and the total return for the first four years after graduation amounted to 65% of the average private investment. The estimated social rate of return for the technical education was 16.5%, assuming a per capita real earnings of 2% a year, and it was 11.7% assuming a zero growth in the income advantage of the graduates (compared to nongraduates). The estimated private rate of return was, respectively, 22% and 16.9%.

Both the social and private rates of return compare favorably with the rates estimated for investments in manufacturing and college education.[13] Although this was only a pilot study, it does agree with previous work that found high rates of return on investments in education.

Although there is still a great need for competent research in the area of evaluation of manpower programs, we seem to know now that investments in this area are worth while and should be pursued. This is especially true since most of the existing studies have concentrated on only earnings and employment improvements; the other possible benefits of many manpower programs (crime reduction, family stability, etc.) have been left largely unmeasured. The construction or improvement of human

---

[11] Glen G. Cain, *Benefit/Cost Estimates for Job Corps*, Institute for Research on Poverty, University of Wisconsin (1967).

[12] Adger B. Carroll and Loren A. Ihnen, *Costs and Returns of Technical Education: A Pilot Study*, North Carolina State University (1966).

[13] The manufacturing and college-education rates have been estimated at 12.0% and 13.0%.

capital through investments made in manpower programs seems to be a very rewarding area for the economy to pursue.

15.5 SOME WORDS OF CAUTION

We should point out here that most of the evaluations that have been done to date on training programs have not dealt with true disadvantaged or poor populations. It may be somewhat misleading to generalize from studies of unemployed trainees to what the results will be when the hard-core poor constitute the main recipients of the training programs. That is, the populations of the poor and of the unemployed are not the same.[14]

Thus, in addition to wanting to know more about the full effects of manpower programs, we are in need of more detailed knowledge of what these programs can and cannot do for different populations in our economy. This is especially true as we start shifting away from the "cream" of the human material available for training and start concentrating on the hard-core disadvantaged. Of course, we have some preliminary data that support the finding that the disadvantaged can receive excellent return from manpower programs (as well as the economy), but more information is needed in this area.

SUMMARY

The evaluation of manpower programs can be viewed as the process of attributing differences between actual and comparative outcomes to programs characteristics, under different conditions of trainee characteristics and other intervening influences, and of making judgments about the value of the program characteristics. In trying to evaluate its complex programs, the Federal government utilizes an integrated management system called Planning—Programming—Budgeting (PPB). The purposes of PPB can be stated as making possible rational choice between objectives; making possible rational choice between programs; facilitating the selection of rational levels of programs; facilitating review and evaluation of program and accomplishments; and providing adequate historic records.

A basic concept of PPB is systems analysis. Systems analysis can help the decision-maker make three types of decisions within the PPB system. These three approaches are called cost/goal analysis, cost/effectiveness analysis, and cost/constraint analysis. The U.S. Department of Labor has recently prepared three pilot studies utilizing these analytic techniques.

The best-developed analytic tool in manpower-program evaluation is the benefit/cost ratio approach. The first step in such an evaluation would be to specify the

---

[14] David O. Sewell, "A Critique of Cost-Benefit Analyses of Training," *Monthly Labor Rev.* Volume 90 (September 1967) was very helpful in preparing this section of the chapter.

objectives of the program. The next phase would be to accurately measure the benefits that accrue to the individual participants, the government, and society due to a particular program. Another critical element in the benefit/cost analysis is to accurately measure the costs of the program. As in the case of benefits, we are usually interested in the costs of the program from the individual, society, and government levels. In order to put these factors together properly, the evaluator has to select an appropriate discount rate, and also examine any third-party and distributional effects.

Many empirical studies have been done recently evaluating different manpower programs. Although there is still a great need for competent research in the field of manpower-program evaluation, we seem to know now that investments in this area are worthwhile and should be pursued.

BIBLIOGRAPHY

Michael E. Borus, "A Benefit-Cost Analysis of the Economic Effectiveness of Retraining the Unemployed," *Yale Economic Essays* (Fall 1964)

Glen G. Cain and Robinson G. Hollister, "The Methodology of Evaluating Social Action Programs," in A. R. Weber, F. H. Cassell, and W. L. Ginsburg (editors), *Public—Private Manpower Policies*, Industrial Relations Research Association Series (1969)

Garth L. Mangum, *Contributions and Costs of Manpower Development and Training*, Policy Paper No. 5 in Human Resources and Industrial Relations, the Institute of Labor and Industrial Relations, University of Michigan and Wayne State University (December 1967)

Jerome Moss, Jr., "The Evaluation of Occupational Education Programs," University of Minnesota Technical Report, Research Coordination Unit in Occupational Education (September 1968)

Program Analysis Manual to Support a Planning—Programming—Budgeting System, U.S. Department of Labor, Manpower Administration, Washington, D.C. (October 1966)

G. G. Somers and W. D. Wood (editors), *Cost-Benefit Analysis of Manpower Policies: Proceedings of a North American Conference, May 14—15, 1969*, The Industrial Relations Centre, Queen's University, Kingston, Ontario (1969)

In the previous chapter we discussed some tools which could be used to evaluate manpower programs. If we look at Chapter 15 as microlevel evaluation, then we can look at the contents of this chapter as macrolevel evaluation. That is, in this chapter we will be concerned with the overall *system* of manpower programs and how it can be improved, rather than the efficiency of any one manpower program.

16.1 THE PLANNING PROCESS

Planning is used by individuals and institutions to approach the future in such a way as to minimize uncertainty and surprise and to eliminate mistakes and waste. In other words, planning is the systematic management of assets.[1] The efficient management of assets, on any level, involves many supporting activities. One such activity is the identification of the primary objectives which the assets will be managed to achieve. Moreover, the management of assets involves the integration of strategic decisions which are necessary if the assets are to be converted into the achievement of objectives. A third supporting activity is the handling of the element of time, since assets are managed for current as well as future incomes.

At the firm level, planning involves the management of the firm's assets, whereas at the economy level, planning involves the management of the nation's assets. In the public economy, government must fill the role of manager (within appropriate limits); and governmental authority in such major areas ⸳s monetary and fiscal policy, defense, foreign trade, and social security give it instruments for inducing behavior on the part of private economic units, such as households, unions, and business firms.

---

[1]See Neil W. Chamberlain, *Private and Public Planning*, McGraw-Hill, New York (1965), especially Chapter 1; and Richard A. Lester, *Manpower Planning in a Free Society*, Princeton University Press, Princeton (1966), especially Chapter 1.

Manpower planning applies this process to the preparation and employment of human resources for productive purposes. In a society such as the United States, good manpower planning aims to enlarge job opportunities and improve training and employment decisions, through informed personal choice and calculated adjustment to rapidly changing demand.

Manpower planning in the United States should work with market forces. It must not seek to restrict individual choice or to replace market processes, but rather it should enlarge choice and help the market operate more effectively by anticipating and arranging for early corrective measures to avoid manpower imbalances, such as restrictive shortages and wasteful surplus.

16.2 NATIONAL GOALS AND MANPOWER PLANNING

In order to intelligently manage any set of assets, one must know what goals or objectives are to be achieved. For the United States economy a great deal of work has been done in the area of national goals. In 1960 the President's Commission on National Goals issued a report listing a series of goals for the United States in fifteen areas.[2] This report was the product of a group of oustanding leaders from different walks of life.

The National Planning Association has taken these goals and done research on both the economic costs of achieving all the goals and the manpower requirements that these goals imply.

16.2.1 DOLLAR COST OF OUR NATIONAL GOALS

Looking at the sixteen areas in which goals have been established, the National Planning Association has projected the dollar cost of achieving these goals by 1975.[3] Unprecedented prosperity in America has existed side by side with a real concern that our resources are insufficient to support an expanding list of national objectives. The problem of matching resources and aspirations is really the problem of priorities, and in a democracy priorities are assigned by political processes and by the decisions of firms, unions, and consumers. Research and analysis are essential if we are to make intelligent choices.

The main results of the research of the National Planning Association's Center for Priority Analysis can be summarized in three statements. First, large increases in expenditures can be anticipated for most of the goals in the decade of the 1970s. The largest increases will be in the areas of consumer expenditures, private plant and equipment, urban development, social welfare, health, and education. Second, the dollar costs projected for all the goals are estimated to exceed the GNP in 1975 by approximately $150 billion, or 15% of the GNP. Third, economic growth is the

---

[2] The list was expanded to sixteen with the addition of space exploration in 1961.

[3] See Leonard A. Lecht, *The Dollar Cost of Our National Goals*, National Planning Association, Washington D.C. (1965).

key variable in increasing the resources available for achieving national goals. GNP growth sets the limits on how close we will come to achieving our goals.

Looking at the sixteen areas somewhat more closely, we find a very large list of goals. The area of *consumer expenditures* includes living standards rising to the limit set by a savings rate of about 8% of disposable personal income; and increases in consumer expenditures from other goals, such as health and education; plus a family allowance system to increase to $3300 the incomes of families below this level in 1975. Goals in the area of *private plant and equipment* include the plant and equipment needed to produce the level of output anticipated in the 1970s plus the additional private plant and equipment projected for specific goals, such as transportation equipment in the area of public transportation, utilities in urban development, etc. Goals in *urban development* include correcting air and water pollution plus installing adequate metropolitan transportation systems, cultural and recreation facilities, public buildings, utilities, and industrial and commercial buildings.

The *social welfare* area includes adequate income-maintenance programs, expansion of coverage of present public and private social-insurance programs, plus a family-allowance system for low-income families. Goals in the *health* area include comprehensive personal medical-care coverage, a major expansion in community health services, and financing of health-related facilities, medical care for the aged, and research. The *education* goals assume an increase in the proportion of students receiving high-school and higher education—amounting to a 50% increase in the proportion for the college group. These goals also allow for a doubling of faculty salaries over a ten-year period, increased teacher supporting staff, expansion of junior colleges, and increased plant and equipment at all levels of education.

Goals in the *transportation* area include transportation equipment and research and development for the projected changes in the use of transportation resources along the lines of President Kennedy's 1962 Transportation Message to Congress. They also include the development of technological advances such as supersonic planes, nuclear ships, etc. *National defense* goals include the maintenance of an adequate national defense system under conditions ranging from partial disarmament to technological advances, such as antimissile missiles and nuclear aircraft carriers. The *housing* area assumes adequate housing for a growing and higher-income population, plus elimination of substandard housing by means of rehabilitation and new construction in urban blighted areas.

Goals in the area of *research and development* project increases in expenditures for basic research, for a research and development extension service for the private economy, and for research and development information systems. The area of *natural resources* includes expenditures for an increase in the supply of, or the development of substitutes for, scarce natural resources. The area of *international aid* includes continuation of public loans and grants to developing nations totaling approximate 1% of projected GNP, and spending for defense support and increased contributions to international organizations.

Goals in the area of *space* include manned lunar landings, exploration of the moon, weather-observation satellites, and expanded research in basic space sciences and space technology. The *agriculture* area includes the continuation of present price-support programs, or land retirement, or direct control of crop output; and it also includes the cost of programs to encourage the movement of low-income farmers into nonfarm employment. The *manpower retraining* goal includes programs for retraining 1% of the labor force a year. The sixteenth area is *area redevelopment*, and it includes programs to create 100,000 jobs a year.

The National Planning Association anticipates that the growth in GNP will be 4.5% a year between 1964 and 1975. This is translated into a GNP amounting to $1 trillion in 1975 (in 1964 dollars). On the other hand, the *gross* expenditures for attaining the goals in the above-mentioned sixteen areas in 1975 amounts to $1.54 trillion (in 1964 dollars). This $1.54 trillion price tag overstates the true cost of the sixteen goals, since it is obtained by adding up the expenditures for the individual goals. It should thus be reduced because it contains overlapping and other double-counting. Eliminating double-counting reduces the costs for the goals in all sixteen areas in 1975 from $1.54 trillion to $1.16 trillion.

Thus the National Planning Association projects that the nation's output in 1975 will be sufficient for realizing most, but not all, of the national goals. The deficit between resources and full realization of the goals in 1975 is projected to be $150 billion in 1964 dollars. The United States can easily afford the cost of only one goal, and the United States can afford the cost of making substantial progress on all its goals. However, the costs of achieving all the goals would exceed the economy's resources by about 15% of the 1975 GNP.

These estimates of deficit emphasize the dilemma inherent in the nation's objectives. Even a trillion-dollar GNP leaves the nation short of achieving all our goals in 1975. Creating a sufficient GNP by 1975 to attain all our goals would entail a growth rate of about 5.8% a year in the 1970s (an unlikely pace). The above projections presupposed an unemployment rate of just under 4% in the 1970s. If the unemployment rate were to be reduced to 3%, the deficit could be reduced from $150 billion to $140 billion.

The relevant question is not really which goals we as a nation will pursue, but rather the question of how much, what combinations, and how soon. This means considering priorities, and as a democracy the United States must decide how we will simultaneously strive to attain all our goals within the constraints imposed by the available resources.

16.2.2 MANPOWER NEEDS FOR NATIONAL GOALS

When a nation pursues a set of goals (such as manpower training), it can add to the supply of manpower at various skill levels. Thus the very pursuit of national objectives has an important influence in determining the volume of employment, the skill composition of employment, and the probability of surplus or bottlenecks in various occupations.

Building on their previous work, the National Planning Association did a study concerned with manpower projections from the perspective of the manpower needed to achieve by 1975 the national goals described in the previous section of this chapter.[4]

Looking at the dollar costs of goals and the deficit between GNP and goal costs can lead to an incomplete picture of the bottlenecks and feedback effects of pursuing a set of goals. For example, the pursuit of the health goal will probably be limited by an insufficiency of skilled medical personnel—doctors, nurses, laboratory technicians, etc. Moreover, each different goal will probably have a different manpower problem.

In their study of manpower projections, the National Planning Association translated the dollar-cost estimates for national goals into expenditures for the output of the industries that contribute to their pursuit. Then the output–employment relationship in each of these industries that existed in the early 1960s is used along with anticipated changes in productivity to estimate the total employment in the different industries in the mid-1970s needed to produce the output each industry would contribute to the various goals.

The major conclusions of this manpower study can be summarized in four statements. First, full achievement of all the national goals by the mid-1970s would require an employed civilian labor force of more than 100 million, which is 10 million more than are projected to be in the civilian labor force in 1975. Second, this projected shortage in manpower, if the national goals are pursued, will probably result in problems of upgrading through education and training, making better use of existing manpower potentials, and improving mobility, Third, substantial progress toward achieving all our national goals could be a major factor in creating better job opportunities for the nation's underutilized human resources: nonwhites, women, older workers, and the handicapped. Fourth, the nation's choice of priorities will have a significant influence on the kinds of jobs the economy will need in the 1970s. Thus, assigning a high priority to the health or education goals will primarily increase the demand for white-collar workers, whereas assigning a high priority to the urban development or transportation goals will primarily increase the demand for blue-collar workers.

The above suggests that manpower planning is needed to make possible the increases in manpower supply that are necessary for realizing national goals receiving a high priority without creating bottlenecks elsewhere in the economy.

Looking at the National Planning Association's study somewhat more closely, we find a projection of 101.2 million people employed in 1975 to fully achieve all the goals in the sixteen areas previously discussed. However, the projection of the expected employment level for labor in 1975 is 87.7 million, and this figure is the benchmark for assessing the manpower gap indicated by the larger requirements for the national goals.

Table 16.1 contains the National Planning Association's manpower projections

---

[4]See Leonard A. Lecht, *Manpower Needs for National Goals in the 1970s*, Frederick A. Praeger, New York (1969).

TABLE 16.1 Employment by occupation—1964 and 1975 projections

Occupational group	1964	Projected number employed (in millions)		Average annual growth rate (%)	
		1975 bench-mark estimate	1975 for national goals	1964 — 1975 bench-mark estimate	for national goals
Total civilian employment	70.35	87.65	101.20	2.0	3.4
White-collar occupations	31.15	41.80	48.90	2.7	4.2
Professional and technical	8.55	12.40	15.80	3.4	5.7
Clerical workers	10.70	14.70	16.70	2.9	4.1
Sales workers	4.45	5.30	5.80	1.6	2.4
Blue-collar occupations	25.55	29.55	34.05	1.3	2.6
Craftsmen and foremen	9.00	10.70	12.80	1.6	3.3
Operatives	12.90	14.55	16.60	1.1	2.3
Service occupations	9.20	12.80	14.65	3.0	4.3
Farm occupations	4.45	3.50	3.60	−2.2	−1.9

Source: Leonard A. Lecht, *Manpower Needs for National Goals in the 1970s,* Frederick A. Praeger, New York, 1969, page 33. (Reprinted by permission)

for major occupational groups and a few selected minor occupational groups. As in the 1947—1964 period, the professional and technical occupational group is expected to increase at a greater rate than the other occupational groups. The clerical worker and service worker groups also show sizable increases, and employment is projected to decline only in the farm occupations.

16.2.3 PURSUIT OF NATIONAL OBJECTIVES: OPPORTUNITIES FOR NON-WHITES AND HIGHLIGHTS FOR SOME GOALS

Pursuit of specific national goals can have a significant effect on job opportunities for nonwhites. The current occupational distribution for nonwhites is still characterized by overrepresentation in the low-skill, low-income, and unemployment-prone occupations. However, the National Planning Association's study demonstrates that the goals for education, health, social welfare, consumer expenditures, housing, and urban development provide the best job opportunities for nonwhites. The pursuit of national objectives in housing and urban development would be responsible for much of the projected increase in nonwhite employment in blue-collar occupations, especially in the skilled crafts.

　　If rebuilding the cities is given a high priority, then it will be difficult to meet the large increases needed in many of the skilled building trades unless substantially more opportunities are created for Blacks and Puerto Ricans to gain admission to the training programs and to union membership, which are prerequisites for entering these occupations. Thus more active pursuit of goals such as urban development could constitute a major program for coping with poverty, especially nonwhite poverty.

Looking at Table 16.2, we can see the manpower implications of pursuing some of the national goals.

TABLE 16.2 Employment requirements associated with selected goals

Occupational group	Projected increase in employment associated with goal, 1964–1975 (%)					
	Health	Education	Housing	Social welfare	Transportation	Urban development
All occupations	105	95	58	83	54	60
White-collar occupations	95	98	67	104	54	67
Blue-collar occupations	40	63	56	54	55	59
Service occupations	133	90	62	111	47	67

Source: Leonard A. Lecht, *Manpower Needs for National Goals in the 1970s*, Frederick A. Praeger, New York, 1969, Chapter 6. (Reprinted by permission)

Each goal will have its own unique manpower pattern. Pursuing the health and education goals will depend heavily on growth in white-collar occupations such as dentists, nurses, physicians; and teachers, librarians, and secretaries. On the other hand, expenditures on the housing goal generates half its employment in the construction industry. Thus about a third of the total employment for the housing goal is composed of skilled craftsmen and foremen.

Pursuit of the social-welfare goal will depend heavily on social workers, and white-collar and service occupations, especially in occupations related to health care. The transportation and urban-development goals will have a heavy effect on blue-collar occupations. The transportation goal will have its greatest effect on a white-collar occupation group (airplane pilots and navigators), and great effects on blue-collar occupations such as auto-service attendants; deliverymen and routemen; excavating, grading, and road-machinery operators; and automobile mechanics and repairmen. Pursuit of the urban-development goal, more than of any other goal, involves large increases in manpower needs in many skilled crafts.

If the United States does pursue most or all its national goals in the 1970s, we will see a rapid growth in the technician occupations. And this in turn will probably speed the shift in emphasis in vocational education from nontheoretical skill training in high schools to two-year post-high-school institutions offering programs combining basic education with scientific and technical studies. Moreover, the future is likely to make general education even more important in job preparation. It will take new manpower programs, expanded facilities in higher education, and a new direction in vocational education to ensure that we as a nation can pursue many goals with an adequate supply of skilled labor.

The work of the National Planning Association demonstrates that fear of automation leading to mass unemployment in the near future overlooks the consequences of a more ambitious pursuit of national goals. Pursuing our goals will mean manpower shortages in the 1970s.

16.3 MATCHING JOBS WITH WORKERS

In order to develop an efficient manpower-planning system, projections of manpower change, such as we discussed in the last section of this chapter, are absolutely necessary. However, once we have some good information about the demand for labor, and once we have an educational system to supply skilled manpower, a crucial assignment is to match the available jobs with the best available workers. In the United States the state employment service system plays an important role in matching jobs and workers. In this section we will look at this role of the state employment service and discuss some recent development which promise to have an important impact in the 1970s.

16.3.1 JOB BANK SYSTEM

In the last few years increased attention has been paid to the application of computers to help solve the problem of finding the best workers for jobs and the best jobs for workers. The U.S. Department of Labor has supported research in this area with the state employment service in California, Florida, Maryland, Michigan, New York, Utah, and Wisconsin. The states of Maryland and Utah had developed two different systems by late 1969.[5]

The Maryland State Employment Service has developed a job bank in Baltimore. The job bank concept was developed to provide all interviewers of the employment service and cooperating agencies with all job openings given to these organizations in the metropolitan area, to eliminate excessive and wasteful referrals of workers to employers, and to eliminate excessive and wasteful job-solicitation visits to employers.

Each morning about 30 sets of the job bank book are distributed to Baltimore central local offices and to outreach stations at key points in the metropolitan area. Moreover, cooperating community agencies have access to the central office books. The job bank book usually contains about 10,000 current job openings arranged in Dictionary of Occupational Title (DOT) sequence. Training slots and other orders are also included. In order to ensure that the job opening is in fact current and that workers do not waste time going to interviews which should not have been scheduled, a phone call is made to a central telephone control before a referral is made. This also keeps the number of referrals within the limits set by the employer.

---

[5]See U.S. Department of Labor, "Status Report: National Computer-Assisted Job Bank," mimeographed, 1969.

Each evening facts concerning referred workers are fed into the computer, as well as facts concerning filled, canceled, and new job orders. New openings received during the day are always exposed to same-day action; but if they remained unfilled, they are key-punched after the offices close.

The Baltimore system uses an IBM 1401 computer which permits overnight updating and resorting of job openings and applicant information and prints the result as a master book. This book is duplicated and automatically assembled in 28 copies.

This job bank system has been in operation since June 1968 and seems to have at least eleven positive values.

1. It has eliminated the previous competition that existed among manpower agencies in their attempt to gather job-openings data. This competition had led to the harassing of employers to the point of a threatened employer boycott against all the public and private nonprofit employment agencies.

2. It has generated a greater body of job orders and openings more suitable to the available labor supply than the employment service has been able to establish and sustain in the past.

3. The job bank concept has led to an extensive decentralization of the employment service staff into the neighborhoods in which the problem populations live, without any significant increase in staff or loss of quality of supervision.

4. There has been an increase from less than 20% to more than 55% in referrals and placements of disadvantaged job-seekers, with no significant loss in the volume of total placements (except in professional and clerical placements).

5. There has been an effective planning, redirection, and coordination of employer relations and job-development effort.

6. The job bank idea has generated a system of management and supervisory controls over the volume and quality of order-taking, selection, referral, and verification by the use of computer printouts of data on individual interviewer and office performance (on a daily, weekly, and monthly basis).

7. This concept provides current information about jobs and job opportunities to be tapped into the ghetto neighborhood grapevine, manpower planning, planning for vocational education, etc.

8. There has been an improved level of community acceptance from employers, job-seekers, and political, economic, and social power structures of the community.

9. There has been a greatly improved acceptance of the employment service by the inner-city population due to the decentralization.

10. The system has made creative use of community aides in outreach among the inner-city residents.

11. There has been a sustained high-level interest and support for the employment service in all the news media (radio, television, newspaper).

16.3.2 MAN—JOB-MATCHING SYSTEM

The Utah State Employment Service has been developing a more advanced system of the job bank, which they call the man—job-matching system. This concept was devised to utilize a computer to match applicants to job openings and openings to applicants. Moreover, the system is designed to provide information on the labor market, improve relations between employer and worker, and supply a management-information system.

Video data terminals and terminal printers are located in three local offices of the Utah State Employment Service. These terminals are linked with a computer at the central office of the Utah Department of Employment Security. Nine types of messages are programmed to be sent from or to appear in either video or paper print, or both, at terminals in the three local offices.

1. List application
2. List job order
3. Is applicant on file
4. Match order to available applicants
5. Match applicant to available job openings
6. Remove order-pending status
7. Remove applicant-pending status
8. Mail out call-in card
9. Request complex search

Other local offices in the Utah Employment Service can mail job orders and applicant information to the central office, where they are matched overnight. Moreover, these offices can telephone urgent requests to the computer center (or to one of the three terminal offices) for immediate access to the data bank. The effect of this is to make *all* job openings and applicants available to the state employment service (unless they are filled or referred during the day of intake) be exposed to *all* applicants and opportunities in the statewide system.

This system also allows for management and substantive supervision over the entire operation by having the computer automatically prepare six daily reminder notices.

1. A selection has been pending three days
2. A call-in has been pending three days
3. A referral has been pending three days
4. An individual has been selected five times but never referred
5. An individual has been referred three times but never hired
6. An individual has been in the active file ten working days with no activity

Moreover, all the local offices and cooperating public and nonprofit manpower agencies are supplied each week with a printout of all unfilled openings in order to widen the area of recruitment and information about job opportunities.

The key element in a computer match of workers and jobs is the strategy used to compare job requirements with applicant characteristics. The Utah design has two basic matching strategies, the DOT Search Strategy and the Complex Search Strategy. The former strategy takes a job order and then reads every mini record (an applicant record abbreviated for search purposes) which has the same DOT code (up to nine digits) as the job order. As each mini record is read, the program first checks up to three "must" factors specified by the job order. If the individual meets these factors, then his record is scanned for up to 33 other selection factors. For every individual who meets the must factors, a count is made of the times the individual's character-istics met order specifications. The job order specifies the number to select, and the individuals are ranked according to the number of selection factors matched. If the nine-digit DOT search does not uncover as many referrals as are called for in the job order, then the program degrades the DOT code to the first six digits and follows the same matching and ranking techniques. This broadening of the search proceeds in this manner until the correct number of referrals are made or until all the files with at least the same first digit DOT code specified on the job order are searched.

The Complex Search Strategy differs from the above in that the DOT code is ignored. Every single mini record is scanned and the entire applicant file is compared to job-order specifications and ranked on the number of matches. The "must factor" provision is still followed. In this program, as with the one above, ties among appli-cants are decided by the chronological age of the applicant record. Both these strategies utilize RCA Spectra 70/45 equipment.

Looking again at the Baltimore and Utah concepts, it becomes obvious that the job-bank system will probably be installed before a man–job-matching system. The job bank is an essential first step in developing a matching program; and since it uses the computer to process only job openings, it provides an easier transition to the more complex computer-dependent matching system. Moreover, once a job bank system is developed, it can help with the important problem of the employment of the dis-advantaged in the cities, and at the same time provide the necessary groundwork for the more sophisticated matching systems. Thus in the 1970s we can expect to see the development of a job bank system throughout the United States as a prelude to a nationwide computer man–job-matching system.

16.3.3 COMPUTER LIMITATIONS AND MATCHING JOBS AND WORKERS

Once the United States Employment Service begins to utilize a nationwide computer-matching system, it may be possible to draw even more heavily on computers to make the matching of workers and jobs still more efficient. Professor Charles C. Holt in a recent publication[6] suggests that there are two very different aspects of the matching problem that need to be handled jointly. The worker is looking for specific things in a job to maximize his satisfaction, and the employer is concerned with finding a worker with maximum productivity. In matching jobs and workers, only if both parties satisfy their different objectives will an offer be made and accepted.

Since interviews can be very costly, Professor Holt suggests putting a large part of the preliminary search on the computer. Thus, with fairly complete information on the workers' qualifications and preferences and the employers' requirements and inducements, the computer can do more than just match workers and jobs; it can simulate a hypothetical interview and predict its outcome. It is hoped that the computer would screen out those interviews that are not likely to result in offers or acceptances and thereby leave more time for interviews that are likely to be promising. In order for this to take place, empirical studies will have to be undertaken to make quantitative estimates of worker satisfaction and productivity. One approach might be to make empirical studies of the variables that influence the probabilities of job offers and acceptances, using data on actual interviews and placements.

Thus, although the use of computers can easily expand the breadth of job-market search (the number of candidates screened per interview recommended), an equally important role can be performed by computers in expanding the depth of search (the accuracy of the prediction that is made of the outcome of each of the job—worker matches that are analyzed). This could be the third step in improving the job market search—the first two steps being the job bank system and the man—job-matching system. Fast information should not be the major criterion of success for any worker—job-matching system. One may hope that such a system would eventually improve the breadth and depth of the job-market search and thereby improve the quality of interviews and the quality of labor market decisions. Of course, this third step will have to be supported by a great deal of new research, and it will be the most difficult step to achieve.

16.3.4 MANPOWER PLANNING AND THE EMPLOYMENT SERVICE

In addition to operating a nationwide system of worker—job-matching, there are many economists who believe that the employment service should be the main operating agency in any program of manpower planning and its implementation.[7] It could be the key institution for the collection, analysis, dissemination, and ap-

---

[6]Charles C. Holt, "How Helpful Can Computers Be in the Search for Jobs and Employees?" in Neil A. Palomba and Edward B. Jakubauskas (editors), *An Interdisciplinary Approach to Manpower Research*, Industrial Relations Center, Iowa State University, Ames (1968). A revised version of this paper was published under the same title as *Firm and Market Workshop Paper 6809*, Social Systems Research Institute, University of Wisconsin, Madison (1968).

[7]The major proponent of this idea is Professor Richard A. Lester. See Richard A. Lester, *Manpower Planning in a Free Society*, Princeton University Press, Princeton (1966), especially Chapters 3 and 4.

plication of manpower information; as well as the major leader in programs for the development and efficient use of the nation's manpower resources.

Such a role for the U.S. Employment Service would mean more emphasis on research, planning, counseling, training, and retraining; and more stress on services to school youth, to employers with manpower problems, and to the community in the development and use of its labor resources.

To achieve this role, the employment service will have to continue its drive to improve its staff. This drive can be aided by including client representation in their top policy making and management. This would bring in new viewpoints, interests, and channels of communication. Moreover, the employment service could develop extensive programs of training and executive development much like the programs of large business concerns.

16.4 COOPERATIVE AREA MANPOWER PLANNING SYSTEM

Just about every serious student of manpower planning recognizes that the recent development of new manpower programs has caused problems such as confusion, duplication, and gaps in the services offered to the target populations. Thus the intended beneficiary might find himself at a disadvantage in his attempt to locate and participate in the program best suited to his personal needs.

In order to alleviate such problems and to promote serious inter-agency coordination at all levels, the Federal administrators of major manpower development programs agreed in 1967 to engage in joint planning and implementation of program activities.[8] Although the focal point for this joint effort is the local area in which manpower services and clients come together, the Cooperative Area Manpower Planning System (CAMPS) is national in scope and provides all agencies concerned with manpower an opportunity to engage in a dialog with their peers about manpower problems and activities and their impact on agreed-upon goals. It furnishes a means for a systematic exchange of information among agencies about available resources and a means for rational adjustment of responsibility for providing services to particular groups. The aim of CAMPS is to maximize the number of persons served and to better match the services offered with the requirements of individuals. Moreover, it should overcome the problems of unfilled program slots and high drop-out rates. CAMPS should contribute to a significant decline in structural unemployment.

Under CAMPS, overall coordinated plans of operation for the upcoming year are developed in concert by the participating agencies. In 1967 committees started work in 67 major labor areas. New areas are added as programs develop, and by 1968 the President of the United States had called for committees in more than 400 local areas, including every major city.

---

[8]This section is based on information about the Cooperative Area Manpower Planning System (CAMPS) supplied by the Manpower Administration of the U.S. Department of Labor, Washington, D.C.

16.4.1 AGENCY PARTICIPATION IN CAMPS

A recent representative list of the Federal manpower and manpower-related programs participating in CAMPS would cover a large number of programs in nine major areas of the Federal government. This list would include the following programs:

Department of Labor, Manpower Administration—programs that provide work preparation and training, place workers in steady jobs, and give special help to those who live in areas of high unemployment.

Department of Health, Education, and Welfare—programs that provide remedial and vocational education, manpower development and training, and vocational rehabilitation.

Department of Commerce, Economic Development Administration—a program to promote economic growth in depressed areas.

Office of Economic Opportunity—programs to provide job training and other manpower-related services for disadvantaged youths and adults in both rural and urban areas, including special emphasis programs for migrants and Indians.

Department of Housing and Urban Development—programs that create model neighborhoods, and provide decent housing and other facilities for low-income families, and jobs for the unemployed in urban renewal and housing projects. Also included are training programs for government personnel engaged in community-development fields, as well as public-service training and jobs in community-development activities.

Department of Agriculture—programs that provide training and jobs in conservation work, in distributing food to the needy and school children, in forest services, and in supplying low-cost electricity and telephones to rural people, as well as programs that assist farmers and rural communities through housing loans, educations, and other services.

Department of Interior—programs to provide training, jobs, and other services for needy Indians, and to train workers for water pollution control projects.

Civil Service Commission—provides information on Federal job needs, and the types of training that are needed to prepare people for Federal jobs.

Special Interagency Plan—a comprehensive program to provide training, relocation assistance, jobs, and other services for migrant farm workers and Indians.

16.4.2 THE PLANNING SYSTEM

Inter-agency planning is achieved through the medium of inter-agency coordinating committees at all administrative levels. All participating agencies are represented on the national and regional committees, and 100% representation is encouraged on area and state committees. Responsibilities and functions in developing plans and procedures for review and approval and in coordinating implementation of plans were set forth in 1967 at the national, regional, state, and area levels.

At the national level, each participating agency appoints a representative to a Federal coordinating committee which is responsible for developing overall direction and policy recommendations for CAMPS; developing annual national manpower goals and guidelines, and preparing documents for the field staffs engaged in developing operating plans (these documents include an analysis of expected economic developments and trends and of manpower problems and needs, and a statement of goals of national manpower programs with budget estimates and estimated distributions among states and suggested program linkages); coordinating the preparation of instructions and technical assistance to field staffs to ensure the strengthening of inter-agency manpower coordinating committees, and to guide other activities relating to developing and implementing area and state plans; and reviewing the operation of the system, and revising it in the light of experience.

At the regional level, each participating agency appoints a representative to its inter-agency coordination committee, which is responsible for developing expertise in the planning system and advising the national committee on the formulation of policy and national goals and guidelines; reviewing and approving state plans in light of national goals and guidelines; providing technical assistance to states in organizing committees and developing state plans; reviewing and monitoring program activities; and arranging with the chairman of the Manpower Administration Regional Executive Committee for the review of the state plans by the Regional Manpower Advisory Committee.

At the state level, the participating agencies have state counterparts designate representatives to an inter-agency coordinating committee. These exist in each of the 50 states (and other areas such as the District of Columbia). These committees invite participation from any statewide urban development planning agencies and the governor's office. The responsibilities of state coordinating committees include receiving national planning guidance and translating it into area terms for the area committees; supplying technical assistance to areas in constituting committees, preparing plans and progress reports, and amending plans; reviewing area plans, negotiating any needed revisions in the plans, ensuring conformance with national goals and guidelines, and ensuring that the total proposed program levels do not exceed those which can be supported by the available resources; combining area plans and plans for the balance-of-state into a clear state plan, transmitting area and state plans to the appropriate regional inter-agency coordinating committee for review and approval; reviewing area reports of progress and recommending revisions in area plans, and reviewing and revising state plans at regular intervals.

At the area level, in every selected local area for which plans are to be developed, each participating agency has local counterparts designate a representative to an inter-agency coordinating committee. The responsibilities of these area coordinating committees include formulating a comprehensive area manpower development plan for the upcoming fiscal year in accordance with policies and guidelines transmitted through the state coordinating committee; transmitting the agreed-upon plan to the appropriate state coordinating committee; coordinating the implementation of the plan by the participating agencies during the year; and preparing periodic progress reports and proposed amendments to plans for transmission to the state committee.

Wherever a local area crosses state lines, a coordinating committee is organized for each part of the interstate area and communication between them is maintained. The committee for the larger portion of the area receives the plan for the smaller portion, and combines it with the plan of the larger portion. Thus the total area plan appears in the plan of the state in which the major part of the area is located. Moreover, special balance-of-state committees (or selected area committees) are responsible for developing the balance-of-state plans covering the geographical areas of the state not covered by the established local area committees.

The above system brings forth an annual comprehensive area manpower plan which is a description of the total program of manpower development and service activities that the agencies participating in CAMPS propose to implement during the upcoming year. Components of the total program are clearly identified, and their coordination through carefully developed linkages is shown. These plans identify major manpower problems and set forth the projected deployment of available resources to solve these problems. Problems of unemployment, poverty, skill shortages, civil unrest, etc., are described and the implication of the program are suggested.

These plans make an assessment of how much of the overall manpower needs can be handled by the resources to be employed in the programs. Moreover, the plans explain the rationale for the overall deployment of resources in regard to priorities among manpower needs, economic development expectations, and their relation to overall national goals.

One of the main purposes of the comprehensive area manpower plans is to avoid duplication of services and to concentrate services in selected areas in which the needs are very great. Moreover, the plans describe linkages among programs showing the actual means whereby coordination is to be achieved.

The area plans are formulated within the framework of economic trends, manpower objectives, and estimated program resources furnished by the state committees. The state plans reflect the planning guidance furnished by the national committee, and they are summations of the local area plans and the plans for the balance of the state.

16.5 A STRATEGY FOR MANPOWER DEVELOPMENT

As the decade of the 1960s closed, the development of CAMPS stood as a giant step in rationalizing our manpower programs into a comprehensive and cohesive strategy for manpower development. As the 1970s unfold, many manpower specialists believe much further development is needed to advance such a strategy.[9] They argue that,

---

[9] This section of the chapter draws heavily on the analysis in Sar A. Levitan and Garth L. Mangum, *Making Sense of Federal Manpower Policy*, Policy Paper No. 2 in *Human Resources and Industrial Relations*, Institute of Labor and Industrial Relations, University of Michigan and Wayne State University, Ann Arbor and Detroit (1967), especially pages 20–42.

although coordination can help to institute a manpower-development strategy, it cannot *alone* solve the major problems of the current proliferation of manpower programs. These problems include the delays in review and approval of proposals due to multiagency administration of particular programs; the confusion at the local level caused by the variety of programs, which in turn means that the less-sophisticated, and often the most needy areas, fail to get their full share of available resources; the uncertainty or delays in refunding, which can cause the disintegration of efficient staffs and programs; and the increased overhead costs.

In order to cope with the problems of program proliferation and multiplicity of funding sources, many students of manpower argue that in addition to a system such as CAMPS we need the consolidation of all the manpower program authority and budgets into a single manpower agency. This consolidation of all Federal support for manpower programs into a single agency can be a very effective complement to more effective coordination.

Bringing all the overlapping (and sometimes conflicting) programs into one agency will force Congress and the Administration to examine the interrelationships and to explicitly confront the overlaps and gaps. This would dissolve the current individual programs but continue their aims and functions in a single integrated program.

The gains from an integrated Federal manpower agency can be quite worthwhile.

1. All the current functions could be supported with less administrative overhead and with more effective administration.

2. There would be an end to inter-agency competition and a reduction in intra-agency competition. The benefits from competition could probably be maintained by research, experimentation, and demonstration projects.

3. There should be a reduction in personnel requirements due to the reorganization, and these savings could be used to supply high-quality staff for the demanding roles of evaluation, monitoring, and technical assistance.

4. A single source of funds for the Federal manpower program would change the current Federal influence from encouragement of proliferation to encouragement of local rationalization and consolidation.

5. With the financial support for all manpower programs being provided by a single agency, the question of the relative effectiveness of various programs is much more likely to be raised and confronted. The application of benefit/cost analysis could become much more useful with manpower programs no longer scattered among various agencies.

Although there are many programs that could be placed into a Federal manpower agency, one good approach might be to consolidate the programs now under the Manpower Administration of the U.S. Department of Labor, the job creation and training programs of the Office of Economic Opportunity, the manpower research activities of the U.S. Bureau of Labor Statistics, and the vocational education and vocational rehabilitation departments of the U.S. Department of Health, Education and Welfare. If something like this was done, the resulting agency should probably be placed within the U.S. Department of Labor or housed in an entirely new department (although the latter suggestion is probably not feasible on political and maybe economic grounds as well).

16.5.1 A FUNCTIONAL MANPOWER POLICY

With the placing of Federal support of manpower programs in a single agency, there would probably occur a comprehensive review of the functions of the various programs and a redesign of the manpower services on a more rational basis.

One possible approach to a functionally structured manpower program (suggested by Professors Levitan and Mangum) would divide manpower activities into four categories: preparation for employment; placement and supportive services; job creation; and experimentation, demonstration, and research.

Preparation for employment includes prevocational training, adult basic education, vocational training, remedial skill training, and on-the-job training. The level and quality of general education are probably the most important determinants of future employability; and although our present high-school system serves the college-bound fairly well, we should probably expand Federal support for broadening the exposure of noncollege-bound students to occupational choices. One goal can be to have a training center in or close to most population centers which would provide technical training, less-skilled vocational training, adult basic education, and prevocational orientation.

Placement and supportive services includes outreach, recruitment, testing and counseling, job development and placement, and mobility assitance. Here the U.S. Employment Service would be the logical key institution. With a complex computer-assisted information system, the employment service could develop workers to fit jobs, as well as match already qualified workers to jobs.

Job creation includes work experience, on-the-job training, public service employment, and job creation for the disadvantaged. However, wherever possible, job creation should be coupled with adequate education and training opportunities so that there is also the possibility of occupational advancement.

Experimentation, demonstration, and research includes innovative projects, labor market data, program evaluation, and manpower research. One Federal manpower agency should mean a better system to establish research priorities, eliminate gaps and duplications, secure better cooperation among research groups, and give wider dissemination to research findings.

16.5.2 AN UMBRELLA AGENCY CONCEPT

Even if some sort of Federal manpower agency were established immediately, there would still remain the problem of proliferation of manpower programs and agencies at the state and local levels. Moreover, many manpower specialists believe that our present manpower system has a lack of state and local participation in program planning and that states are not permitted enough flexibility in the allocation of resources among manpower programs. Controls over most manpower funds remain at the Federal level. For example, except for some institutional training components, the states may authorize the use of only 20% of the funds available under MDTA (if they have an approved CAMPS), and the remainder of the funds are under the control of the national office and the regional manpower offices.[10]

Thus some solution like a Federal manpower agency would be only one step in creating a comprehensive manpower system. A second step could be the development of a single formula for the geographic apportionment of manpower funds. The criteria would include relative sizes of labor forces, unemployment rates, and proportions of disadvantaged people, but some flexibility could be permitted so that manpower policy could be varied to reflect changes in the national economy.

But even more important than this second step would be a third step of sharply increasing state and local participation at the key planning and administrative points of the manpower system. This suggestion goes beyond CAMPS and would create manpower advisory bodies, for both state and metropolitan areas, which were subject to the highest elected executive office. These bodies would include representatives of employers, unions, the public, and the client groups to be served, as well as representatives of the state, local, and private agencies that administer manpower programs. These advisory bodies would act as consultants in assessing the manpower needs of their areas, and in formulating comprehensive plans for the allocation of program resources to meet those needs.

Administrative decentralization could be achieved by having each governor designate one "umbrella agency" as the state prime sponsor to plan and administer all manpower activities. The composition of the state sponsor would probably vary, but the employment service should always be among the agencies included. The elected officials of local governments would designate their own prime sponsors. These local sponsors would draw up the comprehensive manpower plans in consultation with the area advisory bodies. These plans would then be integrated by the state prime sponsor and its advisory body for submission to the U.S. Secretary of Labor. Once the plan was approved, Federal funds would be apportioned directly to the state and local sponsors on a bloc-grant basis. The sum of these grants could total as much as 80% of the manpower budget. Prime sponsors would have the authority to administer these funds in accordance with their approved plans by entering into contracts with public (and private) manpower agencies for the delivery of the manpower services.

Such an umbrella agency concept on the local and state levels (with or without a similar concept at the Federal level) should have several advantages.

---

[10]This section of the chapter draws on a talk by Dr. Joseph A. Pichler entitled "Toward A Comprehensive Manpower System," delivered in June 1969 at the third annual summer manpower research institute sponsored by the Industrial Relations Center at Iowa State University. At the time Dr. Pichler was special assistant to the Assistant Secretary of Labor.

1. The formulation of comprehensive plans by local bodies would assure that manpower needs have been evaluated by those with the best knowledge of local labor markets.

2. Administering funds through a single prime sponsor would allow greater coordination among the various manpower projects within each area.

3. Bloc grants should increase flexibility by allowing state and local bodies to determine the mix of services (counseling, training, etc.) to be provided in their respective areas.

4. The substitution of service packages for categorical programs would permit standardization of enrollee benefits in a local area or state.

The total effect of the umbrella agency concept would be to develop a comprehensive strategy for manpower development which included serious state and local participation in manpower planning and administration. We could thus look at the umbrella agency concept, either in conjunction with a single Federal manpower agency or alone, as a revision of the present CAMPS into a more integrated manpower planning system.

16.5.3 THE FUTURE

It seems clear that the proliferation of manpower programs in the 1960s will be rationalized into a comprehensive and cohesive strategy for manpower development in the 1970s. Whether this is done by expanding CAMPS, or by creating a single Federal manpower agency, or instituting an umbrella agency concept in every state and local area, or some combination of these three, or even by some other as-yet-unborn approach is not clear now, but will become so as the 1970s evolve. But regardless of the method used, any manpower strategy will have training programs, program evaluation, manpower projections, the employment service and its worker—job-matching system, etc., as key elements.

SUMMARY

Planning is the systematic management of assets. In order to intelligently manage any set of assets, one must know what goals or objectives are to be achieved. For the United States economy, the National Planning Association has researched the economic costs and the manpower requirements of a set of sixteen national goals. The dollar cost projected for all the goals are estimated to exceed the GNP in 1975 by approximately $150 billion. Moreover, full achievement of all the national goals by 1975 would require 10 million more employed civilians than are projected to be in the labor force by that date. The nation's choice of priorities will have a significant influence on the kinds of jobs the economy will need in the 1970s.

In developing an efficient manpower planning system, we need a good system to match the available jobs with the best available workers. The United States Employment Service has begun to apply computers to this area, and is developing a job bank system and a man–job-matching system. The former will probably be installed in every employment service office before the more complex computer-dependent matching system is installed. Some economists have suggested that computers can expand the depths of job-market search as well as the breadth.

In order to alleviate such manpower-planning problems as duplication and gaps in offered services, the Cooperative Area Manpower Planning System (CAMPS) was developed. CAMPS furnishes a means for a systematic exchange of information among manpower agencies about available resources, and it provides a means for rational adjustment of responsibility for providing services to particular groups. Inter-agency planning is achieved through the medium of inter-agency coordinating committees at all administrative levels.

The development of CAMPS was a giant step in rationalizing manpower programs into a comprehensive and cohesive strategy for manpower development. Many manpower specialists believe much further development is needed to advance such a strategy. In order to cope with the problems of program proliferation and multiplicity of funding sources, it has been suggested that we should consolidate all manpower program authority and budgets into a single Federal manpower agency. Moreover, to eliminate the proliferation of manpower programs and agencies at the state and local levels, it has been suggested that each state designate one "umbrella agency" to plan and administer all manpower activities.

BIBLIOGRAPHY

Neil W. Chamberlain, *Private and Public Planning*, McGraw-Hill, New York, 1965

Leonard A. Lecht, *The Dollar Cost of Our National Goals*, National Planning Association, Washington, D.C., 1965

Leonard A. Lecht, *Manpower Needs for National Goals in the 1970s*, Frederick A. Praeger, New York, 1969

Richard A. Lester, *Manpower Planning in a Free Society*, Princeton University Press, Princeton, 1966

Sar A. Levitan and Garth L. Mangum, *Making Sense of Manpower Policy*, Policy Paper No. 2 in *Human Resources and Industrial Relations*, Institute of Labor and Industrial Relations, University of Michigan and Wayne State University, Ann Arbor and Detroit, 1967.

Joseph A. Pichler, "Toward A Comprehensive Manpower System," in Neil A. Palomba and Edward B. Jakubauskas (editors), *Creativity and Innovation in Manpower Research and Action Programs*, Industrial Relations Center, Iowa State University, Ames, 1970

PROPOSALS FOR
COMBATING POVERTY   17

Our present welfare system is far from perfect. Many observers feel that, although perfection may not be a possibility, we could certainly get a little closer to it than we currently are. This chapter will review some of the problems which plague our current welfare system as well as alternatives to this system that have been widely discussed.

17.1 THE CURRENT SYSTEM[1]

In this section we will discuss our current welfare system, which consists of income supplements and income-protection programs.

17.1.1 INCOME SUPPLEMENTS

Two major United States programs are designed to provide cash payments to the poor. The public assistance program provides payments to the aged, the blind, the permanently and totally disabled, and families with dependent children if they are poor and meet other eligibility criteria. This program accounted for about $5.3 billion of Federal expenditure in fiscal 1969. A second program, veterans' disability benefits, accounted for another $2.1 billion.

These two programs provide what might be called income-supplementation transfer payment. They provide cash transfers to persons without regard to previous working experience. They supplement incomes recognized as inadequate.

Although some complain benefits are not high enough, others claim that many on welfare could find jobs if they wanted to. Whichever is true, welfare rolls are

---

[1]See Henry J. Aaron, "Income Transfer Programs," *Monthly Labor Rev.*, Volume 92, Part I, February 1969, and U.S. Department of Labor, *Manpower Report of the President*, U.S. Government Printing Office, Washington, D.C., March 1970, pages 139 to 158.

growing. Between 1963 and 1969, the number of Aid to Families with Dependent Children (AFDC) recipients rose by over two-thirds, from 3.9 million to 6.6 million,[2] and AFDC annual outlay more than doubled, rising from $1.4 billion to $3.2 billion.[3]

One of the most glaring defects of the income-supplement program is that it provides payments for only certain categories of the poor. Almost half of our poor families are headed by an employed or unemployed head, yet cash benefits are generally not payable to families headed by an employed or unemployed male or an employed female.[4]

Besides the tendency to encourage desertion of the family by the male head of the household, another very serious problem is the tendency of our current system to discourage work effort. Until 1968, payments under AFDC were reduced a dollar for each dollar of earnings. Now this implicit tax rate has been reduced from 100 to 70% with a $30 exemption. Even with the new provision, work might not be extremely attractive to welfare recipients. If jobs are temporary, difficulties and delays in returning to welfare rolls are likely. Likewise, the costs of child care, transportation, clothing and other items can loom large in the mind of a welfare mother.

In addition, benefit levels under our current system vary widely from state to state, encouraging migration unrelated to the chances of employment. Many states fail to pay benefits that meet their own needs, standards which in turn are frequently below the poverty thresholds.

Too much of what is spent goes to pay administrative costs, which are estimated at 10¢ of every welfare dollar. It was only in June of 1968 that the Supreme Court outlawed the wasteful practice of welfare workers knocking on the doors of welfare mothers during the night to make sure a male was not living with the family. Yet house-to-house calls have revealed fraud on the part of only one-half of one percent of welfare recipients.

17.1.2 INCOME PROTECTION

Income-protection programs are designed to deal with either catastrophes or other events which reduce a family's income below previously satisfactory levels. This would include such events as unemployment, old age and retirement, as well as

---

[2]This growth in the number of AFDC families is explained by population factors (the number of women of childbearing age increased greatly during this period), as well as by the increased encouragement given by OEO and others to eligible families to apply for welfare.

[3]See "Welfare and Illfare: The Alternatives to Poverty," a *Time* editorial, December 13, 1968, reprinted in *Welfare Reform: Problems and Solutions*, The University of Wisconsin, a compilation of articles, recent mimeograph.

[4]Cash payments are made to some of these groups in those states which have adopted the Unemployed Parent Program under AFDC. The Unemployed Parent Program exists in 29 states, but eligibility criteria are very rigorous. Federal assistance for the program is available only for payments to families of unemployed fathers who have had prior work experience.

death or disability of the principal breadwinner in the family. Income-protection programs are thus designed to maintain previously satisfactory income levels.

Social Security is our largest program of income protection, accounting for over $26 billion in fiscal 1969. Although the bulk of its payments are designed to maintain previously adequate income levels, social security provides more cash assistance to poor people than does other public assistance. In fact, in 1967—68 OASDHI accounted for half of the total Federal outlays on all welfare programs, including education and housing.[5] More than one-third of social security benefits goes to poor households, and 40% to households which would be poor if they did not receive such benefits.

It is because of the large share of social security benefits which go to the poor that the social security program should be mentioned in a chapter which deals with combating poverty.

17.2 REFORM

What can be done to more effectively aid the poor? Although the main emphasis in this chapter will be on negative-income-tax proposals, some of the other alternatives will be briefly considered.

17.2.1 OVERHAUL OF THE CURRENT SYSTEM

Some critics feel that, although our current system does have problems, it is worthy of saving. Income-supplement programs could be vastly improved by basing eligibility on *need* rather than on arbitrary criteria. There seems to be no cogent reason why a poor employed person and his children should go completely unassisted simply because the breadwinner has a job. Thus the public-assistance program could be broadened to include employed persons and even non-aged poor with no children. Excessive residence and asset criteria could also be relaxed.

Second, tax rates, at least for those who have work prospects, should be made low enough to encourage work effort. It has even been suggested that payments to the working poor be positively related to the number of hours worked.

Finally, national standards concerning eligibility and benefit levels would help eliminate the wide differences which now exist between states.

The fact that a public-assistance program already exists makes it a plausible place to start building a system to adequately provide for our poor. Some feel, however, that it would be too cumbersome a job to try and alter the existing program which, they point out, already has a deep stigma in the minds of the poor.

Reformers differ as to what, if any, role social security should play in a revised welfare system. Social security is not designed primarily for the poor. Some feel,

---

[5]Mary Jean Bowman, "Poverty in an Affluent Society," in *Contemporary Economic Issues*, edited by Neil W. Chamberlain, Richard D. Irwin, Homewood, Illinois, 1969, page 85.

however, that what aid it does give the poor could be enhanced. Full benefits, for example, could be paid to those who retire early because of illness or disability. The latter are often among the poorest of the poor. Increasing minimum benefits would also be effective, since about half the increase would accrue to poor households.

It is not impossible, for that matter, to conceive of social insurance being extended to cover the risks to a child's security involved in a family breakdown. In Australia and New Zealand, a separated or divorced woman and her children are treated in principle as if the woman were widowed.

17.2.2 FAMILY ALLOWANCES

Family-allowance plans call for payments to all families with children, in proportion to the number of children in the household. Payment would be a matter of right unrelated to family income. The payment received per child may vary by the number and/or age of the children in the family. Schemes differ as to whether the allowance is taxed or whether income-tax deductions for children continue.

Proponents of family-allowance plans point to their widespread use in Western Europe as well as in Canada. They point out that such plans are simpler to administer than plans in which payments are related to income. They note that family-allowance benefits are specifically directed at children—a group which could not possibly be responsible for their own poverty.

In 1968 there were more than 10 million children classed as poor, yet the average number of children on AFDC was 4.3 million. A family-allowance plan would have aided all the poor children.[6]

Other observers see family allowances as being more equitable than other plans, since all families would receive them.

Experience in other countries indicates that family-allowance plans do *not* cause dramatic increases in the birth rate, since they usually cover only a small part of the cost of raising a child. Nevertheless, family allowances have other drawbacks. They are an extremely expensive means of fighting poverty. One scheme, which would allow $50 per child, would cost $42 billion annually, although other estimates are as low as $12 billion. Only about 20% of the outlays on family allowances would accrue to poor families. Since approximately four-fifths of all children do *not* live in poverty, payment to these families would do nothing to reduce the poverty level. Some feel that allowances meant for the children may be spent on other members of the family or just unwisely. Evidence from other countries on this point is lacking. Finally, since payment of family allowances is related to the number of children, aged poor and childless poor will not receive any aid unless additional programs are provided.

---

[6]U.S. Department of Labor, *Manpower Report of the President*, U.S. Government Printing Office, Washington, D.C., March 1970, page 154.

17.3 NEGATIVE-INCOME-TAX PLANS

In this section we will discuss some of the negative-income-tax plans that have been presented as proposals to combat poverty.

17.3.1 FRIEDMAN PLAN

Professor Friedman[7] has termed his device for helping the poor a *negative income tax*, since this stresses its identity in concept and operation with the present income tax. His essential idea is to extend the income tax by supplementing the income of the poor by a fraction of their unused income tax exemptions and deductions.

Under our present law, a family of four is entitled to exemptions of at least $3000. If the family has an income of $3000, it pays no tax. If its income is $4000, it pays a positive tax on the last $1000 earned. If it has an income of $2000, however, it has unused exemptions and deductions of $1000. Friedman would consider this as a *negative* taxable income of $1000. Payment to the family under the negative-income-tax plan would vary, depending on the tax rate applied to the $1000 of negative taxable income. If the tax rate were 75%, it would *receive* $750; if the tax rate were 50%, it would *receive* $500. In the first example, the family's total after-tax income is $2750; in the second it is $2500. With a zero pretax income and a 50% tax rate, the family would receive $1500.

For each size of family the plan defines a *break-even income*, at which the family pays no tax and receives no payment—$3000 in the above example—and the *minimum guaranteed income*—$1500 if the tax rate is 50%. Both the break-even income and the minimum guaranteed income would be higher, the larger the size of the family. (See Table 17.1 for figures based on a 50% negative tax rate.)

Payments could be made at regular intervals throughout the year, based on estimates of anticipated income. Friedman feels that no computational problems, for example definition of the family unit, would arise that do not already arise under the positive income tax. It has been estimated that Friedman's plan would cost between $7 and $9 billion.

17.3.2 TOBIN PLAN

A negative income tax, as Tobin[8] points out, would make our present income tax into a system providing three alternatives: The citizen owes something to the government, the citizen owes nothing to the government, the government owes something to the citizen. The latter alternative would be a right of national citizenship symmetrical to the obligation to pay taxes.

Tobin's plan is similar to Friedman's, although the two plans differ in specific

---

[7]See Milton Friedman, "The Case for the Negative Income Tax," *The Republican Papers* ed. by Melvin R. Laird, 1968.
[8]See James Tobin, "The Case for an Income Guarantee," *The Public Interest*, Summer 1966. Reprinted in *Welfare Reform: Problems and Solution*, University of Wisconsin, Mimeographed.

TABLE 17.1 Incomes by family size
             under Friedman's
             negative-income-tax plan

Family size	Minimum guaranteed income	Break-even income
1	$ 450	$ 900
2	800	1600
3	1150	2300
4	1500	3000
5	1850	3700
6	2200	4400

Source: Milton Friedman, "The Case for Negative Income Tax," reprinted in *Welfare Reform: Problems and Solutions*, University of Wisconsin, mimeographed.

details. Tobin proposes that the government pay the "taxpayer" $400 per member of his family if the family has no income. The allowance would be reduced by $33\frac{1}{3}$¢ for every dollar the family earns. Thus the family will retain the incentive to improve its income. The family improves its income by two-thirds of each dollar it earns.

In contrast to Friedman's proposal, the break-even income for a family of four under the Tobin plan presented above is $4800. They receive no allowance nor pay a tax at this income level. The minimum guaranteed income is $1600. Since the allowance would be reduced by $33\frac{1}{3}$¢ for each dollar earned, the suggested tax rate is $33\frac{1}{3}$%. [9]

Data on Tobin's plan are presented for a married couple with three children in Table 17.2. The first two columns show how the present tax schedule treats a family which qualifies only for the standard deduction. The middle columns superimpose a hypothetical public-assistance program onto our present tax system. The public-assistance program is assumed to provide $2500 to a family of five which has no income. Assistance is then reduced a dollar for each dollar earned. The last two columns show how Tobin's plan of integrated taxes and allowances would affect the family. Comparison of columns 5 and 7 illustrates the improvement in the incentive of the family to earn income under the Tobin plan.

As Tobin points out, designing a successful negative income tax plan requires balancing three objectives.

1. Providing a high basic allowance for families with little or no earnings

---

[9]Note that the tax rate mentioned here refers to the rate at which the allowance is reduced as income is earned. In the discussion of the Friedman plan, the tax rate was the rate applied to the negative taxable income to determine the amount to be paid to the family.

TABLE 17.2 Illustration of impact of proposed income allowances: married couple with three children

(1)	(2)	(3)	(4)	(5)	(6)	(7)
	Present tax schedule		Present tax schedule with public assistance		Proposed schedule	
Family income before Federal tax or allowance	Tax (−)	Income after tax	Tax (−) or assistance (+)	Income after tax or assistance	Tax (−) or allowance (+)	Income after tax or allowance
$ 0	$ 0	$ 0	$ + 2500	$2500	$ + 2000	$2000
1000	0	1000	+ 1500	2500	+ 1667	2667
2000	0	2000	+ 500	2500	+ 1333	3333
2500	0	2500	0	2500	+ 1167	3667
3000	0	3000	0	3000	+ 1000	4000
3700	0	3700	0	3700	+ 767	4467
4000	−42	3958	−42	3958	+ 667	4667
5000	−185	4815	−185	4815	+ 333	5333
6000	−338	5662	−338	5662	0	6000
7000	−501	6499	−501	6499	−333	6667
*7963	−654	7309	−654	7309	−654	7309
8000	−658	7342	−658	7342	−658	7342

*Income level at which the present and proposed methods of calculating tax coincide; above this income the present tax schedule applies.

2. Building in a strong incentive to earn more

3. Limiting the budgetary cost of the scheme, particularly limiting benefits to those who do not need them

Raising either the minimum allowance or lowering the rate at which the allowance is reduced as income is earned to say 20% or 25% would make it harder to confine the program to the poor. It would raise the budgetary cost of the program and extend its coverage to those who have higher before-tax incomes.

Alternatively, a higher minimum guaranteed income could be combined with a higher tax rate, say 50%, to keep budgetary costs constant. Raising the tax rate would, however, lower the incentive to increase one's before-tax earnings.

The relationship between the present tax system and Tobin's negative-income-tax plan can be illustrated graphically. Figure 17.1 depicts Tobin's plan for a family of four with two adults. A 33⅓% tax rate is assumed.

When the family's income is zero, it receives the maximum negative tax payment, $1600 a year. As the family's income rises, it receives 33⅓¢ less for each dollar it earns, until it reaches middle income brackets and pays a conventional tax.

Under our conventional system, the family would be required to pay taxes when its income reached $3000. With the addition of the negative-tax plan to the conventional tax system, however, conventional tax payments would be waived. The family would pay no taxes until its income became greater than the break-even income of $4800. At the break-even income of $4800, its negative tax would be zero and its positive tax would be completely waived.

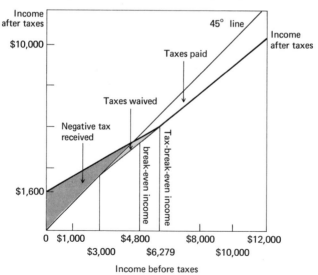

FIG. 17.1 Relationship between the Tobin negative tax plan and the present tax system. Source: James Tobin, Joseph A. Pechman, and Peter M. Mieszkowski, "Is Negative Income Tax Practical?" *Yale Law Journal*, November 1967, reprinted in *Welfare Reform: Problems and Solutions*, University of Wisconsin, mimeographed.

Above $4800 a year, the family would begin meeting some of its conventional tax liability. But to avoid inequities and to prevent any weakening of incentive, some portion of these taxes would be waived. Otherwise a family earning $4801 would suddenly be faced with paying the full conventional income tax, leaving it in a worse position than the tax-free family earning $4800.

At an income of $6279 a year, the partial waiver of taxes would cease. This income level is called the *tax-break-even income*. There are four important areas in Fig. 17.1. Between incomes of $0 and $3000, negative tax payments are made. Between $3000 and $4800, conventional taxes are waived and negative tax payments are made. Between $4800 and $6279, positive taxes are paid, but are less than conventional taxes would be. Above $6279, conventional taxes are paid. The program outlined above is estimated to involve a cost of about $14.3 billion a year, and would, of course, necessitate either negative tax payments or tax waivers to families now well above the poverty line.

17.3.3 LAMPMAN PLAN

Another proponent of the negative-income-tax concept is Professor Robert J. Lampman.[10] Since most of the poor persons not on assistance are in families with a worker, Lampman suggests integrating a negative-rates plan aimed at the "working poor" with our already existing public-assistance programs. Since the "working poor" ordinarily have at least some income, Lampman feels that the level of allowance in the event of no earnings would not have to be high. In fact, setting the maximum size of the basic allowance far below the subsistence level would make it clear that we expect this group to work. The marginal tax rate should also be low, 50% or less, feels Lampman, because it is the working poor, rather than the aged or disabled, in whom we must preserve a strong incentive to work. Table 17.3 presents the details of Lampman's plan for a family of four persons. Larger families would receive larger amounts.

Under the plan, the allowance is unchanged as preallowance income rises from zero to $1500. Thus the marginal tax rate in that range is zero. From $1500 to $3000 of income, the marginal tax rate is 50%.

Lampman calculates the net cost of his plan at $4 billion. This is figured as $6 billion less about $2 billion reduction in public assistance. His plan differs from Friedman's in that the poverty-income gap, rather than unused exemptions and deductions, is used as the criterion for family aid. Lampman feels that this makes out tax system more effective in achieving welfare goals.

The Friedman, Tobin, and Lampman plans all have elements in common. Each has a minimum guaranteed income, a break-even income at which both negative tax payments and positive tax liabilities would be zero, and—implied by these two elements—each plan has a rate at which negative tax payments are reduced

---

[10]Robert J. Lampman, "Statement," hearings before the Joint Economic Committee, U.S. Congress, June 1968. Reprinted in *Welfare Reform: Problems and Solutions*, University of Wisconsin, mimeographed.

TABLE 17.3 Net allowance for four-person
families under a negative-rates
plan for the working poor

Family income before allowance	Net allowance	Income after allowance
$ 0	$750	$ 750
500	750	1250
1000	750	1750
1500	750	2250
2000	500	2500
2500	250	2750
3000	0	3000

Source: Robert J. Lampman, "Statement," reprinted
in *Welfare Reform: Problems and Solutions*, University of Wisconsin, mimeographed.

as earned income increases. Further, each plan stresses family income as well as
family size in determining eligibility for financial aid.

The relationship between the three elements mentioned above can be illustrated
algebraically:

the break-even income	×	the rate at which negative tax payments are reduced as income is earned	=	the minimum guaranteed income

For example:

$6000	×	25%		=	$1500

If $6000 is the break-even income at which tax payments are neither paid nor
received, and the minimum guaranteed income is $1500, then the rate at which
negative tax payments are reduced as family income is earned is 25%.

This follows because if the family earned $6000 and its allowance were reduced
25¢ for each dollar earned, its allowance would be reduced by $1500 and it would
receive no negative income tax payments. It would just break even.

In addition to the negative-income-tax plans discussed above, there is another
form of guaranteed-income plan: social-dividend taxation. Social-dividend taxation plans differ from negative-income-tax plans in that the former would provide
payments to all families, to the rich as well as the poor. Family-allowance plans,
which base payments on family size rather than need, are a type of a social-dividend
plan. Other social-dividend plans call for the payment of a basic independent income to all.

The cost of the social-dividend plans is, of course, quite high.

One way to lower the cost would be to confine the programs only to the poor

and to fill only part of their income gap. This is the essence of negative income taxation.

17.3.4 ADVANTAGES AND DISADVANTAGES OF NEGATIVE-INCOME-TAX PLANS

Professor Friedman[11] lists several advantages to negative-income-tax plans. For
one thing, they concentrate payments on the poor, unlike our present social-security
and farm programs. Second, they do not treat the poor in a degrading manner. True,
they do ask the poor to report their incomes, but income is a far more impersonal
criterion for welfare than whether or not the husband is living at home.

Although the cost of Friedman's plan, with a 50% tax rate, has been calculated
at between $7 and $9 billion a year, Friedman feels that this could easily be paid
by the savings realized by eliminating the current public-assistance program, now
costing us $7 to $8 billion. In fact, says Friedman, we may come out ahead if the
greater incentive to earn income provided by the negative-income-tax plan reduces
poverty in the economy. Likewise, we should save from the elimination of the
expensive welfare bureaucracy that is required for present programs. And, although the effect on workers' incentive under the negative-tax plan may be question-
able, it certainly would be less detrimental than the 100% tax rate implied by our
current tax system.[12]

Friedman also evaluates several objections to the negative income tax. Some
critics incorrectly observe that the negative income tax would destroy incentive.
This criticism is true with respect to plans which call for payment of 100% of the
poverty gap, but it is not true of the negative-income-tax plans which pay only
some fraction of the poverty gap.

Others feel that a national negative income tax cannot be adjusted to the
specific needs of poor families, which vary from state to state. However, there is no
reason why high-cost states cannot pay supplemental benefits.

The objection has also been raised that, as compared to social-dividend plans
including family allowances, a negative income tax would divide the economy
between those who receive checks and those who do not. Family-allowance proponents argue that the extra cost of the plans they favor could be recovered from
higher-income families in the form of additional taxes. The latter statement is
correct. However, sending checks to ten persons in order to really help one or two
seems like a rather cumbersome way to achieve the elimination of poverty.

Friedman feels the most serious objection to the negative income tax is the

---

[11]See Milton Friedman, "The Case for Negative Income Tax," *The Republican Papers* ed. by
Melvin R. Laird 1968, reprinted in *Welfare Reform: Problems and Solutions*, University of
Wisconsin, mimeographed.

[12]In some states the family is allowed to keep part of the income it earns. This introduces
an inequity into the system, since two individuals holding the same job at the same salary
may have different total incomes because one was on welfare before getting the job while
the other was not.

possibility that it might just be added to our already numerous existing programs. However, there is so little support for our present public-assistance program, even among those who administer it, that the chances of its retention simultaneously with the introduction of a negative tax is small.

Friedman also feels that in spite of some observers' belief that the negative income tax might foster political irresponsibility, it is *less* likely than other programs to generate a large bureaucracy interested in expanding the program.

17.3.5 THE PROBLEM OF WORK INCENTIVE

The incentive decision presented by negative-income-tax plans can be illustrated graphically. The new choice situation presented by the negative-tax plans is represented by Fig. 17.2. The figures for the graph are presented in Table 17.4. The table assumes a basic allowance of $1500 and a 50% tax rate.

After the negative tax plan with a 50% tax goes into effect, a family which continues to earn $2000 would have its allowance reduced by $1000. It would receive a net allowance of $500 and its after-allowance income would be $2500. However, if its income target were $2000, it could now attain this total by working less. It could earn $1000 and collect an allowance of $1000.

The range of income possibilities originally open to the family can be illustrated by line *ABC*. The range of income possibilities open to the family after the introduction of the plan is illustrated as line *ABD*. (The exact slope of line *ABC* will be determined by the wage rate which the family would earn for each hour of work.)[13]

TABLE 17.4 Lampman negative-
tax plan for a four-
person family

Family income before allowance	Net allowance: 50% tax rate
$ 0	$1500
500	1250
1000	1000
1500	750
2000	500
2500	250
3000	0
3500	0
4000	0

Source: Robert J. Lampman, "Statement," hearings before the Joint Economic Committee U.S. Congress, June 1968, reprinted in *Welfare Reform: Problems and Solutions*, University of Wisconsin, mimeographed.

---

[13]Note that the minimum-income guarantee is illustrated by the height of the line *DC*. The income-tax rate is illustrated by the slope of the line *BD*.

The family must decide how much of the time to allocate to leisure and how much to work. It will reach its optimum level of satisfaction where the line which shows its income possibilities (*ABC* without a negative income tax; *ABD* with a negative-income-tax plan) is just tangent to an indifference curve. The point of tangency represents the highest indifference curve, and therefore the highest point of satisfaction that the family can reach.

The introduction of new choice possibilities by the plan will cause many families to change their allocation of time between work and leisure. The new choice possibilities line, *ABD*, will ordinarily be tangent to an indifference curve different from the one to which *ABC* was tangent. One family's evaluation of work versus leisure may lead them to increase their hours of work, while another family may choose to reduce theirs. For example, the family represented in Fig. 17.2 is led to increase its hours of work.

17.4 IS A NEGATIVE INCOME TAX PRACTICAL[14]

Even if everyone were agreed that a negative-income-tax plan is the ideal plan for distributing welfare to the poor, there would still be many practical problems.

One major problem is how to define the family unit and relate basic allowances to its size and composition. How should the basic allowance rise as the number of persons in the family increases? Since there are economies of scale in family consumption, the allowance should rise with increases in family size, but not proportionately. However, any incentive to split large families into smaller units must

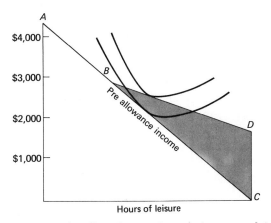

FIG. 17.2 The effect of a negative tax plan on work incentive

[14]See James Tobin, Joseph A. Pechman, and Peter M. Mieszkowski, "Is Negative Income Tax Practical?" *The Yale Law Journal*, vol. 77, No. 1, November 1967.

be avoided. For example, the allowance for the first two adults in a family should be the same so that there will be no incentive for a couple to define themselves as two single individuals.

Definition of the family unit seems to present some difficult problems. Some cases are easy—parents and children, husband and wife. But how do you handle the case of fathers who support children but do not live with them, married teenagers, children who live with grandparents, and other cases? Before a negative-income-tax plan could be made operable, these definitional problems would have to be resolved. Tobin suggests that negative-income-tax payments should be made to adults and to young married couples with inadequate income even if they reside with a family of high income.

A second major set of problems revolves around the question of how to define income. To avoid paying benefits to those who are not needy, the definition of income should be comprehensive. No exemptions or deductions in computing income should be allowed, since the basic allowances already reflect the size of the unit and standard costs of living. Likewise, to avoid inequities between those who do and those who do not own homes, the value of the services of owner-occupied homes should be included as income.

Tobin recommends that transfer payments based on need should not be included in income for calculation of the negative income tax. However, payments based on deferred compensation for previous work, such as pensions or unemployment compensation, should be included. At least some fraction of transfers from friends, family, or private charities should also be included in the definition of income.

Tobin feels that states should be encouraged to maintain public-assistance programs as supplements to the national negative-income-tax system. Such supplemental programs should be made consistent with the national plan and should be designed to provide work incentive.

It seems advisable to include the aged and the disabled in the negative-income-tax plan rather than to try to set minimum social-security benefits high enough to provide income assistance. Possession of wealth above a certain level should probably reduce negative-income-tax payments by some amount. An offsetting tax should thus be imposed on capital as it is on income, though at a lower rate.

A final set of problems concerns the method of payment. The calendar year should be the basic accounting period, but payments should be made weekly or twice a month. This would be analogous to the positive income tax which is regularly withheld for most wage earners. Payments could be made automatically to all families while offsetting taxes were collected. A less cumbersome plan would be to make payments only to families who declared that their expected income would entitle them to such payments. Over-claiming of benefits could be discouraged through an interest penalty.

17.5 THE NIXON FAMILY-ASSISTANCE PLAN[15]

Seeking a break with the past, Nixon's family-assistance plan (FAP) emphasizes structural reform.

The plan would provide assistance to all families with dependent children under 18 whose incomes are below specified minimums. This would include the working poor. The plan would replace the present Federally assisted AFDC program. The other categorical assistance programs applying to adults would be combined into a single program for the aged (65 and over), the blind, and the permanently as well as temporarily and severely disabled. Adults without children would not receive assistance unless they qualified for categorical assistance.

A family with no income would qualify for a basic Federal allowance for $500 per year for each of its first two members and $300 for each additional member. The family would also be able to buy food stamps which, for a family of four, could amount to an effective net increase in its spending power of up to about $870 a year. The total of $2470 from the Federal government would provide slightly over two-thirds of the income needed to bring a family of four above the poverty line.

Those states in which AFDC assistance levels exceed the proposed basic FAP allowances would be required to supplement FAP benefits for families eligible for AFDC under their present rules. In this way no families would be worse off under the new plan.

The FAP places great stress on work incentives and work requirements. All adult recipients except mothers of very young children and certain other groups[16] would be required to register for suitable employment or training. A large expansion of subsidized child care is also planned. This would permit employment of mothers.

If an adult family member fails to register or refuses, without good cause, to accept a suitable job offer or to participate in suitable training and related manpower activities, he would be denied benefits under FAP. However, benefits would continue to the rest of the family.

An "employability plan" would be prepared for each adult registered with the employment service, covering his vocational problems. Training opportunities and skill upgrading would be provided where appropriate. Although lack of education and job skills might prevent some FAP recipients from achieving immediate self support, the plan is designed to reach this goal for as many families as possible.

The FAP has been designed to ensure that work is profitable to the family. The

---

[15]See U.S. Department of Labor, *Manpower Report of the President,* U.S. Government Printing Office, Washington, D.C., March 1970.

[16]Mothers of preschool children (under age 6); mothers of older children if the father or another adult is present in the family and registered with the employment service or working full time; sick or disabled people or those caring for them; as well as those working full time will not be required to register with the employment service.

first $720 earned each year ($60 per month) and half the earnings above this amount would be disregarded in computing FAP benefits. A family of four would receive some benefits until its total income reached $3920 a year.

Reception of Nixon's plan has not been entirely favorable. For one thing, the program does not aid most childless poor adults. Nor does it abolish categorical assistance.

The major criticism of the plan is that work incentive is not adequately provided. True, the first $720 of earnings may be kept by the family as well as 50¢ of each additional dollar. However, food-stamp payments as well as supplemental state payments are also reduced as earnings increase. Thus the family is really left with only about 60% of the first $720 of earnings and only 20¢ out of each additional dollar. Professor Friedman suggests that the basic cash allowance be increased and the food-stamp plan be eliminated.

17.6 THE NEGATIVE-INCOME-TAX EXPERIMENTS

Eight negative-income-tax plans have been experimented with in New Jersey. The plans differ in their basic allowance and in the tax rate at which earnings are reduced. The $1200 low-income urban families included in the experiment are all headed by a non-aged male, and each includes an employable family member. Each family will receive a regular cash payment for three years. The amount will vary with family size, current income, and the plan to which the family is assigned. (Table 17.5 illustrates the nature of the eight plans in use.) Payments will be made every two weeks.

Some conclusions can already be drawn based on the New Jersey experiments. Most of the poor families have been able to handle the paperwork well. Likewise, the experiment has been run with a small staff, even with the necessity for interview administration and calculation of monthly payments. Finally, there was no noticeable "impact effect." Some thought that introduction of the program would cause many to just quit their jobs, but this did *not* occur.

Data also indicate no evidence that work effort declined among those receiving income-support payments. In fact, there is an indication that the work effort of participants receiving payments (the experimental) increased relative to the work effort of those not receiving payments (the control). See Table 17.6 for details.

17.7 THE FUTURE

With so much discussion and interest, the future should bring change. Ideally, the future will see assistance more broadly extended to those in need. Criteria will be family size and composition, as well as income and other resources. Earnings will be taxed at below a 100% rate in order to preserve work incentive. All assistance will be paid in cash. These are features of most negative-income-tax plans.

The Nixon plan differs from the ideal in that no assistance is provided to single persons or families without children. Also the Nixon plan would pay some assistance

TABLE 17.5 Negative-income-tax plans in the New
             Jersey experiment (× marks plans in use)

| Guarantee levels | Tax rates: rate at which allowance is reduced as income is earned | | |
	30%	50%	70%
0.50 poverty line ($1650)*	×	×	
0.75 poverty line ($2475)	×	×	×
1.00 poverty line ($3300)		×	×
1.25 poverty line ($4125)		×	

*Numbers in parentheses are guarantee levels for a family of four.
Source: David N. Kershaw, "The Negative Income Tax Experiment
in New Jersey," a paper presented at the Conference on Public
Welfare Issue, New Brunswick, New Jersey, April 1969, page 19.

as food stamps. Nevertheless the Nixon plan can be considered a first step toward
the ideal situation.

What if the Nixon plan does not pass Congress? There is still some cause for
optimism. Even the welfare system in the progressive states has moved a good way
toward the negative income tax. Many states now provide assistance to "unemployed
and underemployed" parents and others tax income at a rate of $66\frac{2}{3}\%$ rather than 100%.

It thus appears that welfare reform is moving us in the right direction. It must

TABLE 17.6 Negative-income-tax experiment:
             actual work-effort behavior

Percent of families whose earnings:	Control	Experimental
Increased	43	53
Did not change	26	18
Declined	31	29

Source: *Preliminary Results of the New Jersey Graduated Work
Incentive Experiment*, Office of Economic Opportunity, February
18, 1970, page 11.

be remembered, however, that more than just money is needed if poverty is to be eliminated. We owe our citizens training, education, equal opportunities, and jobs without dead ends, as well as public assistance. It might also be pointed out that none of the plans reviewed close all of the poverty gap. (Lampman estimates that it would take $25 billion to close a $10 billion poverty gap.) Only part of the gap is closed under the plans discussed, in spite of the fact that some part of the payments often go to the nonpoor. The latter seems to be necessary if the incentive to work is to be adequately provided.

SUMMARY

Our present welfare system provides for both income supplementation, cash transfers to persons without regard to previous work experience, and income protection, payments designed to maintain previously satisfactory income levels.

The income-supplementation program has been criticized for providing payments to only certain categories of the poor. It has also been criticized for discouraging work effort.

Suggestions for welfare reform are many and varied. Some feel that overhaul of the current system is the best approach. Eligibility could be extended to all those in need and the tax rate could be lowered to help preserve work incentive.

Family-allowance plans have also been suggested. Such plans call for payments to all families with children, in proportion to the number of children. Only about 20% of the outlays on family allowance would accrue to poor families.

Most attention has been focused on negative-income-tax plans. The Friedman plan calls for a payment to the poor based on its unused positive tax exemptions and deductions. The Tobin plan is similar to Friedman's plan, although the two differ in specific details. Both plans specify a break-even income at which the family pays no tax and receives no payment, and a minimum guaranteed income, the amount received by families with zero earned income. The plans also either specify or imply a rate at which the allowance is reduced as income is earned.

Professor Robert J. Lampman is also a proponent of the negative-income-tax concept. He has suggested aiming such a plan at the working poor. He also suggests that both the minimum guarantee and the marginal tax rate be low, so that work incentive is kept as high as possible.

Negative-income-tax programs are attractive to many because they concentrate payments to the poor without treating them in a degrading manner. Likewise it preserves at least some work incentive.

Questions of practicality must be considered. The family unit must be defined and basic allowances must be related to its size and composition. A comprehensive definition of income must be developed.

President Nixon has introduced a plan to Congress which would provide assistance to all families with dependent children under 18 whose incomes are below specified minimums. Assistance would provide the family with cash as well as the opportunity to buy food stamps. With some exception, adult recipients would be required to register for suitable employment.

The major criticism of Nixon's plan is that work incentive is not adequately protected. The New Jersey negative-income-tax experiments indicate no evidence that work effort declined among those receiving income support payments.

BIBLIOGRAPHY

Henry J. Aaron, "Income Transfer Programs," *Monthly Labor Rev.*, February 1969.

Mary Jean Bowman, "Poverty in an Affluent Society," in Neil W. Chamberlain (editor), *Contemporary Economic Issues*, Richard D. Irwin, Homewood, Illinois, 1969.

David N. Kershaw, "The Negative Income Tax Experiment in New Jersey," a paper presented at the Conference on Public Welfare Issue, New Brunswick, New Jersey, April 1969.

"Preliminary Results of the New Jersey Graduated Work Incentive Experiment," Office of Economic Opportunity, February 1970.

Welfare Reform: Problems and Solutions, The University of Wisconsin, a compilation of articles in the welfare area (recent mimeograph).

CONCLUSION   Part V

An economic system has as one of its primary goals the maintenance of a level of "full employment." This is defined in terms of a specified welfare function, which includes economic growth, price levels, unemployment, balance of payments, and wage—productivity as a few of the significant variables which a policymaker considers in reaching for full employment.

The policymaker is able to optimize the attainment of one variable only at the cost of less welfare generated in another. He is involved in various "trade-offs."

Given a constrained level of full employment, the policymaker must then decide optimum investments in various groups or individuals in widening occupational—employment opportunities. These are provided by development of skills, more efficient job information and utilization of manpower, and by conserving manpower resources through health, welfare, and other programs.

MANPOWER AND EMPLOYMENT PROBLEMS AND POLICIES: A SYNTHESIS

18

In our previous chapters we have discussed various aspects of the labor market, problems of market imbalances (unemployment, poverty, etc.), and program approaches to solving these problems. We would now like to look at manpower and employment policies and synthesize them into one conceptual model. We will also suggest how this model can be placed into a general plan of economic development.

18.1 MANPOWER AND EMPLOYMENT POLICIES

The reader will recall the discussion in Chapter 10 of the structural-transformation versus inadequate-aggregate-demand controversy of the 1950s and 1960s. That discussion indicated that both sides contributed something to the understanding of labor-market problems.

The insufficient-aggregate-demand school stressed what we will call employment policies. These are macro-oriented. They are aggregative and generalized in nature and involve monetary and fiscal policies to create jobs. The institutions primarily responsible for employment policies are the Council of Economic Advisers, the U.S. Treasury, and the Federal Reserve Board. These groups are concerned with the level of taxes, the rate of change in the money supply, and the level and composition of government expenditures. Their instruments are used to attain various levels of jobs—or labor demand.

The structural-transformation school stressed what we will call manpower policies. These are micro-oriented. They are disaggregative and particularized in nature and involve training and relocation policies to prepare workers for jobs. The institutions primarily responsible for manpower policies are the U.S. Department of Labor and the U.S. Department of Health, Education, and Welfare. These groups are concerned with basic education, training, and retraining programs and mobility

284

programs. Their instruments are used to prepare individual groups of workers to fill available job vacancies.

18.2 SPECIFYING A WELFARE FUNCTION: EMPLOYMENT POLICY[1]

Just what does full employment mean? Full employment does not mean maximum employment. At any point in time there are a certain number of workers who are between jobs due to the dynamics (or frictions) of real-world labor markets. Thus a good definition of full employment must take into account such factors as job openings (or vacancies), and available (or unemployed) workers.

One of the oldest definitions of full employment is the one proposed by William Beveridge in his *Full Employment in a Free Society.* He defined full employment as an excess of job vacancies over the number of unemployed workers. Recent economists have argued that this definition was too extreme and propose that full employment should be defined as a condition of *equality* of job vacancies with unemployment.[2]

The problem with these definitions is that they do not specify the composition of the vacancies and of the unemployed. Vacancies could be in one area (skilled jobs in the Far West) and the unemployed may be in an entirely different area (unskilled people in the South). In a situation in which the unemployed and the job vacancies are in different areas, the two will not get together no matter how many vacancies exist.

Other definitions of full employment are specified in terms of a certain percentage change .in price level (perhaps 1% or 2% a year) associated with a certain level of unemployment (perhaps 4% or 3% of the labor force unemployed).

18.2.1 CONCEPT OF CONSTRAINED FULL EMPLOYMENT

To have a fully developed concept of full employment, we must specify a welfare function. In an economy as complex as that of the United States, society is concerned with a whole series of goals. The main economic variables which concern society are the overall unemployment rate, the rate of growth in output, and the rate of change in the overall price index. Thus society would be concerned with maximizing a welfare function of the following form: $Z = f(u, \dot{x}, \dot{p})$. Society's welfare is represented by Z; u stands for the overall unemployment rate; $\dot{x}$ is the rate of growth in output (GNP); and $\dot{p}$ is the rate of change in the overall price index. Z is inversely related to u and $\dot{p}$, but directly related to $\dot{x}$. Society will try to achieve the combination of u, $\dot{x}$, and $\dot{p}$ which will make Z as high as possible.

---

[1]The analysis in this chapter is similar to that of Robert A. Gordon, *The Goal of Full Employment,* Wiley, New York, 1967.

[2]For one example, see Arthur F. Burns, "Economics and Our Public Policy of Full Employment," in Edgar O. Edwards (editor), *The Nation's Economic Objectives,* University of Chicago Press, Chicago, 1964.

This welfare function is subject to several constraints, which include the balance-of-payments problem, and the wage—productivity relationship. In recent years in the United States there has been increasing concern with the level of gold reserves. This concern forces extra attention on the domestic price level, especially as compared to the price levels of foreign countries. In order to keep our balance of payments at a reasonable level and our gold reserves secure, the price level of domestic goods (especially goods which move in international trade) must be kept very close to (or perhaps below) the price of the foreign goods they compete with. The wage—productivity relationship measures the difference between the rate of change in wages and productivity. If wages go up at a rate which is greater than the change in productivity, then there will be inflationary pressure in the economy. Other constraints include limited resources, a given level of technology at any point of time, etc.

Thus, although society does try to maximize its welfare (Z) by attempting to change the u, $\dot{x}$, and $\dot{p}$ variables, it can change these variables only within the limits of the constraints mentioned above. The level of u reached when society's welfare (Z) is at a maximum, given these constraints, will be called the *constrained full employment level.*

18.3 PRICE AND UNEMPLOYMENT TRADE-OFFS

Although our knowledge of economic growth is less than ideal, we can safely assume that economic growth (a positive $\dot{x}$) and full employment (a low u) are complementary goals. Economic growth, in fact, is probably much faster at a low level of unemployment than at a high level. Thus we can simplify our welfare function (at least for the purposes of this chapter) by omitting $\dot{x}$. The welfare function would then take the form of $Z = f(u, \dot{p})$.

Welfare is now maximized by decreasing u and $\dot{p}$ (within the given constraints) and full employment is that unemployment rate which maximizes Z allowing for the welfare effects of the rate of change in the price level associated with that level of unemployment.

18.3.1 PHILLIPS CURVE

The Phillips curve[3] is a graphical presentation of the relationship between the unemployment rate and the rate of change in wages ($\dot{w}$). It illustrates the possible combinations of u and $\dot{p}$ open to the society. The Phillips curve (see Fig. 18.1) is negatively sloped and nonlinear. This means that as the unemployment rate falls, the rate of change in wages increases and at an increasing rate. Thus, at a very small u, the $\dot{w}$ in the economy would be extremely high.

For our analysis we will use a modified Phillips curve. We will assume a

---

[3]See A. W. Phillips, "The Relation Between Unemployment and the Rate of Change of Money Wages in the United Kingdom, 1861–1957," *Economica* (November 1958).

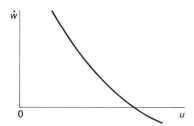

FIG. 18.1 Phillips curve

relationship between $\dot{w}$ and $\dot{p}$ in order to draw a relationship between u and $\dot{p}$. We will assume that if productivity is rising by 3% a year, then $\dot{w}$ should be able to rise by 3% a year, while prices remain stable ($\dot{p} = 0\%$). If $\dot{w}$ is greater than the rate of change in productivity, then $\dot{p}$ will be greater than 0% by the amount of the excess of $\dot{w}$ over the rate of the productivity increase. Having made this wage—productivity—price assumption, we can translate the relationship between $\dot{w}$ and u into a relationship between $\dot{p}$ and u. We shall call a graph of this relationship a *modified Phillips curve* (Fig. 18.2).

We should note that the $\dot{p}$—u relationship is not always fixed, but can shift over time. The exact position of the modified Phillips curve will depend on the amount of frictional and structural unemployment in the economy (among other things). A recent estimate of a modified Phillips curve for the United States indicates that it would take an unemployment rate of 5.5% to get a completely stable price level.[4]

In addition to our representation in Fig. 18.2, it is possible that the true modified Phillips curve looks more like the one in Fig. 18.3.

Figure 18.3 illustrates a situation in which decreases in the unemployment rate to levels below A are associated with increases in the price level ($p > 0\%$), but increases in the unemployment rate above A leave the price level unchanged ($p = 0\%$).

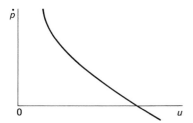

FIG. 18.2 Modified Phillips curve

---

[4]See P. A. Samuelson and R. M. Solow, "Analytical Aspects of Anti-Inflation Policy," *American Economic Review: Papers and Proceedings* (May 1960). For another empirical study, see G. L. Perry, *Unemployment, Money Wage Rates and Inflation*, M.I.T. Press, Cambridge, Mass., 1966.

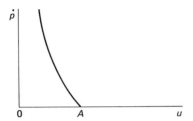

FIG. 18.3 Modified Phillips curve (no price deflation)

18.3.2 POLICYMAKER'S INDIFFERENCE CURVE

Both u and $\dot{p}$ are discommodities—society wants *less* of each and not more. Figure 18.4 displays a policymaker's indifference curve. Each indifference curve shows combinations of u and $\dot{p}$ which would leave society at the same level of welfare. The curves are smooth and concave to the origin. Thus, at high levels of u, the policymaker would be willing to accept quite a bit of inflation in order to get even a small reduction in the unemployment rate. (On curve $Y_5\,Y_6$ he would trade an increase of DE in inflation for a reduction of EF in unemployment.) However as the economy approaches 0 unemployment and high inflation levels, the policymaker would only accept a large reduction in unemployment for a small increase in the rate of inflation. (He would trade AB for BC in Fig. 18.4.)

Indifference curves which are closer to the origin represent higher levels of welfare, since the ideal position is that of no unemployment and no inflation. Although this is the policymaker's goal, he is constrained in the real world by such things as the modified Phillips curve. What the policymaker can do (Fig. 18.3) and what he wishes to do (Fig. 18.4) must be considered together if an equilibrium position is to be determined.

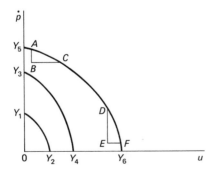

FIG. 18.4 Policymaker's indifference curve between $\dot{p}$ and u

18.3.3 OPTIMUM PRICE AND UNEMPLOYMENT LEVELS

The policymaker maximizes society's welfare (Z) by selecting the optimum level of unemployment and inflation, given the real-world constraints. We can graph this (in Fig. 18.5) by presenting the policymaker's indifference curves between $\dot{p}$ and u with a modified Phillips curve. The optimum levels of unemployment and inflation are represented by the point of tangency between the modified Phillips curve and the indifference curve with which it is tangent. At this point society's welfare Z will be at a maximum.

At point A (the tangency between $x_1 x_2$ and $Y_1 Y_2$ in Fig. 18.5) society maximizes its welfare by selecting an unemployment rate of u_1 and a rate of inflation of $\dot{p}_1$. This rate of unemployment (u_1) will be called *aggregative full employment*. It is the level of u at which Z is a maximum, given our modified Phillips curve.

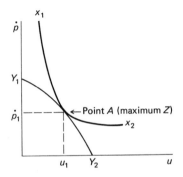

FIG. 18.5 Maximizing Z

Aggregative full employment means that, given the modified Phillips curve $x_1 x_2$, society will not try to lower unemployment further because of the higher inflation that would be associated with the lower u. However, the modified Phillips curve assumes a given level of frictional and structural unemployment. If we could lower this level of frictional and/or structural unemployment, the modified Phillips curve would shift to the left and society could choose a lower level of u and $\dot{p}$. It is only if we cannot, or will not, shift the modified Phillips curve to the left that the unemployment rate (identified by A in Fig. 18.5) is society's full employment rate.[5] But how does one shift the modified Phillips curve to the left? The answer lies in manpower policies which will be discussed below.

---

[5] Although our discussion has indicated that price stability occurs only when $\dot{p} = 0\%$, it is possible that price stability occurs when $\dot{p} = 1\%$ or even 2% a year. This might be true because the *quality* of goods and services is increasing but is not always reflected in our price index. If this is true, then aggregative full employment might occur at a fairly low rate (say 4% or 4.5%).

18.4 THE GOAL OF MANPOWER POLICY

Once we have reached aggregative full employment through the best possible application of fiscal and monetary policies, we have accomplished all we can with aggregative
and general measures. We must then move to manpower policies (disaggregative and
particularized measures) in order to shift the modified Phillips curve toward the
origin.

In Fig. 18.6 we see a representation of successful manpower policy. The modified
Phillips curve $x_1 x_2$, which existed before the use of manpower programs, has been
shifted to the left. The level of frictional and structural unemployment associated
with curve $x_1 x_2$ has been reduced to yield a new modified Phillips curve $x_3 x_4$. The
aggregative full employment level u_1 (and its associated inflation level $\dot{p}_1$) has been
reduced to yield a *higher* level of social welfare. The final equilibrium values u and
$\dot{p}$ are both lower than those at point A—u_2 is less than u_1 and $\dot{p}_2$ is less than $\dot{p}_1$. Thus
society's "constrained" full-employment level occurs at a lower level of u (u_2) than
does society's "aggregative" full employment level (u_1).

In Chapters 13 through 15 the various manpower programs that have been developed in the United States to attack the problems of frictional and structural unemployment have been discussed. These various programs utilize manpower as well
as occupational projections.

On the supply side, manpower administrators require information on their
target groups. This means they must obtain reliable estimates and projections on
nonlabor force members, the unemployed, and the underemployed. (Both quantitative and qualitative estimates are needed.) These people must then be divided
into fairly homogeneous target groups so that programs may be tailored for each
group.

On the demand side, program administrators seek information on occupational

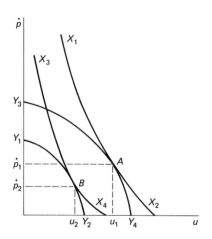

FIG. 18.6 Effects of manpower policy

needs. One approach is to utilize a base-year industrial-occupational matrix[6] of the economy. Projections of industrial employment are made to some target year, and then the industrial-occupational matrix is projected. These two projections are used with the base-year matrix to yield projections of occupational needs in the target year.

An alternative (on the demand side) is to consider the occupational-employment structure of another economy and use this as a target. A given occupational structure reflects a certain level of technology—the relationship between value added by an employed person in a given industry and the occupational composition of the work force in the same industry. For example, Puerto Rico might assume that the occupational structure of the United States in 1950 for a number of industries[7] will correspond to the Puerto Rican economy's occupational structure in 1975.

Manpower policy involves decisions as to investments in "human capital," and choices among alternative occupations for training.[8] This involves:

1. Choosing the occupations and industries to receive the scarce investments in human resource development

2. Choosing among the manpower target groups which should receive the investments

For a developing economy (and perhaps even for a developed economy) the best investments would probably be made in export industries, since these industries help to build foreign reserves, and to develop the economy through multiplier effects. Thus the hypothetical economy described in Table 18.1 would be wise to concentrate human resource investments in the export industries (let us say i_1, i_2, i_3, and i_4) in which it has a comparative advantage. Selecting the industries for investment determines which occupations will receive training money. The second area of decisions (selecting the target groups for investments) should be made in such a way as to maximize investment returns. The economy should consider all the non-labor force, plus unemployed and underemployed people, and invest in those with the best opportunity for increases in productivity.

18.5 MANPOWER POLICY AND INVESTMENTS IN HUMAN CAPITAL: A STRATEGY FOR MANPOWER DEVELOPMENT

The ultimate aim of manpower policy is to make selective investments in manpower target groups in order to make possible a reduction in unemployment without an increase in the price level.

---

[6]An industrial-occupational matrix consists of the occupational structures for the industries which make up an economy.

[7]See Morris A. Horowitz, Manuel Zymelman, and Irwin L. Hernstadt, *Manpower Requirements for Planning*, Vol. I, and Statistical Tables, Vol. II, Department of Economics, Northeastern University, Boston, Massachusetts, 1966.

[8]See Chapter 2 of this text for a discussion of investment in human capital.

TABLE 18.1 Hypothetical industry–occupation matrix

	Industries					
Occupations	i_1	i_2	i_3	i_4	$\cdots$	i_n
J_1	$J_1 i_1$	$J_1 i_2$	$J_1 i_3$	$J_1 i_4$		$J_1 i_n$
J_2	$J_2 i_1$	$J_2 i_2$	$J_2 i_3$	$J_2 i_4$		$J_2 i_n$
J_3	$J_3 i_1$	$J_3 i_2$	$J_3 i_3$	$J_3 i_4$		$J_3 i_n$
J_4	$J_4 i_1$	$J_4 i_2$	$J_4 i_3$	$J_4 i_4$		$J_4 i_n$
$\vdots$						
J_m	$J_m i_1$	$J_m i_2$	$J_m i_3$	$J_m i_4$		$J_m i_n$

One manpower development strategy would entail arraying all the occupational employment gaps with the target groups. The next step would be to estimate the total costs of manpower development for each target group for each occupation. These costs would include training costs, relocation costs, health improvement costs, job matching costs, etc. Then we would have to estimate and discount to the present the earnings stream of each potential investment. If we equated the total costs to the discounted earnings stream, we would get an internal rate of return (r) for each investment:

$$C_T = \frac{R_1}{1 + r} + \frac{R_2}{(1 + r)^2} + \frac{R_3}{(1 + r)^3} + \cdots + \frac{R_n}{(1 + r)^n},$$

where C_T are the total costs of any investment, $\Sigma_1^n R$ is the earning stream due to the investment, and n is the length of time of the investment. In other words, we can get the internal rate of return for training each manpower target group for each employment gap (each occupation, J, in each industry, i). Thus, for each target group, we would have an array of internal rates of return for each trainable occupation (in each industry):

$r_{J_1 i_1} = x_1\%$

$r_{J_2 i_2} = x_2\%$

$r_{J_3 i_3} = x_3\%$

.

.

.

$r_{J_m i_1} = x_n\%$

The rational policymaker will then choose the highest r's for priority investment in order to maximize his returns. One possibility that can occur with such a strategy is that the highest rates of return may be only attainable by the higher-skilled—or the "better"—classes of employed (and nonlabor force and unemployed) workers. The strategy can still be pursued, however; and we can then uplift the other manpower target groups by placing them in the slots (in the labor force) that will be opened by the upgrading of the "better" workers through the manpower programs.

No matter how aggressive manpower policy becomes, there may still be target groups that cannot achieve a high rate of return from manpower-training programs. (Certain mentally and physically handicapped persons might be included here.) For these target groups, government transfer payments may be the only solution.[9] An economy as rich as that of the United States can certainly afford to assign a small portion of its wealth to aid those citizens who cannot earn a minimum income through normal endeavors in the labor market.

18.6 INTEGRATING EMPLOYMENT AND MANPOWER THEORIES AND POLICIES

We can attempt to integrate employment and manpower policies by considering two welfare functions. Society's welfare (Z) can be envisioned as a function of employment policies (Z_1) and manpower policies (Z_2):

$$Z_1 = f(u, \dot{x}, \dot{p})$$
$$Z_2 = f(r_{J_1 i_1}, r_{J_2 i_1}, r_{J_1 i_2}, \ldots, r_{J_m i_n})$$

In order to maximize Z_1, society uses the employment theories and policies at their disposal to move from points such as C and D in Fig. 18.7 to the more optimal position of point A.

Society can then use manpower policies to maximize Z_2 by shifting the modified Phillips curve toward the origin and allowing society to attain equilibrium point B (which is superior to points A, C, and D).

In this way employment and manpower policies can both be used to achieve

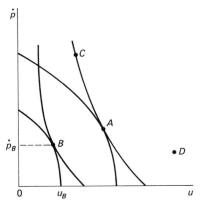

FIG. 18.7 Employment and manpower policies

---

[9] See Chapter 17 for a discussion of such payments.

the highest possible level of social welfare. Full employment in such an economy is at level u_B—the level attainable after both employment and manpower policies are used, and the level of u which gives an acceptable level of price inflation ($\dot{p}_B$).

18.6.1 DISAGGREGATING THE FULL EMPLOYMENT GOAL

If the United States economy should employ an optimal amount of employment and manpower policies, what would be the value for u_B and $\dot{p}_B$ in Fig. 18.7? One good estimate of these values is that u_B would be about 3% and $\dot{p}_B$ would be about 1.5% to 2.5%.[10]

What would a u_B figure of 3% imply for the various subgroups in our population? The estimates of Professor R. A. Gordon of what the various subgroup unemployment rates could be if the United States economy maintained an overall unemployment rate of about 3% are given in Table 18.2, which also shows some actual unemployment rates for the years 1953, 1956, and 1965. A close examination of Table 18.2 reveals that an overall unemployment rate of 3% (in fact *any* overall unemployment rate) covers a wide spectrum of unemployment rates, depending on what segment of the population is being examined.

An overall unemployment rate of 3% would probably leave our teenagers with unemployment rates of 6 to 8% (depending on sex and race) whereas the older males would have unemployment rates of about 3% or less (depending on age and race). Females, of course, would tend to do a little worse than males. An overall rate of 3% would mean a much smaller unemployment rate for white-collar job holders (1.7%), and about twice as high a rate for blue-collar and service job holders (3.6%).

Looking at the actual unemployment rates for selected years in Table 18.2 shows us how far we have to go if we are serious about attaining a 3% overall unemployment rate. The young and the nonwhites have been especially far behind the target rates in recent years.

18.7 THE FUTURE

This text had dealt with basic elements of the labor market, the problems that arise due to imbalances in the labor market, and some approaches to these problems. It is clear that quite a large investment in resources will be needed before these problems are eliminated. The optimal mix of employment and manpower policies to do the job is still an unknown for the United States economy; but with enough research in the 1970s, we should be able to determine, or at least approximate, what this optimum mix ought to be. The future can hold both low unemployment *and* low price inflation if we plan for it with both employment *and* manpower policies.

---

[10] See Robert A. Gordon, *The Goal of Full Employment*, Wiley, New York, 1967, especially Chapter 7.

TABLE 18.2 Target unemployment rates (3% overall rate)

Characteristics	Actual unemployment rates, %			Target unemployment rate, %
	1953	1956	1965	
Males				
14–19 years	7.3	10.2	13.1	6.0
20–24 years	5.0	6.9	6.3	4.0
25–44 years	2.1	2.9	2.7	2.1
45–64 years	2.5	3.2	2.8	2.5
65 and over	2.4	3.5	3.5	2.5
Females				
14–19 years	6.8	10.8	14.3	6.0
20–24 years	4.3	6.3	7.3	4.3
25–44 years	2.9	4.3	5.0	3.2
45–64 years	2.4	3.6	3.1	2.4
65 and over	1.4	2.3	2.8	2.0
White:				
both sexes, 14–19	7.0	9.5	12.2	5.8
males, 20 and over	2.3	3.0	2.9	2.4
females, 20 and over	2.7	3.7	4.0	3.0
Nonwhite:				
both sexes, 14–19	7.9	17.4	25.3	7.7
males, 20 and over	4.5	7.3	6.0	3.2
females, 20 and over	3.7	7.8	7.4	4.0
White-collar jobs	1.4	2.0	2.3	1.7
Blue-collar jobs	3.5	6.1	5.3	3.6
Service jobs	3.2	4.8	5.2	3.6
Farm jobs	1.1	1.9	2.6	1.7

Source: Robert A. Gordon, *The Goal of Full Employment*, Wiley, New York, 1967, various tables in Chapter 7. Basic data are from *Manpower Report of the President*, March 1966, Statistical Appendix, target unemployment rates developed by Professor R. A. Gordon, (Reprinted by permission)

SUMMARY

Employment policies are *macro*-oriented, aggregative, and generalized in nature, and involve monetary and fiscal policies to create jobs. Manpower policies are *micro*-oriented, disaggregative, and particularized in nature, and involve training and relocation policies to prepare workers for jobs.

Both these programs can be used to achieve full employment, and full employment can be defined fully only if we specify a welfare function. This welfare function (Z) would depend on the overall employment rate (u), the rate of growth in output ($\dot{x}$), and the rate of change in the overall price index ($\dot{p}$). Thus the level of u which is reached when society's welfare is at a maximum, given certain constraints, is the (constrained) full employment level.

The above welfare function can be simplified to take the form $Z = f(u,\dot{p})$, which means that society's welfare depends primarily on the price-inflation versus unemployment-rate trade-off in the economy. This trade-off can be expressed in a modified Phillips curve, and the policymaker can maximize society's welfare by selecting the optimum level of unemployment and inflation, given the real-world constraints of the modified Phillips curve and of the policymaker's indifference curves between u and $\dot{p}$.

The rate of unemployment selected by the above process can be called aggregative full employment (the level of u at which Z is a maximum, *given* our modified Phillips curve). However, if, through the use of manpower policies, we can shift the modified Phillips curve to the left, then an unemployment rate *lower* than the above aggregative full employment rate could be achieved. Thus successful manpower policies can lead to a "constrained" full employment level which is lower than the aggregative full employment level. Moreover, manpower policies can be used to advantage in a general plan of economic development.

If the United States should employ an optimal number of employment and manpower policies, it has been estimated that an unemployment level as low as 3% could be achieved with an inflation rate of between 1.5 and 2.5%. Of course, an overall unemployment rate of 3% would cover a wide spectrum of unemployment rates, depending on what segment of the population is being examined.

BIBLIOGRAPHY

Robert A. Gordon, *The Goal of Full Employment*, Wiley, New York, 1967

G. L. Perry, *Unemployment Money Wage Rates and Inflation* M.I.T. Press, Cambridge, Mass., 1966.

A. W. Phillips, "The Relation Between Unemployment and the Rate of Change of Money Wages in the United Kingdom, 1861–1957," *Economica* (November 1958)

P. A. Samuelson and R. M. Solow, "Analytical Aspects of Anti-Inflation Policy," *American Economic Review: Papers and Proceedings* (May 1960)

INDEX

INDEX

Supply of labor
  aggregate level, 53
  and discouraged worker, 52
  firm level, 54
  and income effect, 51
  industry level, 53
  and substitution effect, 50
  and work—leisure choice, 46—52

Underemployment and poverty, 163—164
Unemployment
  concepts, 124
  definition of, 7—45
  and the dispersion index, 149—151
  as an economic concept, 130—132
  generalized vs particularized, 142—146
  historical perspective, 125—126
  and job vacancy, 138—139
  patterns, 152—161
  structural or inadequate demand, 146—
    149

types of, 133—135

Vocational Education Act, 210
Vocational rehabilitation, 212—213

Wage determination
  bargaining theories, 85—88
  monopsony—long run, 84—85
  monopsony—short run, 83—84
  perfect competition—long run, 81—83
  perfect competition—short run, 78—81
Wage differentials
  and demand and supply, 105—109
  equalizing, 104—105
  and noncompeting groups, 105
  nonequalizing, 105
Wage rigidities, 27—29
Welfare system
  current system, 263—265
  reform, 265—266
Work rules, 9